Artistry in Training

Thinking
differently
about the way
you help people
to learn

Respectfully,

Stephanie Burns

Business & Professional Publishing Pty Limited
Unit 7/5 Vuko Place
Warriewood, NSW 2102

National Library of Australia
Cataloguing-in-Publication data:

Burns, Stephanie.
 Artistry in training : thinking differently about the way you help people to learn.

 Includes index.
 ISBN 1 875889 07 8.

 1. Adult education. 2. Adult learning. 3. Employees - Training of. I. Title.

374.11

Cover and text design by Steve Miller, Snapper Graphics.
Indexed by Caroline Colton & Associates Pty Ltd.
Printed and bound in Australia by Star Printery Pty Ltd on 100% recycled paper

10 9 8 7 6 5 4

Distributed in Australia and New Zealand by Woodslane Pty Ltd. Woodslane Press books are available through booksellers and other resellers. For further information contact Woodslane Pty Ltd, Australia on (61) (2) 9970 5111 or Woodslane Ltd, New Zealand on (64) (6) 347 6543.

Why does a training program work with one group but not with another? Why do some learners respond to training and others reject it? Why do some managers succeed in implementing change when others fail?

You already know that there are differences between learners. Now Stephanie shows that it is those differences between trainers, combined with your training preferences, style and range of behaviours, that make or break your training. And she shows that you can use your understanding of this diversity to communicate more effectively.

Drawing on groundbreaking research, *Artistry in Training* gives you insights that will change how you train. It enters the world of the top professional trainer and reveals what makes them outstanding. It shows you how to use their experience to educate or influence in any training situation. Digging deeper than traditional training text into how and why adults learn, it explains how emotions help and hinder your communication.

Easy to read and full of training anecdotes, *Artistry in Training* confirms Stephanie Burns as Australia's leading training and presentation practitioner.

In 1987 **Stephanie Burns** came to Australia from the US, where she had been a military instructor for the US Army, a trainer in various technical fields and had NASA as her first client. Since arriving in Australia she has conducted her Learning to Learn workshop in every state, with resounding success. Today she teaches - how to influence others to learn and ultimately how to influence others to change.

To Mrs Noble, Mr Burns and
June De Toth

As teachers you taught me the value
and long-term influence of
holding high expectations for
those we teach

contents

7 Going real-time — responses to frequently asked questions and solutions to common problems   187

acknowledgments

There have been so very many people who have been instrumental in my career as a trainer—far too many to mention all by name. I am most grateful to my students, those individuals who have entrusted me with some small part in the development of their own training skills. Thank you for giving me the reason for writing this book.

For introducing me to the notion of artistry I am grateful to my dear friend Hilary Austen and teacher Dr Elliot Eisner. I still have far to go to ever do justice to your profound distinctions involving this concept, but know that your work has encouraged me to make my very best attempt to achieve the essence of artistry in my own performances.

In the early years of my training career I was influenced and encouraged by many people, most notably J. B. Cornwell, who gave me my first corporate training position with Searle Diagnostics. I learned so much from that experience. I am especially grateful to all of my early training clients who gave me—an unknown and untested entity—the opportunity to do what I could do and to improve my practice as a trainer.

I would like to thank Pam Chambers and Larry Wilson for the opportunities you provided me during 'the big transition'. Without your support, Pam, I never would have had the audiences to play with. Larry, your support provided me time to study and learn and experiment with a whole new idea about adult learning. I would also like to thank Marvin Oka. Without your inspiration I would never have returned to training, not ever. My times with you on stage count among my most cherished memories.

I am also grateful to all of the researchers whose years of dedicated investigation has provided the grounding for my own perceptions. Although I have not had the opportunity to meet most of you personally, it does not in any way diminish the indebtedness I carry with me. The names Robert Cialdini, Morris Massey, Marva Collins, Malcolm Knowles, David Boud, Ruth Cohen, Jack Mezirow, Phillip Candy, Richard Feynman, Antonio Damasio, Joseph LeDoux, Tad James and Allan Parker are a few of many whose names are spoken aloud by me to audiences many times throughout each year.

For allowing me to continue to work by providing encouragement in a personal sense, and audiences in a business sense, I cannot find the words to express my appreciation for the work of my promoters and supporters. I am especially grateful to Peter Johnson, Suzi Dafnis, Sharon Whiteman and all of the assistants and staff at Pow Wow Events. Also Diane McCann, Robert Mathews and the entire gang at Accelerated Business in Adelaide—what would I do without you? You have introduced me to thousands of people within that community and convinced me that my work has value in places I never would have looked. I would also like to thank the organisers and members of the Australian Institute of Training and Development, and the National Speakers Association of Australia, for their continued support of my work. Of course, I owe a special thanks to Reg Polson and Robert Owen. The two of you have brought so many opportunities into my life without even knowing that you have done so.

Needless to say, this book would not exist without the encouragement to write it. Tim Edwards of Woodslane, you are solely responsible for convincing me, and continuously reminding me, that this book was a good idea. Thank you to the staff of Woodslane who have taken part in this project, especially Paul Franklin and Gavin Heaton, for getting me through the nightmare stages of editing.

Many people in my life have expressed their belief in me; I have dedicated this book to three of these people. These people matter to me still because they did not express their belief in easy-to-come-by acknowledgments. Each in their own way were demons to me—people who expected everything I could give—and rightly so. It was hard to tell if you even liked me, but you truly hit the mark: I was and still am motivated to perform my best for you. First, my junior high school math teacher, Mrs Noble. You were so hard to please. You expected so much. But when my work could win that little wry smile, I knew I was on to something. I worked hard for as many of those experiences as possible. I didn't get many, but I got just enough. Second, to Mr Burns, my military instructor. You, too, were tough as nails. But I noticed that for as much as you expected of me, you expected even more of yourself. Without you, I would never have been motivated to graduate in the top of that class and, hence, today I would be a drill sergeant instead of a trainer. Last, but by no means least, thank you June De Toth, my piano teacher in Santa Fe. You made me the best student I have ever been. Your influence on my thinking was profound. You taught me the value of formality and the danger of familiarity. I will be indebted to you for making me a student again.

And finally, I would like to thank H for what love, truth and sanity exists in my life.

author's note

THE STORY BEGINS

On a hot, sticky morning in August 1974 I woke on my bunk to a familiar cacophony—one that could only be produced by thirty women soldiers living in close proximity. Sounds of a blow dryer mixed with Mexican ballads came from the bay to my right; elsewhere, Minnie Riperton's screeching voice sang *Loving You* in competition with Barry White's Love Unlimited Orchestra; Barry Green's *Rock The Boat Baby* emanated from somewhere on my left. And unbelievably, an alarm clock blared for someone still asleep in the back corner of the barracks.

My bunk mate sat, dressed in fatigues, on her foot locker, eating a bag of potato chips while teasing her hair. The bass to her munching melody came from a floor buffer grinding along the corridor as it slowly followed two Privates who were on hands and knees dripping hot wax from a tin which they kept melted with a cigarette lighter.

I was agitated and nervous. I hadn't been sleeping well for the past few nights. It wasn't the noise; I had long ago forgotten that I disliked music or any other kind of noise in the morning.

I carefully dressed in my summer uniform—a lightweight blue-green regulation-length skirt and a heavily starched, perfectly creased, board-stiff blouse-jacket, with too few stripes and one measly medal. The brass on my collar sparkled from its daily encounter with Brasso and a soft rag. I had perfectly positioned the brass the night before, using a tissue to keep my fingerprints from showing. I clipped on my orange throat scarf, representing the colours of the Signal Corps to which I belonged. I looked at my feet and could see my reflection—I'd spent hundreds of hours spit-shining my shoes.

Last, I clipped a round, engraved, silver badge onto the bottom of my name tag. It was a new ornament on my uniform, presented to me in a ceremony just the day before. It was also the source of my anxiety. It reminded me, and announced to everyone else, that I was now Specialist Burns, Military Instructor. I had just celebrated my nineteenth birthday, and it was the first day of what would be a long career as a trainer.

A BIT OF HISTORY

For the past twenty-one years of my professional career I have, in one form or another, been involved in the arena of 'training'. On reflection, I have found that my experiences fall neatly into two distinct categories: my experiences as a practitioner—someone who stands up, presents training to others and is paid for it; and my experiences as a student and researcher—someone who studies the theoretical literature, does research and then lectures on the findings.

Over the years, I have conducted several thousand training events. I have taught in many different environments: classrooms, ski resort lodges, hotel conference rooms, garages, convention centres, churches, university lecture halls, boardrooms, living rooms, a few tents and even once, on a boat. To some groups I have lectured for just one hour, delivering a keynote address; other groups have required seven days of intense skill development; still others I have trained for a few hours each week for many months. I have been both a sideshow in someone else's conference and the main event.

I have stood in front of small groups of twelve, and larger groups consisting of thousands. I have delivered lectures on new research into human brain function, trained engineers to use computer design tools, taught teenagers to take notes more effectively, provoked teachers to raise their expectations of their students, explored drawing skills with prisoners in the Hawaiian women's prison system and even taught guitar to fifty beginners at one time so that they could all play *Rock Around The Clock* with the back-up band at the end of the first lesson. I have taught old people to juggle, young people to think and a lot of people (amazingly, a lot of nuns) to use personal computers. Today, I mostly teach others how to teach more effectively and explore issues related to the training of adults—how to influence others to learn and, ultimately, how to influence others to change.

Like many trainers I meet, it is not a career I sought, nor one I would have chosen. When I was young, lying in a field of grass dreaming about my future, I never once—not once—fantasised about becoming a trainer. For most of us, entry into this career stems from existing circumstances. Many times we are selected because someone else has identified us as an expert on a certain topic. In my case, having graduated at the top of my computer engineering course, logic dictated that I should be a good instructor of other budding engineers. In other words, there is an assumption that a good guitarist should be a good guitar teacher; a good salesperson should be a good teacher of sales techniques. That most trainers do not choose their career, but stumble into it based on their competence in a particular area, is in itself a fascinating phenomenon.

As a military instructor, I had little experience to draw upon for my training technique—only memories of how my teachers taught in school. My style was therefore very much based on what I had seen others do, along with my personality and the circumstances I found myself in. But the starting point for my commitment to students' achievements—and the inventiveness (sometimes sheer craziness) of the methods I used—goes all the way back to those first days standing in front of a classroom of students: all males, all of them older than nineteen, most with more stripes on their sleeves than mine. It was most definitely appropriate in that context that I took the blame, or blamed my own inadequate experience, for anything less than successful results. It was equally appropriate that I did whatever it took (bar cheating) to ensure my students succeeded.

THE THREE PHASES OF MY CAREER AS A TRAINING PROFESSIONAL

Computers and technology

I have primarily taught three different subjects during the twenty-one years of my training career. The first phase centred around technology. I taught my military students basic electronics and computer design, and how to write simple software routines. After leaving the military, I taught service engineers in Chicago how to install and troubleshoot nuclear medicine imaging and cardiology equipment. I travelled extensively for another company, teaching its clients (all from diverse engineering companies) how to use the company's newest microprocessor design tools. In 1979, I made what at the time felt like a risky move—I started my own training company, in Los Angeles. The first private training contract I procured was with NASA, which called for me to train a number of engineers to use microprocessor design tools. I conducted the training in a small computer room at Edwards Air Force Base, in the California desert. I spent one morning a week for ten weeks working with brilliant aeronautic-computer engineers and made enough money to live comfortably for three months. I felt reasonably confident I would find another training contract before my money ran out. Fortunately, I did—with ABC-TV. Others soon followed.

As it turned out, I was in the right place at the right time to catch the rising industry demand for computer literacy and computer applications training. Companies and individuals were buying any old computers, with no idea how to drive them. For perhaps the first time ever, there were not enough training hours to meet industry demands. That led to large-audience lectures—sometimes 500 people, split into 100 five-person teams, each team with its own computer station, with me literally jogging from station to station during the hands-on exercises. The rising interest in computers and the attention it drew to adult learning and training led to my participation in television programs and interviews, radio interviews and press conferences at computer shows.

Two important things happened in my career as a trainer at that time. The first was a request to give lectures—one-hour stand-up routines in front of large audiences. Sometimes the topic was computers in general, sometimes it focused on the effect they were having on industry, sometimes it was about the phobic response some employees exhibited. I quickly learned that lecturing is very different from teaching and requires a different set of skills.

Along with this recognition came another observation, this time more to do with the trainees than the trainer. When you take competent, otherwise successful adults, and put them back in the classroom, they begin behaving in many ways as they did as six or seven year olds in school. They rock back on their chairs; they doodle on their papers; they avoid eye contact with the teacher. If they do not understand a concept, most will not raise their hand to ask a question for fear of being embarrassed. I learned early on that many people prefer being confused (and suffering the consequences, such as not learning) to being embarrassed. Essentially, my adult students exhibited behaviours that went a long way toward inhibiting their achievement in a learning situation.

Learning to learn

I was fascinated and befuddled: the more I observed my adult learners' behaviours, the more I wanted to understand. In 1983, I disbanded my computer training company and said goodbye to a dedicated staff of trainers, writers, sales and support personnel. The next four years were spent off-stage, studying the literature and working on projects in an attempt to understand more about the process of learning for adults and how we, as trainers, could assist them to learn more effectively.

Those experiences brought me to the second phase of my training career, which centred around teaching learning strategies to adult learners. I transformed from an expert in computer technology to a quasi-expert in learning technology. I designed a program called *Learning to Learn*, which has now been conducted throughout Australia and New Zealand for tens of thousands of adults of all ages, from every level of education and from a wide range of occupations. While teaching this program, I did almost everything a trainer can do on stage and used most methods available to achieve the outcomes. More than anything, I learned a lot about the experience of adults as they re-enter learning situations or choose learning goals to pursue. That work inspired my first articles for publication and even my first book. My knowledge in this area also led me squarely back into the academic environment as I began to train teachers who work with students every day.

The training of trainers

Not long after entering that second phase, the third (and hopefully not final) phase of my training career began to bubble to the surface. I began receiving requests to train other trainers. But being able to do something does not necessarily mean you know how to pass those skills on to others. Once again, I began studying and researching. What was I doing on stage that worked? Did it have a name? And could someone else be taught to do it?

I began seeking out others who had teaching or communication skills that consistently produced excellent results. I found them in a variety of careers: schoolteachers, university lecturers, corporate trainers, consultants, ministers, nurses, therapists and coaches.

For the past eight years I have been teaching these skills in Australia. Once a year, over a four month period, I work with professionals who are exploring adult education and adult learning, with the aim of enhancing their ability to produce consistent results. I am no longer surprised by the variety of careers represented in my courses: psychologists, schoolteachers, radio announcers, business owners and managers, counsellors and, of course, trainers, or those thinking about a career in training. They all have one thing in common: they are responsible for educating, informing or creating change in other people. This book is an attempt to capture the experiences and lessons I have learned from those people.

My life as a student and researcher

Another way I have personally been involved in this industry is as a student and researcher, specifically in the disciplines of adult learning and adult education. Although I've grown to be quite comfortable on stage—most certainly it is how I am best known—on most days I am studying or writing. I like thinking more than talking. I am also a stickler for ensuring that my practice—what I do, or what I teach others to do—has theoretical grounding and is based on rigorous scientific research. I study, design research projects, experiment, discuss, argue and write; but mostly I think. In the end, the goal is to make a contribution: report a new finding, refute an existing theory or develop a new question. By no means am I a scholar, but I am learning with the guidance of others to do scholarly work.

When approached by Woodslane to write this book on training, I was in the middle of conducting three *Training to Train* courses, one each in Sydney, Melbourne and Adelaide. There were 120 students participating in those courses and, as with every other year, they came from diverse backgrounds and industries, and had diverse reasons for doing the course. In addition to this training, I was still doing the occasional short lecture for schools, companies and conferences. But mostly I was in my office studying. I was just reaching the halfway point in my studies for a doctorate degree in adult education. As part of that work, I met with 22 volunteers every three weeks, read hundreds of their written narratives, and spent 88 hours on the phone conducting semi-structured interviews. Together, we explored the effect of emotions on the learning process of adults. Yet, despite all that going on, something told me it was the right time to write this book.

SO WHAT HAPPENED ON THAT FIRST TRAINING DAY?

I climbed the three flights of stairs and walked along the green hallway to my classroom. I entered the room: tables and chairs all in tidy rows, an instructor's podium at the front, computer terminals lining the walls. I knew of nothing important I should be doing, so I waited. I checked that my instructor's manual was in order and double-checked that the reviewer's manual at the reviewer's chair was open at the proper section. It was the first hour of the first day of a four-month course. I opened the windows to the sound of a drill session taking place outside and tried to remember my own experiences as a student in this very room, which had ended only three weeks before. I was shaking, quite uncontrollably, as the chatter of my students grew louder in the hallway as they waited for the morning bell to ring. I prayed it would never ring. It did.

As the students entered, taking seats randomly, I fiddled with my notes and looked at myself in my shoes. The room was quiet and attentive long before I ever noticed. My head was pounding; I could hear my heartbeat in my ears. My lip danced to some odd tune, and my knees moved spontaneously in directions knees were never designed to go, making my skirt do funny things. As I looked up and attempted to speak I began to stutter, not for the first time in my life, but certainly at the most critically important. The harder I tried to control it, the worse it became. The only rational thought that came to mind, as silly as it seems now, was to write my name on the chalkboard. Without yet having spoken a single comprehensible word I turned and walked to the board. I picked up a piece of chalk and with every ounce of effort I could muster I attempted to glide the chalk onto the flat surface. The next thing I remember is choking down chalk dust and hearing a rapid-fire clicking as the chalk slammed repeatedly into the board, shattering into thousands of little pieces. My name had been forever changed to something resembling shots from a machine gun, still firmly ingrained on a blackboard at Fort Monmouth, New Jersey.

When I recovered some many minutes later, turning to face my class, I discovered that my students, out of a mixture of confusion and understanding, had all respectfully left the room.

I say this with all sincerity: given that I have gone on to become a well-respected, highly paid and sought-after trainer since that first experience, forever cemented in my mind is the belief that those with perseverance and a willingness to make all their experiences useful, will without doubt succeed.

CHAPTER

introduction

Trainers, lecturers, presenters and managers hold positions of power and influence. These professionals are responsible for helping other people to become more effective and understand the meaning of their jobs. They assist other people in learning more about themselves, about others, about events and about the world in general. These people have an important role in organisations and educational institutions.

In all my years of training there is just one phenomenon in this industry that still eludes me: I do not fully understand the internal drives, or external pressures, that motivate so many individuals to work in front of an audience, or one-on-one, with the expressed intention and belief that they can in fact educate, inform or change other people. Their motives are hard to understand because of the high-risk nature of the job. It is not risky in a life-threatening sense, like working on a construction site, or on rescue teams or in the police force. It is risky in another way, a very personal way: training is a profession that has the potential to strike dead centre in the heart of an individual's self-esteem. There is the risk of exposure—others can easily evaluate what it is you know and don't know. There is the risk of social disapproval—of not being liked. And there is the risk of inadequacy. Added to this is the ever-present risk of failure. I understand these risks, but I do not understand the motives, not even my own, and often before I take the stage I question why in the world I agreed to the request to train or lecture.

My reasons for writing this book are much easier for me to understand. I have found that much of the literature available to trainers and lecturers, teachers and other professionals who use verbal communication does not speak to my experience with, nor my knowledge of, human behaviour in learning situations. In the literature, several things are missing. I believe that it is time, given the current emphasis on training in industry and the changes facing teachers in the education system, that an appropriate, honest and accurate representation of this profession be expressed.

My goal with this book is to cut to the chase and explore the essential qualities, the essential knowledge and the essential skills necessary to perform successfully in this profession. I want to provide the novice trainer, lecturer or manager with a well-informed set of distinctions about performing well in the training, education and communication professions. At the same time, I also want to create a meaningful representation of training for the experienced professional, presented in such a way that they, too, might consider new distinctions which may lead to improved performances.

In the course of the book I am going to talk a lot about what trainers do, and a little bit about what writers of training technique books tell us to do. Rather than study professional trainers and communicators through theory alone—such an approach can distance the reader from the reality of practice—I hope to bring this complex subject to life through academic research into human behaviour, coupled with real-life stories and observations. Of course, this means that for those of us in this business our behaviours and thoughts are going to have to go under the microscope. We are going to have to take the mickey out of our own behaviours and thought processes if we are going to truly understand what it is we are doing, or what it is we are trying to do. But that's okay; we've all done and said silly things.

THE ORGANISATION
OF THIS BOOK

The hardest part of writing this book has been the ripping apart of the whole complex process of interaction between the trainer, the student, the design, the methods and the environment in which the interaction is occurring. These components are highly interactive and enjoy a reciprocal relationship in the real-time world of training; isolating them has proven especially difficult. To tackle this problem, there are three introductory chapters—each addressing the key topics and building the knowledge base needed to understand in detail the three essential qualities found in excellent trainers. With this knowledge base, we will then be able to adequately, and richly, discuss these components in real-time interactions.

The first of the introductory chapters—Chapter 2—is devoted to building an understanding of the training process from the learner's perspective. It addresses some of the significant factors that contribute to the idiosyncratic nature of the learner—their personality traits, values and preferences, thinking styles and past history. The first purpose of this chapter is to develop our perceptions of the individual members of the audience—this will eventually assist us in making wise choices regarding design and methods. The chapter then addresses the question: What is the experience of learning for the adult who enters a learning situation? This builds upon the preceding discussions of individual differences and allows us to vicariously sit in the seat occupied by our students—both emotionally and cognitively. We will explore the notion that learning, for the individual, is not fun, and in most cases not enjoyable. This argument leads us to a radically different perspective of our students' reality as they participate in the learning process, and will be used to guide our own choice of methods and design.

Chapter 3 focuses on exploring the topics related to the trainer's range and flexibility of behaviour. Four sections in this chapter are directed at unravelling our own behavioural sets—what we do on stage. The first section explores the notion of 'acts' and the means for identifying our current set of acts and their likely effects on different types of students. The second section breaks these behavioural sets into their constituent components. The third section asks: What are the useful acts for trainers? This leads to the fourth section which explores the ways in which we, as trainers, can begin to expand the range of behaviours available to us when working in front of an audience. The chapter ends by building on these discussions in greater detail.

Chapter 4 addresses the last of the knowledge bases involved with the essential qualities of the professional trainer. These are the topics related to the organisation of content knowledge—the program's sequential design. Along these lines it is a natural progression to introduce distinctions about various methods and types of training environments. Trainers do not interact with students in a vacuum, nor without direction. To complete the picture we need to understand the role of these factors on the whole of the interaction between the student and the trainer.

Building now on this dissected view of these three main topics, the final chapters of the book get to the heart of the training profession in real-time. Chapter 5 begins to look at how it all works and how to make it work effectively, and deals specifically with special skills such as constructing meaning and creating relevance. Chapter 6 deals with other issues, such as the unexpected nature of training environments.

If we can use what is learned in the first part of the book to feel comfortable about handling the baffling problems that confound most trainers, we will have achieved a contextualisation of the material such that you can use it in everyday situations. Chapter 7, then, expands our working knowledge of the material presented in the initial chapters by addressing frequently asked questions and problems that trainers confront. This chapter addresses problems and questions related to: getting students to participate; behavioural problems; personal trainer's concerns (such as getting too emotionally involved); design and outcome; and whether to use handouts or other media.

Reading approaches — cover-to-cover, or dip-in?

I would suggest that the book be approached sequentially. In a training session, I have the advantage of linear time: the students cannot jump ahead of where I am in that moment. This avoids confusion. In a book, I relinquish that control. There truly is no mortal harm in skipping about. I would ask however, that if you find yourself questioning the relevance or knowledge that supports some argument that appears late in the book and you have not read the opening chapters, that before you pass out of hand some notion or idea as being false you go back to the foundation that has been developed in the earlier chapters. I wish you a good read.

DEVELOPING A WORKING DEFINITION

There is a key issue that needs to be addressed before we can properly begin: we need to define what we mean by training, and the act of being a professional trainer. The diversity of this industry demands that we attempt to clarify who we are, what our environment consists of, and what the responsibilities of a trainer encompass. This is perhaps the most difficult task.

Any book must begin by defining the subject of investigation. One must know, and let it be known, what one is talking about. In the case of training and the role of the trainer, this is a difficult matter. When I label myself as a trainer, or state that I am going off to do training, what do I mean? What do these statements imply? Much has been written about training, both in academic literature and in popular books, but a search reveals there is little agreement about what should be included in a definition of training or a list of requisite skills for a trainer. The same lack of agreement occurs among those practising in the industry.

That theorists, researchers and practitioners cannot agree on a single definition for training is not to say that theories do not exist, or that there is a paucity of research conducted with published results in reputable journals. The disagreements that exist are understandable: each theorist stresses different aspects and features of the discipline of training, and each makes a unique contribution. Some theorists stress issues related to the process of learning—in other words, training from the learner's perspective. Training viewed from this perspective tries to gain greater insights into the experience of the learner—how the learner behaves and responds within the training environment. We encounter topics such as transformational learning, self-directed learning, the development of autonomy, the effects of cognitive appraisals and emotional responses on performance and so forth. Combined, these insights provide a structure for the trainer's teaching which is sensitive to the learner.

Other theorists focus more specifically on the role and skills of the trainer. Ideas are drawn from fields as diverse as adult education, management and leadership training, experiential education and therapeutic literature. Theorists attempt to devise better methods by which trainers may achieve their outcomes. The focus is on both overt and covert processes used by trainers, and the effects of those processes on the adult learner or the learning process itself.

My own personal view of training and the activities that constitute a trainer's skills are inclusive of many aspects found in leadership, therapeutic, psychological and management literature. It is a larger rather than a smaller construct. I think of the development of skills and artistry of training as an evolutionary process, one that develops over time. I also view training as a lifestyle, a unique way of perceiving and learning from the world at large for the sake of being more effective when working with others. These views have been developed over many years while attempting to grapple with the responsibility of developing others to be effective trainers. The 'map of the territory' I think about when considering this notion of training allows me to explore issues, include viewpoints and entertain ideas that otherwise are ignored in the training and adult education literature.

How, then, shall we know what we are talking about when we use the terms trainer and training throughout this text? Perhaps it is prudent to begin at the beginning, as if we do not know what training is, or what it is that trainers do.

Let's begin by viewing our notions of training and the activities of the trainer from several different perspectives. From each of these perspectives we can discover some new facet of the practice, or a useful set of distinctions. We shall ask questions, such as:

- What do we learn about training and trainers when we analyse the usage of these terms in everyday language?
- When individuals label themselves lecturers, facilitators, coaches, professors and so on, are they talking about the same activity and responsibilities, or are they different?
- If they are different, can and should those distinctions be brought together to define a broader concept of the trainer?
- When a psychologist or salesperson attends a program to develop training skills, what can we learn from their participation and intentions?
- When we observe a trainer who inspires students to (for instance) re-evaluate beliefs that have lead to a fear of computers, where shall we look for the description for that particular trainer's skill and method? In the literature that deals with adult learning, or therapeutic interventions?

This section aims to construct a working definition of the terms "training" and "trainer" to guide us through the rest of this book. A comprehensive definition, if possible at all, can only be reached at the end of this section's inquiry.

What's in a name?

When I started out in this business I was labelled a military *instructor*; when I moved into industry I was called a technical *trainer*; when I delivered information at a computer conference I was described on the brochure as a *lecturer*; when working with teenagers, an *educator*; when working in outdoor experiential events, a *facilitator*; and when working with prisoners and streetkids, a *cracker*! These distinct labels all carry different connotations—they represent labels appropriate to different environments, industries and audience members.

I observe this same phenomenon in the job titles listed on the questionnaire my students fill out before they start of the *Training to Train* course. They use all of those labels, and many others. It seems that people who enrol in this kind of course—or at least my particular program—may not classify themselves as *trainers* at all. These course participants classify themselves as diving instructors, professors, lecturers, coaches, group facilitators, public speakers, presenters, schoolteachers and so on. The question we need to ask is: Are these terms synonyms, or do they in fact define a different set of phenomena? In other words, do we perceive there to be a qualitative difference between the skills and responsibilities of a *teacher* and a *facilitator*? If so, what are those differences, and how do they relate to our notion of trainer?

These labels most certainly have different connotations for the people who filled out the questionnaires. The differences are significant enough for them to differentiate themselves by the use of a specific title. To them, at least, the definition of *facilitator* is different to the definition of *lecturer*. There are two obvious reasons for these distinctions.

First, in some cases the different labels are used to distinguish different environments, content and audience members. For example, the title of professor is usually reserved for someone teaching in a university environment, where the content is of an academic nature and the audience is typically made up of adult learners. Who has ever heard of a professor of volleyball or, for that matter, a maths facilitator or a preschool lecturer?

Second, there is a distinction drawn in terms of time frames for the training. For instance, a public speaker's training presentations might generally be thought of as short, hour-long bursts, whereas teachers are perceived of as spending all day in front of a group.

However, the real question we want to answer here is: Do these different labels connote more than just different industries or time frames? To answer this question, I asked groups of trainers and adult learners to list the attributes and skills associated with these different titles. A short list of responses for two of these terms is provided below for analysis.

Teacher	Facilitator
Establishes social norms	Coaches
Sets boundaries and reinforces through discipline	Creates an experience
	Makes learning easy
Leads toward conforming	Encourages autonomy
Is an authority	Encourages cooperation
Is teacher-centred	Is client-centred
Focuses on content	Focuses on process
Influences attitudes	Encourages interactivity
Holds expectations	Is a resource
Assesses, evaluates and measures	Guides

Of course, these lists are not meant to imply that the attributes and skills are mutually exclusive. However, they do show which attributes the group saw as belonging particularly to teachers or facilitators.

Another interesting insight into this issue of differentiation between the different titles related to training comes from a perusal of any dictionary. For example, the *Macquarie Dictionary* provides the following definitions for some of the labels that individuals use to define their jobs. Compare especially the definition of the verb "train" with the others:

—train

20. to make proficient by instruction and practice.

22. to discipline or instruct... to perform specified actions.

—teach

2. to impart knowledge or skill to.

3. to impart knowledge or skill; give instruction.

—educate

1. to develop the faculties and powers of by teaching, instruction, or schooling; qualify by instruction or training for a particular calling, practice, etc.

3. to develop or train.

—coach

5. a person who trains athletes for games, a contest, etc.

6. a private tutor who prepares a student for an examination.

—lecture

1. a discourse read or delivered before an audience, esp. for instruction or to set forth some subject.

—present

2. to bring, offer, or give, often in a formal or ceremonious way.

7. to bring before or introduce to the public.

10. to bring before the mind; offer for consideration.

To me, when I think of the term *trainer*, it includes all these attributes. In one context or another they are each used by top training professionals. Nevertheless, these definitions do show that there are substantial differences between each term and the way each type of trainer operates. There will most definitely be times when the students and outcomes of a training are best served by specialised methods associated with that of the teacher, of the coach, of the presenter.

The importance of having a diverse viewpoint

I have benefited from, and exposed my training students to, the notion that we are not restricted to the forms of expression and methods found in training-related activities. I have learned more about how to construct a metaphor from Whoopi Goldberg than from any book on training I've read; similarly, I've needed to refer to the skills of a therapist such as Milton Erikson to find the best terms for describing particular methods. I have discovered that top trainers explore many different non-training areas of knowledge to enhance their skills. Let me elaborate...

In analysing the skills of master trainers over the years, I have found adult education literature and popular training books limited in their ability to define and describe the skills of these trainers. I have had to broaden my own scope. In these analyses I have found myself making comments such as, "He has strength like Henry Fonda in *The Grapes Of Wrath*," or "she's as compelling as a Bette Midler when she performs." Such broad associations prompts further observation of professionals in other fields. By analysing the approach a minister consistently uses to help people see a bad situation in a more favourable light, trainers and other professionals may learn how to help students or clients see their situation in a new way, leading to more desirable behaviours. By observing how a film-maker portrays the potential consequences of actions in order to influence our behaviour, we learn how to paint word-pictures and tell stories so that our audience is influenced to think and re-evaluate. A successful counsellor can teach us how to listen, formulate leading questions and instil hope. An excellent trial lawyer can teach us the effect of vocal variety, timing, style and precise organisation of data and facts—skills which, if we too could master them, would enable us to make sense of disparate facts for our audience, yet at the same time hold them in rapt attention.

If we as trainers look only to other professionals from our own field for models, methods and guidance, we limit our ability to make the most of the training situation. The best in each industry are those who learn from the unique communication skills displayed by members of other disciplines. Analysing the performances of a great lawyer, leader, comedian or politician has much to teach any professional about constructing effective communications.

Trainers as leaders, influencers and counsellors

When we analyse the skills of an outstanding trainer, we find that some of the attributes of those trainers do not particularly fall under any of the traditionally defined training disciplines such as those discussed earlier. Three meta-constructs have been instrumental in forming my thoughts about training and what trainers do: leadership, influence and therapy. To my mind, *trainers are leaders, trainers are influencers and are influential* and *trainers counsel and conduct interventions*.

I stumbled upon this thought when trying to analyse trainers' behaviours in the mid-1980s. As I attempted to describe how a trainer assisted a learner in overcoming a mathematics phobia, I realised that this situation was more akin to a therapeutic intervention than to an educational technique. As I attempted to describe how a trainer had inspired a group to suspend their beliefs long enough to consider new perspectives, I found that I had to turn to the literature on leadership for the appropriate understanding of the trainer's behaviour and its consequences.

Acknowledgment of these training functions is not readily apparent in the educational literature. Simply put, many trainers do not conceptualise themselves as leaders or therapists, although there are times when they do lead, and they do intervene.

On the first day of each of my *Training to Train* seminars, I ask participants to think about their associations for these specific labels: *leader, influencer* and *therapist*. (It is an important aside to note that a word such as *leader* is a broad term that contains within it skills and attributes assigned to managers, politicians, ministers and the like.) The participants are asked: In what way do our concepts for those terms relate to our notion of the skills used by some trainers or the skills a trainer would benefit from having?

Below is the list of associations for the terms "leader", "influencer" and "counsellor" elicited from a recent group of trainers.

Trainer as leader	Trainer as influencer	Trainer as counsellor
Is a visionary	Builds rapport with ease	Re-evaluates social norms
Leads by example and inspiration	Appears believable or credible	Encourages self-responsibility
Is passionate	Is confident	Uses questions
Is eloquent	Is authoritative	Places no blame
Emanates personal power and authority	Is enthusiastic and passionate	Shows empathy, is placatory
Excels at work	Is articulate	Is client-centred
Is value-driven	Is easy to like	Encourages autonomy
Is willing to take risks	Is motivating	Resolves issues
Is an initiator		Works meta to own values

The key attributes associated with these three labels are included in my map of a trainer's attributes. They are attributes and skills that all trainers should be able to use competently, because all trainers lead, influence and change others—even if they are incompetent in doing so. The danger is that a lack of competence in these areas works against the trainer when trying to achieve an outcome. You can just as easily lead someone to resist change as embrace it, to fear computers as use them, to teach discrimination as engender empathy for different cultures.

Of course, lists of associations do not constitute a comprehensive description of the trainer's role as therapist, influencer and leader. However, observe how the associations for each differ quite markedly. While it is true that some leaders are empathetic, or know how to *do* empathy, that is not what comes to mind when thinking of the general attributes of a leader. The point is that the attributes of both leaders and counsellors can inform the practice of trainers in adult learning situations. There are benefits for the trainer, and ultimately for the students, if the trainer is able to use both authority and empathy at appropriate times. The trainer teaching Computers 101 to clerks may need to employ counselling skills, for example, if a student fears the new technology. The trainer will need these skills to recognise the reaction and form a strategy for alleviating that fear so that learning can occur. What about leadership? Are there not times when it is beneficial to know how to motivate clerks to see the benefits (say) of boarding the technology bandwagon? Of course, some trainers already use these multi-disciplinary skills in their training sessions, but those who don't have new things to learn.

If we are to rely purely on adult learning and adult education literature, our knowledge of training would be limited. The three training constructs are informed by diverse areas of information: influencing is informed by theories of compliance and sales techniques; leadership by theories of leadership, politics and management literature; therapy by clinical therapies and psychology.

Yet are all those skills and attributes necessary to all trainers at all times? I hesitate here because clearly, even in my work on any given day, not all of those factors play a role in achieving outcomes for the class. On the other hand, over the course of my career I have needed to access each one of them at some time, when it is most appropriate to a given situation. I have needed at times to know how to have control; at other times I have needed to know how to be flexible. I have had to know how to play the inspirator and the disciplinarian; I have had to be the 'good guy' and the 'bad guy'.

The lists above may help you classify some of your own strengths and weaknesses, and thus give you a starting point for development. If, for example, you are not perceived as compassionate, and you do not identify with that attribute yourself, there are steps you can take to develop that attribute so that it is accessible when you most need it. Beyond this, you can also begin to evaluate your own concepts of a trainer, using the lists of attributes to help broaden that concept.

Points of diversity

Having expanded my own thinking about the sources of skills and knowledge about effective communication, I have noticed in recent years that in the *job title* blank on the *Training to Train* questionnaire *more than half* of the program's participants are from disciplines *not related* to training in any normal sense of the word. They work as managers, counsellors, psychologists, therapists, chiropractors, solicitors, salespeople, members of the armed forces, doctors, social workers, astronomers, pianists, nurses, business owners and so on. The question is: How is it that one subject, or set of skills, appeals to such a diverse group of people, with seemingly diverse responsibilities?

First, some professionals in diverse fields may, in some part of their work, have direct training responsibilities, even though it may not be the primary activity of their job. They may make presentations at conferences or in boardrooms, lecture to community groups or tutor apprentices. Second, their effectiveness in their general career may be directly linked to their skills as a communicator: they may need to be able to elicit new clients or contracts, manage the development of employees or convince others to make a decision or to take a risk. The art and skill of such communication resides in the domain of the master trainer. Therefore, these professionals from other fields perceive a benefit from learning about communication from the trainer's perspective.

On a more subtle level there is a fundamental characteristic shared by members of the diverse disciplines with those of the trainer—everyone is in the business of *influencing* or *changing* some aspect of human behaviour. Although the actual content and the ability to express that content may vary, all of us are somehow involved in attempting to influence other people. There is a *shared intention*.

Training professionals may intend to influence others to change their behaviours, or improve their performance by teaching them a new skill; similarly, other trainers may intend to influence an audience to think, or think differently. Professionals from other disciplines influence others to change the computer software they use, to dress differently, to vote in a certain way, to solve a problem in a new way. But first and foremost, the goal is to influence, or change, some aspect of human behaviour—and there are common skills for doing that effectively, regardless of the content or specific outcomes.

Therefore, although the method, environment, tactic, personality or relationship with the audience or individual are variant, professional and casual trainers alike benefit similarly by educating perceptions—being able to 'see' more—by observing and analysing what other professionals do effectively to produce outcomes. Trainers can learn from professionals in other disciplines, just as these other professionals can learn from the skills and artistry of a trainer.

To help define what we call training and what we see as the skills of the trainer, we would do well to examine the diversity of motivations and skills that people bring to the task of training.

Content experts versus expert trainers

Most professionals in the training industry fall into one of two distinct categories (although some may have their feet firmly planted in both camps). First, there are trainers who are better known as *content experts*. They are involved in training because of their expert knowledge of a subject. It must be noted, however, that the development of content expertise does not necessarily lend itself to development of the skills needed to effectively teach others. Most of us have experienced a presentation by a reputable source whose lack of expressive ability managed to put the audience to sleep, or diminished the importance of the content or—worst of all—adversely affected our thoughts about the presenter's credibility.

Other trainers are not content experts at all, but are considered *expert trainers*. They have mastered a set of skills to express information in such a way that it makes sense to others. They most often work with the content developed by experts who either have no interest, or skill, in training itself. Many corporate trainers fall into this category, the expectation being that they will quickly learn the content of the courses they have to teach.

26

The idea of a trainer who has no content expertise may, at first, seem odd. However, the phenomenon is not limited to the training industry. Many singers, for example, are paid to sing because of their quality of voice and expression—but the *content* of their music comes from the songwriter's expertise. Orchestra musicians express music through an instrument, music that is interpreted by a conductor—but again, the content was developed by an independent expert (the composer). Biographers and some writers tell other people's stories—it is what they are good at. Film-makers, too, express other people's ideas. Looking at it this way, it is not so unusual to think that there would be trainers in the business of expressing someone else's expertise and knowledge.

So we can say that training is conducted by *content experts* who dedicate their time to mastering certain knowledge or skills which they then present with some level of effectiveness, or *expert trainers* who focus on mastering the skills of expression, and use those skills to teach the material of a content expert.

Due to this division of the field, the task I have in training trainers is twofold. On the one hand, content experts are looking to enhance their means of expressing content in convincing and compelling ways, and to organise their knowledge so that it is coherent when presented verbally. On the other hand, expert trainers—though they, too, are looking to enhance their means of expression, to be able to do more within the context of training—are also looking for better means to utilise the knowledge that exists in the world, and in some cases to become content experts themselves in some field. Although there is some overlap, each has a different path of development.

Different trainers have different relationships with the audience

Some trainers work consistently with groups who have no prior experience with that trainer or the previous trainer's work. These trainers require different sets of skills than those trainers who lecture or present information to colleagues or peers. Still other trainers may not be known personally to the audience members, but their work, available in books or publications, is previously known. Some relationships are based on age differences, such as a teacher working with young students.

The skills and experience of the individual trainer vary

Unlike other professions, the training industry has no standard for formal education of members. At the most basic level, we know that some trainers have had formal academic, military or commercial training in the skill of training. We also know that some have had no training whatsoever.

Training may be a full-time job or a sideline

For many, training is a career. For some, it is a nine-to-five job, although it is not likely (except perhaps for schoolteachers) that such trainers are in front of groups for all of that time. The time in between may be spent preparing for a class, attending a class or following up with graduates.

Some keep training as a sideline: scoutmasters are a good example. Some people have hobbies and speak to groups about what they know about their hobby. Others may be active in community politics and find themselves addressing groups as part of that role. Others may coach a sporting event on the weekend, or give tennis lessons. Still others may tutor students on piano after work hours. And some are parents who seem to be teaching all the time.

The audience members have diverse backgrounds

Audience members are never blank slates. Each individual enters the training environment with a history that reflects the development of specific skills, knowledge in a variety of domains, beliefs about the subject and attitudes about learning environments—to name just a few.

The trainer's approach should in part be determined by how much the audience already knows about the subject, or can relate to through similar experiences. The delivery should also account for the diversity of backgrounds in an audience—some trainers must work with different ages, educational and work experience, values, agendas, needs and personalities. Whatever the diversity, all must be accommodated.

Sometimes the background and knowledge of the audience will be known. They may be members of a society or institution, in which case something is known of them. At other times, their background can be a mystery. In that case, something has to be done at the start of the training session to determine their level of expertise. There is not much worse than misjudging the prior experience of an audience. It can mean under-stimulation, leading to boredom or disdain, or over-stimulation, causing outright confusion and frustration. Neither end of this continuum serves the learning process very well.

The aims and outcomes of training are diverse

Trainers have different aims or objectives for training. Some people conceptualise training as a process of developing new skills, the outcome being to change others in such a way that they are able to improve or enhance an existing skill, or perhaps learn a new one altogether. For such people, training is the act of changing what people *do*. For other trainers, training is the act of delivering, or helping others to discover, new information or knowledge. This may result in changing what people *know*—giving them richer distinctions about a subject—or changing how people *think*—helping them to see things in a new way. For still other trainers, training facilitates change in how people *feel*—perhaps about a company's new policies, or even about themselves.

The content is variant

Training topics are diverse—there are trainers out there teaching anything and everything. Any industry that requires information to be passed from one individual to another is likely to have some investment in training. People are always eager to learn: from how to cook a specific Italian dish, to identifying varieties of fish species; from how to write a computer program, to learning about the new findings in the neurosciences; from how to be a better parent, to some new information that changes our beliefs about people from other cultures. If someone can do, think or feel something, then there is something for all of us to learn, and for some of us to teach.

There are many methods

How do trainers go about achieving their anticipated outcomes? There are two things to consider: the approaches taken by the trainer, and the props or aids they use. Approaches relate to *how* the educational experience is created. Some trainers use straight chalk-and-talk methods (in other words, I talk; you listen). Others ask questions, use games or conduct role-playing exercises. There is no one correct set of methods, but some methods will be more effective in some circumstances, depending on the trainer's aims and skills.

Props or aids are the devices the trainer brings into the learning environment to assist the learning process. Different trainers need, and are comfortable with, different types of props or aids to get their message across. Some distribute handouts at the start of the course; others hold onto them until the topic is raised. Some provide course notes; others a conference paper. Some use overheads and slides; others a whiteboard on which to write key points as they emerge. Some put on a funny hat whenever they tell a personal story; others wouldn't dare. In one course I attended, I was even handed a basket of lemons for an exercise.

There are many different environments

The environment refers to where the educational experience takes place. Some trainers work in classrooms with a small number of students seated at tables, while others lecture to a large audience filling an auditorium. Still others, such as managers and counsellors, may sit in a comfortable office and work one-on-one. Some trainers have control over the environment in which the training takes place, while others have no control at all.

There are different time frames

Training tasks can extend across different time scales. They can range from one-day sessions to week-long events; from short fifty-five-minute keynote addresses, to training that continues for many months.

Diversity is the norm

No two trainers are the same; we have different past experiences, values, strengths and weaknesses. Not only are we all different, but we teach different things—sometimes skills, sometimes knowledge—sometimes we change how people feel. We also work with different types of people, yet within those general categories, diversity is still the norm, not the exception. Even further, no two audiences are ever the same. Simple training 'techniques' are therefore problematic. There are no 'standardised' ways to train, nor 'simple' fixes for the problematic situations we encounter.

The working definition

So, finally, we have a tentative working definition which sets the stage for what follows. *A trainer is an individual who has an overt or covert intention of influencing change in either the behaviour, thoughts or feelings of one or more other people by using specific, but highly variant, methods of verbal expression and visible gestures.*

There are *no* simple training techniques

I have interviewed many trainers and I have read numerous books on the subject of 'training techniques'. From those two sources, there appear to be some general notions about what 'works' in a training environment—in other words, what trainer behaviours, or activities coordinated by the trainer, get results. But I do not think these notions of training are adequate—indeed, they can be misleading. We need to think differently.

My intention is that this book be a radical departure from most of the current literature available to us as professionals whose careers depend on being influential communicators. The most accessible type of literature on training and communication skills today are those books espousing techniques, the so called how-to of training, presenting and communicating. Such literature is founded on a limited view of training.

In one sense, the notion that there are *simple* techniques is naive—effecting change in human behaviour is a complex process that requires skills in communication. The simplistic notions implied by the idea of 'training techniques' diminishes the value of the skills that excellent trainers and other communication professionals possess. It is an affront to the trainer who knows the amount of effort, risk, time and resources it takes to develop oneself to be competent in this profession—as if making eye contact, speaking clearly, preparing good notes and clear overheads is all that is required to do this job. These do not constitute the *essential* qualities of a professional trainer.

In another sense, a belief that only simple training techniques need be learnt by the new trainer can be misleading, resulting in undesirable student reactions and consequences, such as students walking out before the end of the program, feeling embarrassed or failing to learn.

The act of training does not lend itself well to techniques, formulas, dogma or even logic; *it is a dynamic process of interaction between humans which unfolds over time and is dependent on the elegant execution of complex skills.*

The major problem with the notion of simple training techniques is that it presupposes that there is a set of prespecified actions that:

(1) work for all professional trainers and communicators;

(2) will have the same affect on all learners or employees; and

(3) can be applied in any situation.

These predetermined techniques tell us not to put our hand in our pocket; to make eye contact; to move a little—but not too much—on the stage; to treat all students as equals; and at the same time to be 'natural'. Some trainers, myself included, do not always stick to these techniques. We do put a hand in the pocket; we often find eye contact threatens the dickens out of some students; and we try to make our movements appropriate to the message and comfortable to us as trainers. And most importantly, we realise that students are not all the same.

Going by the book

Recently, I was skimming through a 'how-to' book: a new one with a funny little cover. In a section addressing how a trainer should gain the attention of the audience, several techniques were proposed. The author suggested that the trainer could start with a joke or funny story (neutral, of course, so as to not offend any of the participants). A second suggestion was to use a question-asking technique, noting that "no one wants to be the one who doesn't know the answer." It was suggested that this tidbit of motivational psychology—motivation through fear—could be used to advantage. In some training circles this method is referred to as the "pose, pause and pounce" technique.

Personally, I do not ever want to think that the reason my students or employees are motivated to pay attention is simply because no one wants to be the one who doesn't know the answer or because I tell a good joke. Competent trainers do not tend to tell jokes to gain attention at the start of a lecture. Nor do they find it appropriate to periodically pounce on unsuspecting students to sustain audience attention. Trainers gain the attention of the audience not because of a technique, but because they are interesting to listen to and watch, have a relevant message or have created relevance for their message. They have a pace which motivates, and a means of interacting with the audience that compels the group to stay present and attentive.

In all fairness, I should point out that some 'how-to' books do attempt to include caveats for their proposed techniques. However, I have learned a simple truth in training, or any work involving the change of human behaviour. This truth is summed up by the words *it depends*. Does eye contact work? *It depends*. Should you dress 'up' or 'down'? *It depends*. Therefore, a valid and useful training technique book would be one part technique to ninety-nine parts caveat. To my mind, this is an unrewarding ratio.

To gain or sustain the attention of the audience, trainers may do many different things. There may indeed be times for telling stories that are humorous, and even times for calling on a particular student unexpectedly, but it is important to stress that any technique is only as good as the individual trainer's ability to execute it.

Relying on gut instincts

One of the most important notions to understand right from the start is that when a trainer enters a training situation, be it on a one-on-one basis or in a classroom, they can only convincingly do what is natural for them to do. They perceive the world—those in it and the particular situation at hand—based on their own unique model of the world. This model is dependent on the skills and knowledge they possess from their own past experiences.

I remember a time when I was teaching in the Army. I had a class of thirty students, and this little skinny soldier had an annoying habit of interrupting me with what I perceived as irrelevant and aggressive questions. I was a new trainer, but more importantly, I was young, and had little life experience. At that time in my life, I perceived his behaviour as confronting, annoying and antagonistic. So I tried the two 'techniques' I had been taught in the instructor training course to deal with students who ask argumentative questions. First, I ignored him. I 'put him in my blind spot' so he would not so easily get my attention. The result of my behaviour led to more aggression on his part. To add insult to injury, the other students began siding with him. Now I had a bigger problem than the one I had started with.

34

The second technique I tried was to talk with him privately during a break. I politely told him that his questions were interesting (I was lying—and he knew it—but I was just saying what the manual said I should say), and yet his questions were 'over the heads' of the rest of the group and causing others to feel confused. I offered to meet with him after the class to discuss his questions personally. Now, this may have worked with some individuals, but for this student, it was not an appropriate technique. Having figured out how to get personal attention, his hand waved even more in the next session.

Left out on a limb, with no more 'techniques' known to me, I could only do what was most natural for *me* to do. The next time he raised his hand I quickly and enthusiastically called on him. When he finished posing his question, I thanked him, and said, "That's a very interesting question. Sergeant Brown, would you please answer this young Private's question." Sergeant Brown, confused, stood as military convention required and responded, "Specialist Burns, I don't know the answer to that question." I thanked Sergeant Brown, who was the largest man in the room. This scenario was repeated a few more times in the session. Each time, I redirected the question to Sergeant Brown. On the next break I heard a ruckus out in the hallway. When I looked through the door to see what was happening, I found Sergeant Brown had our little skinny soldier pinned up against the wall, having a 'discussion'. Back in class, the little skinny soldier changed. His questions stopped. He calmed down, became a model student, a good ally, and learned a lot.

Just because this strategy worked doesn't make it a 'technique'. It worked due to several dynamics: I outranked the soldier, he was physically smaller than I and so on. If the situation had been different I would not have taken this course of action. It might have had disastrous effects. The point I want to make is this: when the 'techniques' don't work—and they don't work a lot—your next step will be to do what you would do naturally, as if you were in any other social situation.

Our effectiveness as trainers has everything to do with our general skills and knowledge about how to affect human behaviour in a positive direction. I've learned a lot since those days, and I don't go around terrifying members of my audiences any longer. But in that situation I could only do what I knew to do, based on who I was at that time, filtered through my unique set of life experiences.

A broader approach

On the first day of my *Training to Train* program, I ask participants to come up on stage and take approximately ninety seconds to introduce themselves to the rest of the group. The purpose of the exercise is manyfold, but what is important are the audience comments after the presentations. Members of the group, when not on stage, are asked to note the general characteristics that 'work' for the presenters.

After the first ten or so presentations we talk about what is working well in the presentations. Below is a short list elicited from a recent group:

- when they moved on the stage it kept my attention;
- when they made eye contact I felt they were talking to me;
- when they seemed passionate about what they're saying it made me believe them;
- when their movements looked natural I thought they must have a lot of talent;
- when they disclosed something of themselves I moved closer to them;

- when they were funny I found it easy to listen;
- when they spoke loudly I thought they were confident;
- when they told a personal story I got a sense that they were interesting;
- when they had a pleasant voice they were easy to follow;
- when they used hand gestures it punctuated their message.

Later in the day, another group of ten takes the stage to introduce themselves. The audience is then asked to notice the types of behaviours that do not work particularly well up front (of course, it is done in general terms, and even those in the group who had introduced themselves participate in the exercise).

Again, here is a short list of responses:

- when they moved on the stage it was distracting;
- when they made eye contact I felt uncomfortable;
- when they tried to be passionate I felt they were trying too hard to sell me on what they were saying;
- their natural way of moving didn't seem to match what they were saying;
- when they disclosed something of themselves I felt embarrassed;
- when they tried to be funny, they weren't.

The point is that there is no single set of techniques that work on stage—there are techniques that work in some situations, for some trainers, depending on the content. For example, sometimes personal disclosure helps lead students to share more about themselves, which may be necessary to the desired outcome; at other times it is inappropriate and serves no purpose. Some trainers have developed skills outside training that allow them to get away with certain behaviours on stage—but only because they have become *natural* to that trainer. Humour is a great example: some people have never developed the ability to be funny, and people who are not naturally funny should not try to be so on stage without some development of that type of skill. But whatever behaviours we choose, they need to be appropriate to the content we are teaching. Having a serious tone of voice (which some trainers have naturally) is just not going to work when delivering content which you hope will relax or entertain an audience.

Thus, the behaviours we use on stage, and which will be focused upon in this book, need to meet three criteria:

(1) they must be behaviours that we can execute naturally and comfortably;

(2) they must be appropriate for the situation; and

(3) they must be congruent with the content or message.

THE THREE ESSENTIAL QUALITIES OF THE TOP PROFESSIONAL TRAINER

Whatever it is that a trainer does to capture attention and effectively convey a message, it will be based on the skills and knowledge that form the three essential qualities found in top professional trainers, presenters and lecturers. These three qualities are:

(1) a broad range and flexibility of behaviours—what can convincingly and naturally be done in the communication context;

(2) a heightened sensitivity to, and awareness of, the effects of the trainer's behaviours on the individual learner's experience; and

(3) the cohesive organisation of subject material—in other words, the ability to organise material so that when it is expressed verbally, it makes sense and is made relevant.

These three general qualities have come from my observations and analysis of the experiences I have had working with top professional trainers. Let's take each in turn.

Range and flexibility of the trainer's behaviour

What we as trainers can do on stage, or in front of a class, is based solely on the range of expression and behaviour available to us. Only the behaviours that can convincingly be manifested in everyday situations are those that will be available when working in training sessions. There is no way to be a different person, with different natural behaviours, by coming to a standing position to talk. Uninteresting people will be uninteresting trainers unless they take steps to become interesting people. People whose behaviour encourages others to feel incompetent will become trainers who make many others feel incompetent. If we do not listen to others in our family, we will not likely listen to students in a classroom.

If we observe outstanding trainers, one component of their excellence is the broad and appropriate range of behaviours and expressions they bring from their own experiences in life into the classroom. For example, if you want to become more precise in your gestures on stage, those new gestures need to be developed in your personal life, and over a period of time. It is not enough to explain a physical technique: how to stand, or how to make eye contact. If the behaviours are not natural, they look acted, appear stilted, are sometimes silly and are always incongruent.

One thing I know for certain is that *there is no way to improve your performance on stage while working on stage.* The myth that experience on stage is the best path to becoming a competent trainer simply doesn't make sense. A lot of trainers who confused their audiences twenty years ago are still confusing them today. *Through repetition we only get better at what we already know how to do.* And on stage, you cannot focus on your outcomes and on your performance at the same time. Most of us have, no doubt, had the experience of trying some new 'technique' only to lose everything else that was good about our performance.

What we do, what we can do, on stage merely reflects what we have learned to do in other communication contexts. As I said recently to a group of trainers attending a lecture in Melbourne: If you bore people around the dinner table, you will do that even better on stage.

Knowledge of the learner's experience

There is a marked difference between the trainer who is aware of the effect of their presentation on the learner and the trainer who is blind to it. A trainer who has an appropriate range of behaviours for their training situation, but who lacks awareness of the effects of their presentation on individuals within the audience, will still, at best, be hit or miss with their outcomes. The best trainer is sensitive to, and aware of, the actual experience of the learner—the experience of the individual who is the recipient of the means and methods of the trainer's communication.

A trainer develops this knowledge of the learner's experience in two distinct ways. First, they take time to reflect on their own learning experiences, in order to learn from that perspective. Some trainers even choose to regularly enter learning situations and pursue learning goals simply for the sake of staying in touch with this 'experience of learning' from the learner's perspective. If a trainer remembers the frustration of being confused, they are likely to take measured steps to not create confusion in their own audiences. If a trainer remembers the embarrassment of being called on unexpectedly, they are not likely to unexpectedly call on others.

Second, the inquisitive trainer develops knowledge about the learning experience of others by studying the phenomenon. There is a large and growing knowledge base about human behaviour, much of that dealing with motivation and learning. For instance, we know that an individual's past experiences, personality, values, gender and age—to name only a few—affect how they will respond to the various methods used in a course to deliver content, or to develop new skills.

Coherence

The third essential quality of the top trainer is their ability to organise their knowledge of the content into a coherent message that makes sense. Not possessing this skill can, and often does, lead to confusion and diminished learning. Sometimes even the trainer is confused. Of course, if the trainer also lacks awareness of the learner's experience (as discussed above), they don't even know that the audience is confused. Competent trainers and communicators make sense—they have learned how to organise subject knowledge so that it is logically sequenced, orderly, united and aesthetically whole.

TOWARDS BECOMING
A TOP TRAINER

All the skills in the above domains are difficult to define and talk about, so it's easy to understand why so many attempts are made to boil these skills down to simple 'techniques'. But in this book, we are going to directly tackle the complexities of this profession. We are going to address hard questions and, through analysis, see if we can come up with honest and appropriate answers rather than quick-fix techniques.

To help us begin, I have analysed the performance of successful trainers and communicators—trainers, lecturers, managers, counsellors and lawyers—in order to classify what it is that they know, and do, to consistently produce results. I focused not only on those who exhibit excellent skills, but also on those who have found the means to continue to improve their existing competencies. Observation of these exemplars has helped formulate an approach to training that you can use yourself to become a top trainer.

Do you want to gain and sustain the attention of your audiences? Then you need to be perceived of as an interesting person. You need to have a range of behaviours and expressions that match your message. Your message will need to be coherent, and you will need to gain enough experience with human diversity in learning situations to take action with the appropriate responses. There are no simple answers.

Training skills are evolutionary

Improvements in your skill as a trainer do not happen overnight, nor are they likely to be based on any single new insight. Changes evolve over time and require two simultaneous responses. The first is learning: studying, observing, experiencing, with the express intention of increasing the range of accessible behaviours in social and learning situations, and becoming sensitised to the learning experience of the individual student. The second is practising these new skills: choosing to consciously pay attention to, learn from and try new behaviours in personal interactions, at home, at work and socially. Only then can you truly begin to expand the repertoire of skills and knowledge that you bring to an audience.

What is it that we as trainers could be doing in our lives that might lead us to be better trainers? What do we need to know? What do we need to think about? What are the differences that make a difference? These are questions we need to think about.

LOOKING BACK
BEFORE MOVING ON

In this chapter we encountered all the major themes to be covered in the rest of this book. We first established definitional boundaries, noting that diversity is a multi-dimensional feature of the trainer's world, relating not only the trainer's skills, but also to the audience, environment and type of content we teach. We discussed the problematic nature of simple training techniques, and then introduced the three essential qualities found in top professional trainers and others who use communication skills to manage the learning and change process. And finally, we noted that the skills of a trainer are developed in an evolutionary way. Training is an art that develops over time, as life-experiences and knowledge influence a trainer's perceptions and behaviours. There are no one-time quick methods to gaining mastery as a trainer—but there is a path of development that, if adhered to, can lead to mastery.

The remaining chapters explore the detailed knowledge that can lead to the development of the three essential qualities of the top professional trainer, preparing us to look at how these qualities can be applied in real-time training situations. There's a lot to learn, but with this chapter behind us, we are ready to proceed.

CHAPTER

the learner — the components of individual differences

INTRODUCTION

Professional trainers are in the business of *other people*. They are in the business of *changing or modifying human behaviour*—affecting the skills or actions, the thoughts, and even the emotions and feelings of other people. In the study of human behaviour, the rule is *diversity—people are different from one another*: they think differently, feel differently, behave differently and respond to the same situation differently. This chapter is dedicated to increasing our understanding of human behaviour, and in particular, the behaviour of our students.

The goal of this chapter is to develop a deeper understanding of the behaviours our students exhibit in learning situations by examining some of the factors that relate to the diversity of human behaviour. What is it that makes some students so receptive to experiential learning exercises, while others run for cover? Why can some be held in rapt attention, while others sit picking their cuticles, daydreaming? Why do some never ask questions, while others are thunderously expressive? The intention is to create *sensitivity* to that which motivates both the internal and external behaviour of the student. To achieve this we need to explore the subjective experiences of learning for the students who sit in our classroom. What is it like for adults to engage in learning activities?

But to begin, let's start with a scenario to help describe the complexity of the situation we face as trainers and the puzzle we will later have to solve. A trainer stands on stage. Pick any few moments out of the training day—maybe the start of the session, right after morning tea. Remember, the trainer is a single entity—one person—and one person can only do one thing. Whatever the trainer does, it is seen and heard by every member of the class at the same time. In this instance, imagine that the trainer welcomes the class back from the break, asks them to settle down, and tells them there is a quiz lying face down on their desk that will be used to review what they learned in the morning session. What is intriguing is not what the trainer has just done, but how the students individually respond to what the trainer has just done. A woman in the front row flushes with embarrassment and looks down, a man sits back in his chair and crosses his arms defiantly, another student starts thinking about why she didn't ask for clarity on a confusing point before the break, some could care less about taking the quiz. As the quiz begins, someone calls the trainer over and whispers that he isn't feeling well and needs to leave.

What a multiplicity of behaviours! This is specifically the kind of complexity trainers have to deal with—complexity that arises out of everything they do. An action has one meaning for one student, another meaning for another student.

In an ideal world trainers and students, or managers and employees, would share equal, although different, responsibilities for the change or learning process. Trainers would present accurate, coherently organised information and facilitate exercises that logically lead to the building of new skills. The trainer would have a set of skills to use in order to build and maintain rapport with many different types of people all at one time. The trainer would be responsible for generating and sustaining interest in the subject. They would know how to get all their students to feel comfortable participating in exercises. At all times they would be perceived as credible, honest, intelligent and capable. The student, on the other hand, would be responsible for—and capable of—doing what is necessary to learn. They would listen and take effective notes, they would study the materials for reinforcement, they would ask questions for clarity, they would leave their personal problems at home, they would be respectful when the trainer is talking, and they would practise. *In the student's ideal world all trainers would be competent, and in the trainer's ideal world all students would be the same.*

After all my years of training and of working with trainers, I have learned that we do not live in an ideal world. Some trainers (or all trainers at some time—including me), despite the best intentions, confuse the hell out of some students, put others to sleep and irritate a bunch of others. Some students, despite their need to learn what the trainer has to teach, disrupt the training process with tangential questions, annoy other students who want to learn and won't do their homework. One human being, locked in a room all by themselves, would exhibit more complexity in their behaviours than science can explain. Put any two or more human beings together in any context—let alone a learning context—and the combinations of causes and effects for behaviours escalate beyond imagination. Trainers are smack-dab in the middle of this complexity.

Everything we do, every factor that contributes to our moment-by-moment behaviours—our gestures, facial expressions, posture, tone of voice, words and so on—*impact differently* on each student. In a later chapter we will address how we shall deal with this complexity, but for the moment our focus is on identifying some of the key factors that determine these individual differences.

The benefits of perceiving individual differences

The benefits of being able to perceive the factors driving the individual student's behaviours are manyfold. First, we have a far better chance of building valuable rapport with more members of the audience and achieving a higher percentage of successes in the classroom.

Second, we can be better satisfied that we are accurately interpreting the different reactions of students during the training program; so called aberrant behaviours do not look so aberrant with a well-informed view.

Third, we will have the ability to be more responsive and take better-informed action to influence the diverse behaviours of students. Fourth, we will have a rationale for our choice of methods that is based on an understanding of the effects of those methods on the students. Before we as trainers can ever begin to understand what is right, wrong, good or bad about training methods, we need to understand what is considered to be right, wrong, good or bad about training for the learner.

Lastly, we will have a rationale for our own choice of behaviours and expressions—be they to do with dress, language, references, anecdotes or whatever. The more we are able to 'read' the reactions of the students, and understand why certain responses are occurring, the better we are able to make appropriate choices for our own behaviours. Without knowledge of the effects of our behaviours on the students, we are prone to making many mistakes and creating problems in the training environment, some of which are difficult, if not impossible, to correct.

How shall we approach this subject?

Unfortunately, our experiences are not always the best source of accurate information on this subject—our perceptions, of course, being coloured by our own likes, dislikes, values and personalities. We are looking for objective knowledge that helps us make more sense of our observations of, and experiences with, other people when we are training or teaching. The best source of information to improve our understanding of the differences we observe in our students' behaviours is academic literature. This literature contains rigorously tested and objective theories on the subject of human diversity. To this end, we are going to review some recent theories related to human behaviour.

The study of human behaviour encompasses a vast set of theories from many different academic disciplines. However, there are four central theories relating to individual differences in human behaviour that have been instrumental in developing the effectiveness of top professional trainers—trainers who produce consistent results with diverse audiences, and with little or no resistance from individual students. The concepts springing from these four theories relate to action—what the student will comfortably do, or will avoid doing, in learning situations.

The first are the theories that relate to the study of *personality traits* and the effects of personality on behaviour. Different people have very different biologically, socially and culturally constructed personalities. Your everyday experiences have no doubt led you to the realisation that an introvert will react and behave very differently to an extrovert in a training environment. Of course, introverts and extroverts can and do participate fully in trainings and achieve outcomes, but what gets them there will be different. Theories of personality assist us in developing an understanding of the reactions of our students to our choice of methods and form of expression.

Theories related to *values and preferences* constitute the second critical knowledge factor when developing an understanding of individual differences. Values define what is important to a person, and what in a learning situation the person will decide is right and wrong, good and bad, normal and not normal about the content, the methods or your presentation.

The third set of theories which particularly help us understand individual difference are to do with *styles of thinking*. The theory of thinking styles assists us in understanding the preferred ways in which different students approach learning and use the content we teach in our courses.

The fourth set of useful theories relate to the effects of *past experiences and memories* on the interpretation of current situations. Students enter training environments with rich histories, and those histories filter their perceptions of current situations.

If we are able to interpret our students' behaviours through the lenses of personality, values and preferences, thinking styles and past experience, we have the unique opportunity to accurately assess the effectiveness of our own choice of actions in the classroom environment.

What can realistically be done in this chapter?

I have spent nearly every day of the past three years studying the academic literature on just one small aspect of human behaviour—namely, the phenomenon of emotion. Although I today feel well versed on the theories surrounding that subject, I also know that there are a myriad of other related pieces of work I have not begun to explore. With academic research you learn quickly that you cannot know everything. I also know from experience how much literature exists surrounding our four main topics of interest.

Let me try to give you just a very brief example. One theory of personality is proposed by Myers and is based on Carl Jung's theory of types. In Myer's theory there are sixteen different personality types, resulting from all of the combinations of two ways of perceiving (sensing versus intuition), two ways of judging (thinking versus feeling), two ways of dealing with self and others (introversion versus extroversion) and two ways of dealing with the outer world (judgment versus perception). Then there is Gregorc's theory, which takes a more cognitive approach to types. Gregorc has proposed four main types, or styles, based on the possible combinations of just two polarities—concrete versus abstract and sequential versus random.

Other theories of personality types are context-specific. For instance, the theories espoused by Renzulli and Smith look at personality in the domain of education. They suggest that individuals have various learning styles, with each style corresponding to a method of teaching—projects, drill and recitation, peer teaching, discussion, teaching games, independent study, programmed instruction, lecture and simulation. Holland, on the other hand, has taken a more job-related orientation. He proposed six styles that are used as a basis for understanding job interests—realistic, investigative, artistic, social, enterprising and conventional.

The theories represented here are by no means a full representation of the existing theories within each of these domains—very far from it. There are many, many theories available which benefit our understanding of the learner. One very important point to keep in mind as we continue is that you will interpret the behaviour of the students differently depending upon which theory you use as a perceptual filter. You will interpret a students' behaviour differently if you 'see' them through the lens of the Myers theory instead of the lens of the Gregorc theory. The choice of theories and theorists reviewed here was guided by the objectives of this book, and are those theories that I have found which significantly inform the observations and experience of trainers and lecturers. But to reiterate, it is important to remember that this review is an extremely small subset of the information available to you through a good university library.

But writing like this starts to sound more like a doctoral thesis, and does little to directly educate us in ways that affect our practice as trainers. Therefore, the intention here is not to review the corpus of literature on human personality, values and so on. The aim is to introduce the key factors of these phenomena that relate directly to your experience of students in the classroom. After absorbing the ideas in this chapter, you should be able to say, "I understand why role-playing exercises threaten some students" or "I understand why some students want to express their own ideas during the class session."

PERSONALITY TRAITS AND BEHAVIOUR

The first major factor related to individual behavioural differences is based on the concept of personality. The literature informs us that human personality is developed from influences that are both biologically and environmentally based. Personality traits show up in early infancy, persist later in life, and have a hereditary basis. These traits are highly stable and are not likely to change.

The training job typically requires that the trainer be able to facilitate learning for anyone, regardless of their personality type. The importance for the trainer of understanding personality types lies in its implication for the design of a course, the choice of methods and how they will be perceived by the different personalities in the audience. The student's personality affects how they filter information, what they pay attention to, and how they interpret that information. What one students perceives as fun, another—having a different personality—will perceive as threatening. Remember, *different student behaviours are the norm, not the exception*. We are interested in the kinds of behaviours we can expect from each of the major personality types, and the likely reactions to what it is that we, as trainers, are doing.

Models of human behaviour can be used constructively or destructively

Like any model, personality models are a double-edged sword— they can be used for destructive as well as constructive purposes. On the destructive side, personality typing can be used to 'pigeon-hole' students. One effect of this is that the trainer then holds different expectations for students with different personality types. This would be limiting to the trainer and possibly damaging to the student. On the other hand, the more we understand about what is driving the motivation and behaviour of the individual student, the better equipped we are to make informed choices that enhance the likelihood that all the diverse people in our sessions will learn.

I personally do not test my students for personality type, nor do I recommend the practice. Tests provide information that you really cannot do anything with when you are in real-time training situations; if anything, such specific information about each individual would likely interfere with your performance. It is also a highly simplified way of looking a very complex organism. I have seen trainers get too wrapped up in personality typing as a way of informing their practice. For me, I have used this information only as a set of perceptual filters, a way of 'seeing' my students' behaviours, or likely reactions, to guide my own choices for training. I do not ever apply this information to any particular student.

Jung's theory of personality type and the MBTI

Many personality models have been developed, right from the beginning of recorded history. However, there still is no 'true' model of human personality. Most researchers assume that human personality is too complex to ever be modelled perfectly. And yet, the models that have been developed do seem to approximately and reasonably model human personality to a degree of accuracy that makes them useful and predictive.

The personality system I have chosen to introduce is known formally as "Jung's theory of personality type". It was first developed by Carl Jung in the early 1920s, but it has been recently resurrected and made into a practical instrument by Myers and Briggs. You may have heard of the "Myers-Briggs Type Indicator" or the "MBTI". The MBTI is a particular test that is used for personality typing.

In a nutshell, this model of personality typing essentially assumes that our whole personality can be divided into four independent areas or scales. These are:

- energising;
- attending;
- deciding; and
- living.

Within each scale we have a *preference* for one of two opposites that define that scale. Combined, this makes for a total of sixteen unique personality types.

In each of the four scales, every person usually has a preference for one of the two opposing choices. But this does not mean that they do one at the exclusion of the other—people can go the other way, given the circumstances. *Behaviour is contextual.*

It is important to note that the following descriptions are simplifications—almost over-simplifications—of complex, rigorous, deep and hard-to-understand descriptions presented by Jung. Yet for the purpose of opening our minds to one phenomenon that determines individual diversity they serve our purpose.

In order to 'see' these personality traits in your students, both in what they say, and in what they do, I have assembled a list of preferred vocabulary for each trait. These terms and phrases are associated with each of the preferences on the four scales. By reading the words on the left and right for each scale you will get a sense of the different methods that a student might prefer, or the way in which they would like to have information presented and organised. This list, of course, crosses many of life's contexts; it is not exclusive to the training environment. These lists will also help you to better understand what the four scales actually measure or denote. I have also included the percentages of the total population (in Western society) who hold those preferences. It is also important to note that these four scales are essentially independent (or orthogonal; meaning they lack any statistical correlation).

The four personality scales

Energising relates to whether a person draws energy from the factors found in the outside world of people, activities or things, or by drawing energy from their internal world of ideas, emotions or impressions. The two ends of the scale are denoted by the traits of *extroversion* and *introversion*. Energising is only one facet of this scale, which is actually a measure of a person's whole orientation towards either the inner world or the outer world.

Extroversion–introversion preferred vocabulary

Extroversion, E (75% of population)	**Introversion, I (25% of population)**
sociability	territoriality
breadth	depth
external	internal
extensive	intensive
interaction	concentration
expenditure of energy	conservation of energy
interest in external events	interest in internal reaction
multiplicity of relationships	limited relationships

Attending refers to what a person pays attention to. At one end of the continuum there is *sensing*, used by individuals who have a preference for taking in information through the five senses and noticing what is actual. At the other end there is *intuition*, used by those with a preference for taking in information through the 'sixth sense' and noticing what might be.

Sensing–intuition preferred vocabulary

Sensing, S (75% of population)	**Intuition, N (25% of population)**
experience	hunches
past	future
realistic	speculative
perspiration	inspiration
actual	possible
down-to-earth	head-in-clouds
utility	fantasy
fact	fiction
practicality	ingenuity
sensible	imaginative

The third continuum relates to *deciding*. Some individuals make decisions based on *thinking*. These individuals have a preference for organising and structuring information to decide in a logical, objective way. Other individuals make decisions based on *feeling*. They exhibit a preference for organising and structuring information in order to decide in a personal, value-oriented way.

Thinking–feeling preferred vocabulary

Thinking, T (50% of population)	Feeling, F (50% of population)
objective	subjective
principles	values
policy	social values
laws	extenuating circumstances
criterion	intimacy
firmness	persuasion
impersonal	personal
justice	humane
categories	harmony
standards	good or bad
critique	appreciate
analysis	sympathy
allocation	devotion

Living refers to the lifestyle a person adopts. *Judgment* is the preference for some individuals. These people have a preference for living a planned and organised life. On the other hand, *perception* defines those who have a preference for living a spontaneous and flexible life. The distinction depends on whether the individual prefers an open-ended lifestyle or one that is planned and controlled.

Judgment–perception preferred vocabulary

Judgment, J (50% of population)	Perception, P (50% of population)
settled	pending
decided	gather more data

Judgment–perception preferred vocabulary—continued

Judgment, J (50% of population)	Perception, P (50% of population)
fixed	flexible
plan ahead	adapt as you go
run one's life	let life happen
closure	open options
decision-making	treasure hunting
planned	open-ended
completed	emergent
decisive	tentative
wrap it up	something will turn up
urgency	there's plenty of time
deadline!	what deadline?
get the show on the road	let's wait and see…

Now what does all this mean to us as trainers? Well, first it points to the very complicated task we engage in when we stand up in front of a group with some notion of teaching. Second, it makes us aware that we must somehow accommodate the various preferences that these personality types indicate will be present in different students. For example, if 'judgers' want closure (meaning well-defined instructions, time frames and so on) but it is not the most appropriate approach for achieving our training outcomes, we will need to either change our approach, or get these students to be comfortable with their innate preferences not being met in our classroom. We will revisit this topic in a later chapter and explore our training options to minimise or neutralise the effects of student personality differences.

A thought exercise for trainers

As a means of absorbing the impact of these individual differences, the following is a excellent exercise. Start by using either the descriptions for each of the four scales or the preferred vocabulary lists and ask yourself this question: *What are the needs of a person with this personality and these preferences in a training environment?* For example, you might note that extroverts need time and opportunities to express themselves, whereas introverts might need choices and control over how they will participate. If you do this exercise for each of the eight distinct types, you will develop a good understanding of how individual students are affected by the various methods or approaches to training you use. In this you are not looking for 'right' answers or rules, but a new way of organising what you know about training methods and approaches.

A second thought question is: *What might inhibit the learning process for each of these types?* Think of the methods, material organisation, timing, trainer behaviours and so on that would 'turn off', annoy or threaten each of the personality types. If you do this exercise in earnest you will find that virtually everything you know how to do will 'turn off', annoy, or threaten someone. But take heart! There are ways to neutralise the effects of the various personality traits. (And it will be the subject of Chapter 6.) Even so, you still need to realise that every approach has the potential to interfere with the learning process of someone in your audience.

A third thought question to ask is: *What kinds of behaviours would each type exhibit in a training if their needs weren't being met?* Now, of course, everyone is a blend of their position on all four scales, but this is an exercise. If you had a whole class of introverts, excluding their other personality dimensions, how would they behave, or 'act out', if their needs weren't met? Would they leave, ask questions, become talkative, daydream? What would they do?

A fourth and final question is: *How would a course be designed to best teach a given subject to each of the eight personality profiles?* Would you lecture, use games or processes, do outdoor activities, have reading exercises, do group work, allow independent study or use other methods?

It is important to look objectively at our current training methods and identify who is, and who is not, likely to be served by the approaches being used. And if for whatever reason the methods need to remain the same, we need to ask how we might make those chosen methods appropriate and comfortable for all of the members of the class. Together we will explore these questions, in Chapter 5.

Trainings have personalities too

A sidenote for those who are independent trainers who attract audiences from either the general public or corporate clients. Note that when you write about your courses, you unconsciously are telling the prospective client something about the 'personality' of the training—something about *your* personality. For example, if you mention that the class will use role-plays and games and exercises, you are setting a stage. You will be likely to attract only those students who, prior to coming to your training, feel comfortable with those methods. An introvert will not be likely to show up, because they have no knowledge of how safely these exercises will be conducted. They will not take the risk. I am like this. I do not attend a lot of trainings unless I know that the style of presentation suits my personality style. I do not always want to put myself in a position of being uncomfortable. So although the brochure tells me you will be covering the latest research on human brain function—which interests me—and that the material will be presented with the latest alpha-accelerated-yoga-hoo-ha technology, I will not be there!

You, too, have a personality, and it is reflected in your published materials, trainings and in your approaches. Beware, though: your own personality type can be a liability. Master trainers have learned to understand their own personality traits—their limitations and strengths—and have chosen to increase their flexibility and sensitivity to the values of other personality traits. In my trainings I like my intuitor types: personally, I may not like them in my home, but as a professional trainer I have learned to value their unique way of seeing and acting in the world so I have developed ways of accommodating their unique personality in my classrooms.

VALUES AND PREFERENCES

Another component of the brew of individual differences relates to the notion of human values. Values determine what will motivate the student—how the student wants to, or will, spend their time. According to Woodsmall and James (writing in 1988) "Values are how people choose and evaluate their actions." (p. 11) As researcher Morris Massey would say, values are central to what the individual thinks is good and bad, right and wrong, normal and not normal. People use their values to make judgments—to judge you, to judge what you do, to judge what you say, to judge what they will do in response to you. Their values determine what they believe to be true.

Human values are formed early in life based on our experiences. As trainers we are concerned with what the individual student perceives as normal or not normal in training environments and in the behaviours of the trainer. In this way, values add another dimension to what we have discussed about personality. For instance, you may have an extroverted student in your classroom who is, under normal circumstances, quite outgoing, but who perceives games and activities as *not normal* for a training situation. His or her values might indicate that training is supposed to be performed with the trainer standing behind the podium, reading lecture notes, maybe showing a slide or two, and providing handouts. This is what is 'normal' and 'right' and 'good' about training to that individual. To some people, learning should be 'fun'; to others, having fun is not learning. You may consider that trainings should be fun, but think again: if it is perceived as not normal by half your audience, you have a problem.

Like the subject of personality, the literature available on the subject of values is vast. Again, values influence all facets of behaviour and choice. However, for me personally, the study of values has been most influential in understanding one particular phenomenon observed in the classroom—namely, why students of different ages perceive the training's content, methods and my own performance in such different ways. The researcher who introduced this notion of *generational values* is Dr Morris Massey.

There is no way I know to do justice to Dr Massey's contribution to our understanding of the behaviours and motivation of students in the classroom, so I would recommend that you get the full impact of this information from Dr Massey himself. He has produced a video training session which is available commercially. Each year my *Training to Train* students spend an evening with these tapes; a vibrant discussion always ensues.

The point stressed by Dr Massey, which we would all know from experience, is that we cannot know or generalise values by factors of economics, background or education. People are all very different. But what Dr Massey has shown is that to the degree that people in a similar age bracket have experienced similar significant events in their lifetime—such as world wars, the great depression, landing a person on the moon—there will be a general and common value set. How members of that generation relate to the world will show common themes, although individuals within those groups will vary on many other levels.

Have you ever wondered why audience members of different ages respond to your trainings in different fashions? In regard to training and learning, members of different generations have had certain experiences with education through the school system. This is the source of their values surrounding what is right and wrong, good and bad in learning environments. And the experience of learning and school was very different for those students who went to school in the 1930s than those who went to school in the 1970s. Some generations experienced learning as a passive process, being told what they need to *know*. Other generations were educated at times when experiential learning was emphasised; it was a more active process. They were told what they needed to *do*. So if you suggest to a sixty-five-year-old student that they should meditate before studying to increase their effectiveness, they are likely to think you have lost your mind.

Values affect the students' perceptions of you

How you dress, your gender, your age, your accent, your credentials are all filtered through the values of the members of your audience. If you are lecturing to a group of older students, having a university degree is likely to be important, but so too is where you got your degree. To an audience of younger people, this will not carry the same significance. They have been raised in an environment in which many credible and well-known people do not have university degrees.

Values affect the students' perceptions of the content

Do you know that to some people, in some age groups, computers are not normal? Nor are people who use them. In my generation jet airplanes are as familiar as buses; however, some people from earlier generations just don't trust airplanes. They say things like, "If God had wanted us to fly he'd have given us wings." How a student will perceive the content of your training will be affected by their values. Let's face it, some people believed that using calculators would destroy a generation of those learning mathematics—and they still do!

THINKING STYLES

A third set of theories that educate our perceptions of the learner relate to a person's *thinking style*. Robert Sternberg in 1994 wrote *Thinking styles: theory and assessment at the interface between intelligence and personality*. In this paper, he discusses the notion of thinking styles which are conceptualised as an interface between intelligence and personality. Thinking styles, like personality, vary between individuals and assist our understanding of the different approaches to learning that trainers observe in their students.

In his article, Sternberg specifically addresses the implications of thinking styles for test-taking, but the work is easy to generalise to other learning activities. He argues that approaches to testing "inadvertently reward students who show certain profiles of thinking styles, while punishing students who show other profiles." (p. 169) The same can be said for other methodological and evaluation choices made by the trainer.

An introduction to Sternberg's theory

Sternberg emphasises that a thinking style is not an ability. A thinking style is defined as an individual's preferred way of "expressing or using one or more abilities. Two or more people at the same level of ability may nevertheless have very different styles." (p. 170)

Like abilities, but unlike personality types, these thinking styles are not fully formed at birth. Like abilities, they are, to a large degree, a function of the environment and can be developed. Thinking styles can change with context; some people approach different situations with a different thinking style. Perhaps how they solve problems on the home front is different to how they solve a similar problem while in a work environment. Sternberg also notes that thinking styles may change with age, and suggests that at different stages of life various thinking styles are preferred.

He tells the story of three college roommates. Because these stories translate easily to the types of students we confront as trainers, they are quoted verbatim from the Sternberg paper.

> Consider three college chums (all of them real people). The friends—Alex, Bob, and Charles (only one of the names is unchanged)—seemed to be remarkably similar intellectually when they entered college. All had almost identical Scholastic Aptitude Test scores, similar high school academic averages, and similar strengths and weaknesses in their intellectual abilities. For example, all three were more verbal than quantitative, and better in abstract inductive reasoning than in spatial ability. Thus, in terms of standard theories of intelligence, such as those of Spearman (1927) or Thurstone (1938), the three roommates seemed quite similar. Even in terms of more modern, diversified theories, such as those of Gardner (1983) or Sternberg (1985), the roommates would

not have varied very much. Moreover, today, all three roommates are fairly successful in their jobs and have achieved some recognition for their work. Thus, one could not attribute differences among the three to motivational differences alone.

Yet, looking beyond the intellectual similarities of the three roommates, one cannot help but notice some salient variations that have profoundly affected their lives. Consider some of the differences among them.

Alex, today a lawyer, could be characterized (and would characterize himself) as fairly conventional, rule-bound, and comfortable with details and structure. He does well what others tell him to do, as a lawyer must, and has commented to me that his idea of perfection would be a technically flawless legal document or contract whereby those who sign on the dotted line are bound to the terms of the contract without loopholes, unless they want to pay extra legal fees. In a nutshell, Alex is a follower of systems, and follows them extremely well. Even in school, he showed the same tendencies. He was happiest when given assignments and tests that were well-structured and clearly circumscribed. He was less happy in his senior year when working on a senior project that he, rather than his teachers, had to structure, in which the boundaries of the assignment were only vaguely circumscribed.

Bob, today a university professor, is quite different stylistically from Alex. He is fairly unconventional, and unlike Alex, dislikes following or even dealing with other people's rules. Moreover, he has relatively few rules of his own. Although he has some basic principles that he views as invariants, he tends not to take rules very seriously, viewing them as conveniences that are meant to be changed or even broken as the situation requires. Bob dislikes details, and generally is comfortable working within a structure only if it is his own. He does certain things well, but usually only if they are things he really wants to do. His idea of intellectual perfection would be the generation of an idea and a compelling demonstration that the idea is correct, or at least useful. In brief, Bob is a creator of systems, and has designed various psychological theories that reflect his interest in system creation. In school, as well, he was happiest with independent assignments and projects, and liked the least highly structured assignments and tests. The more freedom he was given to pursue his own interests and ways of doing things, the happier he was.

Charles, today a psychotherapist, is also fairly unconventional. Like Bob, he dislikes others' rules, but unlike Bob, he has a number of his own. He tends to be indifferent to details. He likes working within certain structures, which need not be his own, but the structures have to be ones that he has adjudged to be correct and suitable. Charles does well what he wants to do. His idea of perfection would be a difficult but correct psychological diagnosis, followed by an optimal psychotherapeutic intervention. In sum, Charles is a judge of systems. He showed his interest, perhaps passion, for judging early in his career, when, as a college student, he constructed a test (which we called the "Charles Test") to give to others—especially to dates—that judged the suitability of their values and standards. Charles was also editor of the college course critique, a role in which he took responsibility for the evaluation of all undergraduate courses at the college. In college, Charles was happiest doing analytical essays, especially those that allowed him to point out the strengths and weaknesses of various ways of approaching intellectual problems.

What we can see from these examples is that three students with almost identical levels and patterns of abilities nevertheless have very different preferred ways of expressing these abilities. (pp. 171–2)

We can imagine, as trainers, the different ways that Alex, Bob and Charles would respond to our choice of methods, of the 'logic level' of the information we present, and the ways in which they would respond to the types of tests and activities we use to measure their performance. In reading the above vignettes you may have found yourself more easily relating to one of the three characters— the behaviours and thoughts of one of the characters may have made more sense to you personally. You may also have noticed, if you are now a trainer or manager, that your current style might be a problem for one or two of the individuals.

An important notion for all of us to remember when working with other people is stated clearly when Sternberg notes:

People's proclivities toward certain styles must be distinguished from their ability to implement these styles. Someone may like doing things a certain way, but not be very good at it. For example, most of us have had students who want to express themselves creatively, but who seem not to have developed the creative talent to make these expressions all that the student (and we, as teachers) would like them to be. Or people may not want to capitalize on their most outstanding abilities because they do not feel comfortable while exercising them. For example, a potentially creative person may never realize her creativity due to a lack of a desire to stand out from the crowd. Thus, we must distinguish abilities from people's desire to exploit these abilities. (p. 174)

This adds another critical piece of knowledge for our perceptions of the student that assists our understanding of their behaviours in the classroom.

Sternberg's theory of thinking styles—a theory of mental self-government

Sternberg cleverly uses the model of US government to make clear the components of his model of thinking styles. Had he been an Australian researcher he might perhaps have used our government as a model. He calls his process *mental self-government* and says, "At the heart of the theory of mental self-government is the notion that people need somehow to govern or manage their everyday activities, in school as well as outside. There are many ways of doing so; whenever possible, people choose styles of managing themselves with which they are comfortable." (pp. 173–4) However, he also notes that people are to some degree flexible in their use of thinking styles. And they do try "with varying degrees of success, to adapt themselves to the stylistic demands of a given situation." (p. 174)

In classroom situations learners will have a preference for their own style of thinking, and this will affect how they approach the various tasks you set for them. What follows is a brief discussion of the various components of the learner's thinking style.

The three functions of mental self-government

Just as the US and Australian governments' structures have three branches, each with different functions, so too do thinking styles. Each of these functions are represented in the stories of Alex, Bob and Charles. Sternberg uses the terms associated with these functions of government to label the three functions of mental self-government; the *legislative*, *executive* and *judicial*.

(1) The *legislative style* characterises people who enjoy the planning stage of problem solving. These people like to have the chance to establish their own approach to a project. This might include coming up with the project, developing an outline and organising the material accordingly. For the legislative person, the creativity rests in the planning and organising, not necessarily in the implementation of the project.

(2) Individuals with an *executive style* are implementers. These people prefer to follow already established systems. They are more comfortable with, and get more out of, successfully completing a project than generating the topic or determining the scope and organisation of the project. An individual with an executive style will tend to favour structured environments rather than an environment which requires personal initiative.

(3) As the name suggests, the *judicial style* is seen in those people who like to judge things. They prefer projects which require a large degree of evaluation and analysis. The chance to evaluate or compare and contrast alternatives in a project is perfect for the individual of this persuasion.

All three functions are involved with mental self-government and all coexist in most people, but it is important to note that one of these functions is likely to dominate; one function will be preferred over the alternatives.

The four forms of mental self-government

Governments have different forms—monarchic, hierarchic, oligarchic, anarchic. Sternberg uses these terms and their definitions to describe the four forms of mental self-government.

(1) The *monarchic form* can be described as a 'single-minded' approach. People following this form do not notice, or actively disregard, any obstacles that might prevent them from reaching a specified goal. Their approach to problem solving is tightly focused.

(2) The *hierarchic form* can be described as a 'prioritising' approach. People of this form are able to deal with a number of projects or goals at the same time. They realise that not all projects can be completed to the same level of satisfaction, and that some goals are more important than others. Their approach to problem solving is ordered and systematic.

(3) The *oligarchic form* also deals with multiple projects or goals, but does not prioritise them, giving each task the same level of importance instead. Oligarchic people experience difficulty and tension when assigning priorities to tasks. The oligarchic person often does not complete projects, due to an inability to distinguish the priorities of a range of projects and goals.

(4) The *anarchic form* reflects a random approach to projects and goals. Anarchic people prefer unstructured tasks, and are able to think outside of established conventions. They resist and cannot understand the need for authority, structure or regulation.

The two levels of mental self-government

Governments operate on two levels: the global and the local. So too do people's thinking styles.

(1) The person with a global style prefers the 'big' or 'macro' picture, ignoring to some extent, the details of a project. These people enjoy the conceptualisation of tasks but may not understand the detailed construction of the task or project.

(2) The person with the local style has a more pragmatic outlook, preferring to deal with the 'nuts and bolts' of a project. These people enjoy the precision of a project but may not understand the 'big picture'.

The two scopes of mental self-government

Just as governments deal with internal and external issues, so too do individuals.

(1) People with an internal style are more introverted and less confident in a social environment. These people prefer to work alone on projects and will resist cooperative projects.

(2) People with an external style are more extroverted and socially adept than internalists. These people enjoy cooperative work and will often seek out this type of project.

The two leanings of mental self-government

Individuals and governments are often characterised as being progressive or conservative. Sternberg uses this analogy to further examine the concept of mental self-government.

(1) People with a conservative style prefer structured, unambiguous environments. They prefer familiarity in their life and work, and like to minimise the effects of change.

(2) People with a progressive style enjoy ambiguous situations and prefer working and living outside existing regulated environments. These people become bored when a situation or project becomes static, and are therefore always searching out new challenges.

A mix of theories

You may have noticed that there are overlapping themes between Jung's theory of personality styles and Sternberg's thinking styles. If you are familiar with any of the many theories of learning styles you will note additional overlapping material. All of these models contain many similar components, but by arranging these pieces differently we 'see' and interpret human interactions in different ways, each affording a unique contribution. When I design a new course, or prepare myself for a presentation, I think about how my choices will affect, and be perceived by, the various personality types, value sets and styles of thinking that will be present in my audience.

PAST EXPERIENCE

A fourth significant factor that relates to individual differences in our students is their past experience, and specifically, their past experiences in learning situations. No two students come into the classroom with the same set of experiences. In addition to the role these experiences play in the development of a student's values, these past experiences significantly affect the feelings and emotions triggered by the environment you create, their beliefs about their general ability to learn and their perceptions of the difficulty of the tasks you set.

Your training environment and your methods of teaching trigger memories in students—memories of their experiences in learning situations in the past. For some students, past learning experiences may have been unpleasant, boring, embarrassing, even threatening. When they enter *your* environment these memories can be triggered and will affect their behaviour. This is one important reason why techniques such as the 'pouncing' technique discussed in Chapter 1 can be so destructive. For the student who has had the experience of being called out and embarrassed by a teacher, further use of this technique in a training can cause a very strong negative reaction.

For further exposure to this notion, recent research on the effect of memories on goal achievement can be found in Jefferson Singer and Peter Salovey's book, *The Remembered Self*. It is recommended reading for all trainers.

THE SUBJECTIVE EXPERIENCE OF LEARNING

In the preceding sections we have discussed four different phenomena that contribute to the individual differences we observe in our students. An understanding of these types of factors goes a long way towards helping us vicariously enter the actual experience of learning for the individual—the subjective experience. Have you ever been curious about how you would feel if you were a student in your own training session? This is something I've been curious about for many years, and it has led me to study the process of learning from this subjective perspective. How do the students *feel* when they are engaged in learning activities?

My PhD research was based on this type of question. I wanted to discover in what way emotions and feelings were experienced by adult learners as they pursued learning activities, and whether those emotions and feelings affect how they behaved in learning situations. The preliminary findings of that study are showing some interesting patterns, and although the analysis is not yet complete, there is good reason to explore some of the anticipated results with you. To understand how the study was conducted, and what was discovered, you will need just a cursory review of the current theories of emotion.

A brief history of the study of emotion and feelings

If we look closely at the theories that underpin our practice as adult educators and our understanding of the learning process of adults, we find that the source of those theories stem from the psychological sciences. From psychology, they are refined in the sub-area of educational psychology. It is the research in educational psychology that affects how we, as trainers, are taught to educate. In regard to the study of human emotion and feeling, psychology has a long history of failing to consider the effects of these phenomena. And to the degree that psychology has been remiss in studying this phenomenon, our own literature on adult learning and training reflects this same lacking.

This tradition of ignoring the study of emotion is owed in some measure to the work of the seventeenth-century philosopher, Rene Descartes. Descartes' work has had an enormous influence upon the intellectual community generally, and hence the psychological community. Regarding emotion, he argued they were *confusi status menis*—confused states of mind, or confused ideas. To Descartes, emotions as an information system were deceptive. His argument rested on the observation that emotions may lead a person to behaviour that is not in the person's own best interest. This argument diminished the status of emotions for nearly two centuries.

By the second half of the nineteenth century some theorists, most notably Charles Darwin and William James, were formulating rudimentary theories of emotion. This period marks the time when research on emotions began in earnest. Yet, until very recently, the currents of this research were fitful and uneven. The domination of the psychological scene by the behaviourists, led by B. F. Skinner in the middle of this century, further relegated emotions to a back seat in psychological inquiry. They considered that only objective behaviour, that which could be observed, could be studied with any accuracy. Therefore, emotions were placed out-of-bounds for scientific study.

The emergence of the cognitive sciences in the early 1960s was instrumental in turning the attention of psychology toward questions of the mind. During this period psychology was dominated by the assumption that cognition is the primary cause of behaviour. Although this paradigm fostered many advances, it also continued the relative neglect of other processes, such as emotion and motivation, as causes for behaviour.

In the past fifteen years, the fate of human emotions as a focus for research has undergone a sudden and dramatic change. They have come back to the centre stage of psychological inquiry. This trend is now evident in every sub-area of psychology.

What is an emotion?

Defining emotions is highly problematic for researchers—philosophers and psychologists have been trying to define emotions for at least 2,500 years. There are many reasons for this problem, but they are unimportant to our discussion. Yet one common aspect found in some recent theories directly relates to our understanding of the experience of our students. This is, namely, definitions that include the notion that emotions are responsible for directing the flow and type of action our students take. *Emotions are action readiness.* They allow the individual to adapt his or her behaviour to changing external or internal stimuli. In this regard emotions are viewed as the preparation to take action. For instance, fear interrupts ongoing action and makes the individual ready for flight or fight. Fear also directs attention to the environment for signs of danger.

This link between emotion and action is central to the behaviour of our students. If the student perceives the learning situation, or something in that situation, as threatening, they may respond with the emotion of fear or anxiety or embarrassment. This biologically and psychologically prepares them to take action; their behaviour either distances them from the source of the threat (they don't participate, they quit the course or leave their homework materials behind), or minimises the effect of the threat (they daydream, doodle, talk to their neighbour or don't make eye contact).

Where do feelings fit?

Feelings, body sensations and visceral arousal are closely associated with some theories of emotions. According to neurologist Dr Antonio

Damasio, this association is close indeed. He asks the questions: What is a feeling? Why are the terms emotion and feeling differentiated? One reason he notes is that "although some feelings relate to emotions, there are many that do not: all emotions generate feelings if you are awake and alert, but not all feelings originate in emotions." (p. 143) Therefore there are several varieties of feelings; all of these types are experienced by our students, and all of them affect their behaviour and learning performance.

The first variety are based on the five primary emotions. The most basic of these emotions are happiness, sadness, anger, fear and disgust. Damasio reports that "[w]hen the body conforms to the profile of one of those emotions we *feel* happy, sad, angry, fearful, disgusted." (p. 149)

A second variety of feelings is based on emotions that are considered secondary emotions; subtle variations of the five basic emotions. These are the emotions of euphoria, ecstasy, melancholy, wistfulness, panic, shyness and so on. These second variety of emotions are based on experience. We learn over time to make subtle distinctions between our cognitive state and the state of our body. No doubt you have experienced, or seen others experience, primary and secondary emotions while involved in some learning task.

The third type of feeling reported by Damasio is called *background feelings* because they "originate in 'background' body states rather than in emotional states." (p. 150) A background feeling corresponds to the body state that prevails *between* emotions and is related to what we call our *moods*.

What this means to us as trainers is that when our students enter our training environment they do so *feeling* something. They are always feeling something. It may be simply a background feeling that is neither too negative or too positive—the feeling is simply pleasant or unpleasant. Occasionally these feelings conform to the profile of one of the emotions and our students may report feeling anxious, frustrated, excited and so forth. Given the connection between emotions and action readiness, we can also say that *what our students do, or avoid doing, is based on how they feel*.

An important observation noted by Damasio is that "When we have feelings connected with emotions, attention is allocated substantially to body signals, and parts of the body landscape moves from background to the foreground of our attention." (p. 149) For instance, in my work training trainers, there are opportunities for the students to come to the front of the room to give short presentations. Of course, prior to the suggestion they are feeling something, although if they are comfortable these feelings reside in the background and are likely processed unconsciously. However, once the request for volunteers is made, this changes for many students. They report 'butterflies' in their stomach, a 'pounding' heart, sweaty hands, 'rubber' legs and so on. For us as trainers it important to note that these feelings draw upon a student's limited *attentional resources*, which are no longer available for the task at hand. This is one way that feelings affect performance.

What in training and learning generate emotions and feelings?

There are several well researched phenomena known to generate emotions and feelings in humans. All of these phenomena are present in training environments. The first of these are external sensory stimulus. As humans we are biologically pre-wired to respond to environmental stimuli. In training environments these stimuli could be one of a thousand external events: your tone of voice or how you are dressed, some feature of the learning activity, the temperature of the room. The list is endless. Students automatically and unconsciously scan the environment with their five senses and then interpret those features as either threatening or beneficial. In very simple terms, if the stimuli is interpreted as threatening, a negative feeling or emotion is generated; if beneficial, a positive feeling or emotion is generated.

The second trigger for emotions and feelings is based on internal cognitive processes—memories, self-talk and rumination, images of the future and so on. This means that our students generate emotional responses in the absence of any external cause. For example, I have had students report that they are nervous about the possibility of failing the course. Obviously this hasn't occurred yet, but they are imaging some possible future scenario and generating an emotional response. This emotion, if it is allowed to persist, can very much affect the student's performance in the class.

The third trigger for emotions are based on the student's body state. Two such features have been well researched—facial expressions and body posture. Changes in a person's facial expression or body posture can generate an emotional response. For example, studies by Riskind and Gotay showed that manipulations of expansion and contraction postures altered emotion experiences, expectations and task persistence in the expected directions.

The experience of learning

If there is one thing we can say with certainty, it is that *people attend training sessions to learn*—to learn a new skill, to improve on an existing skill or to broaden their knowledge in some subject area. To accomplish these learning goals, we understand that *the learner must take action*; students have to do something, either through internal thought processes or external exercises. We also understand that it is not just action in a singular sense; achieving learning goals requires that the student take consistent and frequent action steps, a series of small steps toward the desired end result. For instance, an individual with a desire to learn how to touch-type will need to do many repetitious exercises in order to achieve competence.

I have been unable to find much research on the nature of these learning actions in terms of what they require mentally and emotionally from the student. But can you say, "This is what you need to do" without a thought as to the actual subjective experience of *doing it*?

If we analyse the learning actions that are necessary to achieve some new learning goal, we observe an interesting phenomenon. We observe that in most cases, learning actions have one or more of the following attributes:

- ambiguity,
- uncertainty,
- unknown,
- frustration,
- boredom,
- confusion,
- mental exhaustion, and
- physical discomfort.

Now, the realisation we must make is that learning actions, those actions required to achieve the learning goal, are fraught with opportunities to experience negative emotions and strong physiological feelings. This says that, for the most part, *learning is not fun* for the student (even if at times it may be considered challenging or interesting). And further, these emotions and feelings will directly affect the action the student decides to take. To ignore the fact that our students have feelings and emotions that are triggered by both their own internal processes and external events and situations is to miss the predominant feature of the learner's experience.

One approach trainers have been trying in recent years is to make their learning activities and events fun, as if to say, "If it is fun, people will learn." But we need to consider this approach to the problem closely. The notion that learning is fun does not match my own experience while engaged in learning actions, nor does it seem to match the experience of many of my students. When I think of the goals I have achieved, that I highly value, they are those which required very hard work. My logic also agrees. For some activity to be fun there needs to be some existing level of competence. We have fun doing things we already know something about. Emphasising ease in training for the sake of making it fun for the student may result in teaching very little that is challenging and therefore useful to the student.

There were two periods for my project volunteers when they thought learning could be given the attribute of fun. Most of them thought the learning process could be fun *before* they began to actually take action toward the goal. They could daydream about achieving the goal, get excited about different facets of the experiences they would have and so on. The second period that could be fun and exciting was at the *completion* of the learning goal. For instance, I remember when I learned to ski. Before I started I was having a lot of fun in my mind with the idea of learning to ski. I imagined all kinds of exciting scenarios. And buying skis and boots and clothes was really good fun. Of course, now that I know how to ski, it *is* fun. However, learning *how* to ski was definitely not enjoyable. It was disorienting, difficult and tiring. Not that there weren't funny stories to tell about the process and a few laughs along the way, but by and large it was hard work.

Recognising and remembering that learning actions are by nature challenging and difficult will go a long way towards understanding the subjective experience of learning for the learner. It provides an important insight that is useful when it comes to making choices about teaching methods and understanding how we as trainers can best support our students in achieving their learning goals.

If we can manage how students feel, we can positively affect their performance

So our situation is this: if there is no way to truly make learning activities fun or enjoyable, and they remain naturally problematic, leading the student to negative emotions and feelings, how shall we support our students in their learning tasks? I believe that this is one very important skill that the top trainers, teachers and coaches seem to possess. It is as if they pull the students along through the confusing, boring, tedious, difficult tasks involved with learning, knowing that motivation, for some personality types, is not high when feelings are low. Rather than try to convince the student that an activity is fun when in fact it is not, they teach the student that these difficulties are a natural part of learning which is experienced by most students. We will explore the types of strategies used by trainers in a later chapter, as we apply our new knowledge to real-time situations. But for the moment this is food for thought.

CONCLUSION

Students' reactions and responses in training situations are very much determined by their personality, values and preferences, thinking styles and past experiences. Perceiving a student's behaviour as 'lazy' or 'out to get me' leads the trainer to a no-win situation for the student. Armed with the information in this chapter, the hope is that you can begin to interpret the behaviour of the student in a way that leads to manageable and fruitful responses. You should now be able to think about alternatives in design, methods and your own behaviours.

Training effectiveness may look much more difficult from the perspective of individual differences. How shall we do the one thing we can do in any given moment and affect, in a positive direction, a student's movement toward learning? Here I will need to ask you to be patient; we will approach this question shortly. You will discover that the more you understand about what makes students react differently the better you will be guided in the use of methods to minimise or neutralise the effects of negative factors.

This chapter introduced you to a lot of detailed information, and you may find it beneficial to read it over again—there are simply too many influences on your perceptions to be managed or attended to at one time. My suggestion would be to start small, and task yourself as you (re)read to simply observe the people around you in your work environment, classrooms or homes for one particular personality trait, thinking style, value or preference. Hopefully, the observations will help you make the transition from the *theories* to the *actual behaviours* you spot as indicators of those theoretical traits, styles and preferences.

In this chapter we also discussed the notion that the activities that students must engage in to achieve learning goals are complex and have many attributes that can lead to negative emotions and feelings. Students engage in mental and physical behaviours to manage their own emotional state. These behaviours can be counterproductive to the learning process.

As a trainer there may be little that we can do directly to minimise the effects of the factors of personality, values, thinking styles and past experience (although we can do some things), but we can and do have a great deal of control over how the student *feels*. And if we can successfully control that factor, there is a chance of truly minimising or neutralising the effects of the other factors. In later chapters, when we discuss the specific issues and problems we confront in real-time training situations, an understanding of the role of human emotions and feelings will be paramount. We cannot discuss the merits of any training design or method without first understanding the experience of the effects of these methods from the learner's perspective. The extent to which a trainer can stand behind a lectern and read their notes to the joy of some participants and demise of others is based on the lack of awareness of the impact of their behaviours on the students.

CHAPTER **3**

79

the development of the trainer

INTRODUCTION

The learner, and his or her internal process, is only one half of the total training equation. The other half of the equation is comprised of all those elements and factors that impinge on the nervous system of the learner. Environmental elements, such as the actual room where the presentation is being conducted, the use of training aids, the food served to the participants for lunch and so on, are just some of those elements. The single most important element affecting the learning environment is you, the *trainer*. Specifically, what is important is what you do, how what you do is *perceived* by the students and how these perceptions *impact* the student's behaviours and learning process. This chapter is dedicated to analysing the behaviours of trainers with the intent to increase awareness of, and sensitivity to, how students perceive and are impacted by the trainer's behaviours.

As trainers, we are a special breed of character. We require a range of behaviours only exceeded by versatile actors. The best trainers are those with a broad and flexible range of behaviours—trainers who can convincingly be a placator, a beggar, a briber, a gangster and a drill sergeant.

In Chapter 2 we explored the complexity of human behaviour. We understand now that no two students are the same, and to deal with this diversity we know that we require enough flexibility to find a thread that can connect with, and influence, every member of the group. Getting people motivated to do what you want them to do is the quintessential skill and art of the top training professional.

An individual's personality, values and past experiences affect their perceptions—what they 'see' and how they interpret what they see. In general, human beings habitually make quick conscious, and unconscious, judgments about the behaviours of other people. In the first moment of meeting someone new, we are observing, listening, feeling, reminiscing, thinking. We notice how the other person speaks, dresses, walks, gestures—every nuance. These observations are filtered through our personality, values and past experiences as we search for a category, or a label, in which to fit that person's behaviours—dull, interesting, funny, cute, smart, aggressive.

A critical element of how students interpret the experience of learning in your training sessions is based on how they perceive you. Within the first few moments of going before an audience (on occasion before you even get to the front of the audience), the participants make decisions—they make decisions about you. You cannot effectively educate others who are not listening to you, who do not perceive you as credible, or who are sceptical because of that 'shifty thing' you do with your eyes. Like it or not, *as a trainer, other peoples' perceptions count for more than your own personal likes and dislikes in that context.*

You may like having behaviours that are perceived by others as serious and studious, but if those same behaviours put participants to sleep, of what value are they to you as a trainer? You may like being thought of as a 'nice guy', but if students walk all over you and are disruptive as a result, the nice guy might need to stay home. You may have a well-developed behaviour of quick thinking and wittiness, but if your wit is perceived by some students as offensive you may end up tangling with a lawsuit. One goal, then, is to find the balance between doing what is *right* for and *accessible* to you as the trainer, while at the same time ensuring that you have enough behavioural choices to select from that are also right for students.

The range of behaviours that have been developed over the course of a lifetime are the primary source of our skills as trainers. They constitute our strengths, our weaknesses and our limitations. The range of behaviours that we can access go a long way towards determining many other aspects of our career, such as what content we can teach, what audiences and clients we can attract, who we can be influential with and the methods we can convincingly use.

In this chapter the first notion we are going to explore is that of *acts*, or behavioural sets; how what we do is perceived and labelled by others. The goal is to describe a process by which trainers can identify the idiosyncratic acts that they access in training situations, and how those acts are perceived by, and what kind of impact those behaviours have on, different students. The process of learning about the effects of our own behaviours is a process of analysis. We need to analyse ourselves, and others, in the communication professions in order to see the effects they have on audiences. When working in front of a class, some behaviours are effective, some clearly are not.

Secondly we will bring to mind the notion that acts are made up of a variety of components, such as vocal and gestural quality, facial expression, gender and age. Sometimes it is a little thing that the trainer does with their hands, their eyes, how they stand, or tuck in their shirt that leads to the perceptual labels the students apply. For all of us there are strengths, weaknesses and ticks. Analysing the components of our own behaviours can be a daunting—but enlightening—process.

We then focus on the methods for changing or adding to our range of acts. We begin by discussing the components of the acts that can easily, and *not* so easily, be changed. This section then enters a discussion of how, realistically, we might go about changing some of our existing acts, or adding new acts to our range of behaviours—behaviours that would allow us to produce better results in our classes, teach different kinds of content or work with different kinds of audiences.

We also list useful acts for the trainer. These lists come from an analysis of the attributes of successful people in various communication industries.

The final section in this chapter discusses other factors that relate to the acts we are most likely to access easily and those which are most difficult. Factors such as our personality and values, gender and age are such factors. For example, if you have a strong desire to be perceived as a nurturing trainer, you may not choose to add an authoritative act to your training style—although I am going to try to make it make sense why you might want to re-evaluate your values about these kinds of issues. Of course, values and personality also influence what content you choose to teach, the environments you work in and the audience you attract.

Underlying this chapter—indeed, the whole book—is the notion that your own past experiences affect the acts that you do on stage. Our past experiences are both significant resources, and significant influences, on our life as trainers.

IDENTIFYING ACTS

Training is one of those rare professions where other people's perceptions of your behaviours matter more than your own. Their perceptions count more than what you think you are doing, or intend to be doing. In many cases, if the audience doesn't 'get' you, you don't get the outcomes.

My recognition that each of us as trainers come to the career with what I have termed behavioural sets, or *acts*, as they will be referred to here, came early in my career. When I was starting to produce consistent results with my students, I would often be approached by other trainers and training managers and asked a simple question: How do you do what you do? In those early days, the only legitimate and honest answer I could give was: I don't really have a clue, but I can do it every time. I really did not know how to describe what I was doing in any way that would be helpful to another trainer. I knew my students were achieving outcomes in the class, I knew they were inspired to try new things and think new thoughts. I even knew that they were entertained and impressed. But I had no categories or labels for what I was doing, and why those behaviours were working.

But I learned. The path to my own understanding had three approaches:

- I analysed videotapes of my performances;
- I listened to critical feedback from both students and other communication professionals; and
- I spent endless hours studying the technical literature.

Each method contributed a unique set of distinctions. Over time, I developed both a sensitivity to my experience on stage, and the means to describe that experience accurately to others.

Defining the term "act"

If a group of people were to observe you performing on stage, they would immediately and automatically apply labels to describe their impressions of you. They might label your behaviours as 'sincere', 'confident', 'intelligent' and so forth. These impressions, once labelled, are your *acts*; in other words, a 'sincere act', a 'confident act', an 'intelligent act'. As trainers we have many acts we use on stage—a 'boring' act, a 'confident' act, a 'professional' act, a 'mother's little helper' act.

Acts are constructions. They are constructed out of a combination of elements—your facial expression, your style of dress, your hand gestures, your vocal quality, your movements. All of these elements combine to say something to your students about you, and help the student label your behaviours in a way that fits their model of the world. Therefore, an "act" can be defined as the *sum of the individual behavioural components that you are engaged in at any given moment, that other people perceive and have labels to describe*. An act is *not* your behaviours, it is how those behaviours are perceived and labelled by others. If I am standing on stage, very rigid, with notes in my hand, shaking like a leaf, with a broken voice, others might label that act as a 'nervous' act—when in fact I might just be coming down with the flu. *What matters to you as a trainer is not what is actually happening for you, but how it is perceived by your students.*

The three caveats about acts

Three caveats must be noted before we go further. The first of these is that *no two people are likely to perceive and label your behaviours in exactly the same way*. What one person might label as an 'intelligent' act, someone else in the audience might label as an 'know-it-all' act. When the audience members evaluate and label (consciously or unconsciously) the acts that you have on stage, they are both right and wrong. Importantly though, they are right for themselves, and that matters. If someone is perceiving your behaviours as 'boring', then that is what matters for them, because it will determine how receptive they will be to learning from you. But they are also wrong to the degree that not everyone would view those same behaviours as boring: others might label the same act 'diligent'.

The second caveat is that *trainers are not their acts*. It is important to note that these acts are sets of behaviours, and when we label them as such, we are focused on the effect of the behaviours; we are not labelling the trainer doing those behaviours. To say someone has a 'little girl' act does not mean she (or he) *is* a little girl. What is being said is that the way the person is behaving, or acting, brings that label to the mind of others. To say someone has a 'boring' act does not mean that they are a boring person, just that someone else affected by those behaviours perceives and labels those behaviours as 'boring'. In another example, I know a lot of people who have a 'confident' act—meaning that what they do leads other people to perceive them as having a lot of confidence—when in fact they do not experience themselves as confident at all. I know many other people who have a 'well-read' act when I know from experience that they have not read a book in years. So acts are other people's perceptions of your behaviours—behaviours which may not be based in any reality whatsoever.

The third caveat is that *acts are contextual.* How people behave will likely be different in different environments, or contexts. Some of the acts I may be perceived of as having by my friends are different than the acts I am perceived of as having by my clients. People are more diverse than narrow in their range of behaviours. In this chapter we are primarily concerned with the acts your audience perceive when you are operating in your capacity as trainer. By no means is it assumed that these behaviours are the sum total of the behaviours you have in all the other contexts of your life.

Analysing our own acts

The first and single most important task I have when working with trainers as students (people, I might add, who are already competent and earning a living in that profession) is to assist them in analysing their own performances, and identifying the acts that they are perceived as having by others. This activity is twofold. First, the task is to assist them in learning how to perceive and label their own acts. If you have never seen yourself as an audience sees you, it is impossible to have any real idea about how you are perceived when working. How else do some trainers with 'boring' acts continue to maintain that 'boring' act? It is because they do not know that that is how their behaviours are perceived by others. If they did know, I have little doubt that they would discontinue those behaviours.

The second task is to give the trainers a safe environment in which they can receive honest feedback from other trainers who have watched them give a presentation on stage. This is a process of critical examination. Trainers who have experienced this process are often pleasantly surprised by the strengths that others perceive in them. For example, most trainers watching their own performance will perceive a 'nervous' act (actually they are not perceiving the act, they are just remembering the real feelings they had during the presentation), and they are surprised to discover that it is not their audience's perception.

By critically evaluating what as a trainer you do on stage, and how other people perceive the acts you exhibit, you can begin to appreciate your current strengths—those acts that are natural to you, and appropriate for your work as a trainer—and your current weaknesses—acts that either are not particularly appropriate for your work as a trainer, or acts that are missing altogether. It is through this analysis that you begin to pull apart your performance and begin to see the gaps that, if filled, would lead to greater successes. Those successes might relate to more consistent achievement of outcomes, or the ability to work with more diverse audiences, or even the ability to earn more money for your time.

As discussed in Chapter 1, different trainers have different types of outcomes, different audiences, different time frames and so on. Individual trainers are also different. The same idiosyncrasies discussed in Chapter 2 can also be applied to the trainer—different trainers have different personalities, preferences, values, past experiences and vastly different sets of behaviours. The outcome I have when working with trainers who want to improve their range of behaviours is to ensure that each trainer follows a learning path that produces the kinds of new behaviours which that trainer feels are important and appropriate for them. Watching the trainers who attend my program at the end of the course is the experience of watching fifty totally different performances. They all achieve their outcome with the audience, but each individual does it in their own unique way—a way that uses what is natural for them to do on stage, and a way that is appropriate for the content they are delivering and the audience they are working with.

So as we begin to look at analysing our own performances it is important to keep in mind that this chapter will mean to you something different than the next reader. What you take from it and what you ultimately decide to do for your own professional development will be your decision.

BREAKING DOWN ACTS INTO THEIR CONSTITUENT PARTS

When we are observed by our audiences, they see the one whole act, and describe it with labels (as discussed in the preceding section). Oftentimes, however, it is not the whole set of behaviours that are leading to the perception, but some small part of it. It might be our tone of voice, or some simple thing we do with our face that leads the participants to make the judgments they do. But likely as not, if we try to change everything at once, we end up replacing one act that does not serve us for another that is equally useless. If we want to seriously consider acts, their impact and the possibility of changing or adding to them, it is useful to break the acts into their constituent parts. Once we know more specifically the component responsible for a particular (undesirable) perception, it is much easier to make changes.

Before we look more closely at these components, we should ask: Does every trainer need to work on this? I would say almost, but not all. The people who are exceptions fall into two categories. One is the content expert. If you have discovered a cure for cancer, people will listen to you and pay attention no matter how you present that information. Some trainers work with such important ideas and information that how they present it matters very little. Some trainers teach important skills and we forgive them their lack of presentation skills because we want to learn from them. The second exception is age. Older trainers and lecturers are viewed differently than young ones. Audiences tend to extend permission for them to have soft voices, slower movements, even ill-fitting clothing (although not all older trainers have these attributes). But for those of us not in either of these categories, acts either enhance or inhibit the student's process of learning. The more we can finetune our performances, the easier the job will be.

If you want to consider adding new acts to your repertoire, or cleaning up some of those that just do not work well, you will need to work on *components* of your behaviours. Every part of you that is available to the participants' senses can contribute to the labelling of acts. How you are labelled depends on everything, from your posture, movements, gestures, facial expressions, eye movements, vocal qualities (tone, pitch, volume and accent), vocabulary, to your gender, age, clothing, hairstyle and your smell—perfumed, smoky, sweaty and so on.

To analyse your acts as a trainer, or enlist the support of others for this process, you need to learn an important question: *What was it about what I did that led you to perceiving that act?* For example, say a few participants give you feedback about having an "unprofessional" act. If that was something you wanted to change, how would you go about it? What would you change? I'd venture to say you would not really know what to do unless you were to go one level deeper and discover what specifically is leading your critics to use this label.

If you asked, they might say something simple like, "It's because your shoes aren't shined and clothes don't fit properly." Those things most certainly can lead people to question your professionalism. Although some skilled trainers will have other attributes that override the effect of scruffy shoes, you may not. With that specific feedback, you have an easy change to make—go home, shine your shoes and get someone who knows about dressing professionally to help.

You might, however, get feedback like, "You sound like you are doubting your own expertise. It is the way you end your sentences with a question." Now this is different. The way you speak naturally is leading some other people to question your professionalism. Correcting this will require something more than a quick shoeshine. Vocal quality can be a big issue for many trainers, especially women. Top professional trainers, like many actors, have taken voice and elocution classes at some time during their career to change their ineffective vocal patterns. The point is: what you will need to change will depend on the specific feedback you receive. The more specific, the easier the problem is to attack.

Remember that you have to be the final judge in all of this. Some feedback is just not useful; you must decide what to disregard. I have had students make comments about attributes that they wish I would change but that personally I have judged are good for me on stage, based on many years of experience. For example, people oftentimes feel I have a 'privacy' act and they would feel more comfortable if I were more open and accessible. For me, that is not appropriate. Not for my personality, not for my outcomes I have with my students.

When I watch students in my *Training to Train* program performing on stage, or reviewing these performances on videotape, I am very sensitive to the components of their acts. What is it that is leading me to the perceptions I have? Sometimes it is a repetitive tick that captures my attention—constant "ums", hand-wringing, rocking back and forth, playing with hair, smiling incessantly and so on. Once identified, these are things are easily changed. Sometimes, though, nothing identifiable stands out. In such cases, I look for the weakest component of that trainer's behaviours. Perhaps they have a voice with little power, or no movement on stage, or limited facial expressions. I know from experience that if the trainer works to improve their weakest, least flexible part of their behaviour, many other things will change along with it. For example, someone who greatly improves their posture will tend to have automatic changes in their voice. Sending someone off to improve their vocal quality can, in turn, affect their breathing, which changes the speed at which they talk and think, and lifts the head upright. The trainer may even begin to make more eye contact, simply from working on their voice.

Imagine you gave a short presentation on stage and at the end of that presentation you were to ask the audience to give you some one, two, or three-word descriptions of their perceptions of you as you work on stage. They raise their hands and give you the following feedback: "I saw an intelligent act," "…an articulate act," "…a caring-if-I-learn act" and so forth. You might feel pretty good about this, and indeed you should, if this is how you hope the audience is in fact perceiving you. What if the feedback you received was: "I saw a waffling-on act," or "…an uncertainty act," or "…a confused act"? These, of course, might not be so pleasing to hear, but they

89

should be appreciated; they tell you something about other people's perceptions of your own behaviours. Would you *really* rather not ever know that this is how people perceive you when you are working your heart out up there?

INCREASING THE TRAINER'S RANGE OF ACTS

This section is about increasing your range of behaviours, not at improving what you already can do. *There is nothing inherent in the act of training that leads to new behaviours.* You can put a trainer on stage every day for ten years and at the end of that ten years they will not have a broader range of behaviours which contribute to the skills and artistry of training. However, the existing behaviours are likely to be better refined and more comfortable to execute.

Every behaviour you bring to the training profession was developed during the course of doing and learning things in life. If, once we are adults, we never take on the task of learning new skills, there will be no change in our training performance. We end up doing what we have been doing all along. We develop just one good set of habits and behavioural patterns. But with a little effort, we can do more.

Selecting new acts to add to your repertoire

How do you decide what acts would be most beneficial to change or add to your existing set of behaviours, and what factors contribute to this decision? First, changes in this area should be based on your future aspirations. If you were to imagine yourself continuing to train on into the future, what kinds of fantasies or goals do you have? What kinds of environments, what kinds of audiences, what kinds of content? To build rapport, generate interest, influence and be credible in those places of your fantasised future, what would you need to be doing differently? The second consideration for your decision should be based on an honest evaluation of your own strengths and limitations.

I no longer know where this quote comes from, but it continues to be a major influence in my life and career: *It's not what you do in public, but what you do in private, that you get credit for.* For me, this quote emphasises on how I spend my time when I am not training. It helps me focus on the activities, experiences, people, reading materials and so on that I engage in, and emphasises that what I am learning might enhance my performance on stage. Even watching television can be educational and useful (though more often it's likely to be numbing and useless). I also take the quote to mean that if I do nothing in private to improve and develop professionally, I will not likely see professional benefits. Today, I pay a lot of attention to how I spend my time in private, and the professional benefits are very apparent. It is important to remember that, as a trainer, you spend far more time off stage than you ever spend on it. This thinking led me to begin considering *training as a lifestyle*.

Everything we do in life has the potential to inform our practice as educators. Without any doubt, what you read, who you associate with, what you watch, has this potential. But in this section we are going to narrow the focus and explore how we can either modify some existing act, or add new acts to our training behaviours by choosing and engaging in new learning goals and challenges.

As has been said before, there is nothing I know of that a trainer can do while working in front of a group that will lead to new behaviours. *Once we walk to the front of the group, what we do is what we can do, and what we can do are behaviours that were developed in other life activities.* When you observe a trainer working in front of a group, analyse the acts they use consistently: you can tell a lot about the what kinds of experiences and activities that person has engaged in elsewhere. Or, at least upon hearing about these experiences, you are likely to not be surprised. You can see the connection between their 'performance self' and their life experiences and activities, by which these acts have been developed.

For example, I used to get a great deal of comments about the articulation of my hand gestures when speaking, and was queried by trainers about how I had learned to do that. Of course, I had little, or no real, awareness of my hands at all when I was training, but videotape analysis helped me observe what my students were commenting on. These were natural gestures for me to make, and seem to match the rest of my communication. I also knew that in a less exaggerated way I used my hands in all communication situations. So how did these gestures develop? I certainly was not born with them, and they were not unique to training situations. On reflection, I was able to identify at least two experiences that related to the development of my hand gestures. The first was through playing the piano and guitar. When I watch myself training on videotape I can see gestures and hand positions that are very familiar. It is not that I am making 'chords in the air', but there is something familiar in the movement, intensity, and articulation that comes from that experience. My hands learned to do different things through that experience that now are transferred to my skills as a trainer. The second experience was as a young child. I was fascinated watching Leonard Bernstein's *Young People's Concerts* on television. To me, the energy and power in his hands was mesmerising. I would walk around imitating these gestures. These are the attributes that my students see coming through when I am working on stage.

Given that what you can do now—all the acts, and all of their components—were developed through the experiences and activities you have chosen in your life, the following point can be made salient. The modification of your existing acts, or the development of new ones, will come by taking on new life experiences and activities.

If, after an analysis of your existing acts, you decide that you want to develop more precision, you will need to consider engaging in some activity in which precision is a by-product. If it is precise body movements, or control, the activity might be a martial art. If it is precise focus and coordination, the activity might be building model boats in a bottle, or flying radio-controlled helicopters. If it is verbal precision you want to develop, the activity might be learning the famous speeches of Dr King, Clarence Darrow, or the court-room speech made by the character Howard Roark in the movie *The Fountainhead*. We talk shortly about other useful activities for trainers.

Distinctions about activities

You will need to decide personally what kinds of activities are likely to have the behavioural by-products you are looking to develop. You will also have to decide how far outside your own comfort zone you want, or need, to go. For a trainer who is already very flexible in their behaviours on stage, meaning they have a broad range of acts that emerge, they may choose activities that are comfortable but will lead to subtle changes. For example, choosing a new physical chal-lenge like preparing to run a marathon, or climbing to base camp at Mt Everest, for some people might not be a huge physical step, but preparing, and then following through, will add small changes to many dimensions of their acts.

For trainers who seem to be missing a whole dimension in their behavioural set, or who over time have become very rigid in their training styles, I would recommend going for the least likely thing they can imagine themselves doing—you know, the 'that's not me' category of experiences. For example, if I have a female trainer whose acts are consistently perceived of as 'stiff', 'serious', 'librarian' and so on, but she wants to find a whole new set of acts to access, I might suggest she go do something like belly-dancing classes. After a few months of that experience she will still be able to access the acts of stiff, serious, and librarian when they are appropriate, but I guarantee that there will be new acts accessible when they too are appropriate and required. You cannot remain who you are, right now, if you tackle new experiences. I was all that I had been, *and a whole lot more* behaviourally, after I prepared for and competed in triathlons.

We are not talking about one-time experiences

The experiences and activities that we are talking about here are different than going off and doing one bungy jump, or one tandem skydive. Such experiences also have their place; they create great stories for trainings that can be used to inspire others. But one-off experiences that take little in the way of preparation do not have the impact of changing the access to new behaviours in trainings. We are talking about experiences and short-term learning goals that take at least three months to develop—for instance, a commitment to three months of dance lessons, or learning to touch-type, or getting a dive ticket and doing one deep water dive, achieving a yellow belt in a martial art, swimming a kilometre, or getting a motorcycle licence and taking a long interstate tour. Remember, you are looking to build a new way of moving, a new way of behaving. If it can be done in a one-time experience, it is likely an activity that is built on skills you *already possess*. You do not have to learn to do anything new to get strapped to the chest of a skydive master and be thrown out of a plane. That experience might have other effects, but it would not have behavioural change effects that you can count on when working on stage.

Does this activity have to be long-term?

This activity does not have to become a long-term part of your life. The point here is not to become a master musician, or competitive dancer, unless you find you really enjoy the activity to make the commitment to devote the time to it. The point is to give yourself a new experience that will lead to a new way of moving, of thinking, of acting, of standing, of relating, for a long enough period of time that these new ways become comfortable, become a part of you.

Practising new training acts: how and when?

The simple answer to this question is: anywhere but on stage. Once in front of a group, you have to use what comes naturally.

Experimentation in that situation with new skills that are still weak can lead to disastrous results. I never consciously try to do anything different on stage. These new behaviours will show up automatically when they have become a part of my behaviours. But you can, and should, practise these new behaviours in other life communication contexts. Life is a playground for practising training skills. Any inter-action provides an opportunity—with your children, your partner, your business associates or whoever serves you in the grocery store.

Do I really have to do this?

Well, of course not. But if you want to improve your performance on stage, I know of no other truly successful way of achieving the same dramatic outcome. You might want to consider also the many other benefits to opening yourself up to these new experiences.

First, the more you experience in life, the more you will be able to relate to your audience, and the greater empathy and understanding you will have for their processes. Second, you continually make refinements in your understanding of the learning process. Even a failure in one of these attempts will assist you in understanding the failures of your students. Third, the more you do, the less you will fear doing in the future. A fourth benefit is that the more physical skills you engage in, the more flexibility and strength you will have for performing with greater stamina—and the longevity of your career is enhanced. As you no doubt already know, training is a very physically demanding job. Fifth, you will end up with great stories and metaphors that can be used in trainings to punctuate your lessons. Somehow these stories show up at the most unusual times, but perfect for the moment. You have to have had the experience to have the story. Lastly, you become an inspiration to others. Trainers are very much leaders in the way of ideas and possibilities. You get to congruently say, "If I could do *that*, then you can do *this*."

Learning goals chosen by trainers to increase their range of behaviours

In my years as a trainer of other trainers I have seen all kinds of learning activities chosen with the intention of increasing a trainer's range of behaviours. I have very little to do with these choices, just the odd suggestion if someone gets really stuck. These choices are truly left up to the student to make. This is because the activities chosen need to make sense to them personally—the person involved is going to need a reason for engaging in the activity or they will likely never get started. The goal needs to be realistic and achievable. The student is the only one who can accurately assess the goal. The student is also the only one who can judge that they have the resources of time, money, family support or whatever to begin and sustain the process of achieving the new goal.

List of activities for trainers

The list of potential activities provided below for you to consider is by no means exhaustive. My comments about the benefits of those activities are not necessarily the only benefits either. But they are the activities I can say have been chosen by other trainers, and they are benefits that I personally have seen take place after just a few months. Remember, too, that most of these activities require classes and teachers, so you get the benefit of watching another trainer work, and can use that experience to further your understanding of the effects of the trainer's behaviours on your learning process.

Particularly physical activities

There are literally hundreds of general physical activities that trainers have chosen. They are usually personal challenges and all of them build various levels of strength and flexibility. One year, half of my *Training to Train* class banded together to prepare to run in their first *triathlon*. Some of them did not even know how to ride a bicycle, and others were afraid of the water. Together, they met, hired a coach, inspired and motivated each other, and shortly after the completion of our course, all competed in their first triathlon.

All forms of *gym work* can be good, so long as the trainer has some specific goals in mind, like lifting a particular weight, or losing weight or inches. Without a specific goal gym work may feel like an endless path going nowhere. *Aerobics* and *weight training* can be like this. Activities such as *ice skating, running, swimming, rollerblading, skateboarding, surfing, snowboarding* and *skiing* are also prone to this "for what purpose" problem. But the difference, and hence the value of these activities, is the steep learning curve at the beginning. They are great short-term challenges. The problem only occurs once you reach a stage of competence—if you are not going to compete or join a club for some adventures, then interest may fall off quickly.

Other gym activities like *boxercising* can be great fun and lead to fast gains. The fact that there is an instructor and several others in the class can be very motivating. Also, it is focused and teaches new body movements, including balance.

Activities such as *pistol* or *skeet shooting* or *archery* are also excellent activities for trainers. These teach discipline, focus, concentration and extreme control of the movements of small muscles in the body—your feet have a lot to do with hitting a target. There are clubs in most major cities, and again the social network and instructing facilities allow you to observe another trainer, their process and the process of learning for others in the group.

Doing full courses that have long-term learning processes are excellent. *Martial arts*, which teach increasing levels of flexibility, strength, technique, discipline and self-esteem—which in turn leads to higher grading levels—can be very motivating as a long-term activity. You can do a martial art for a few months and gain benefits, but you can also do it for twenty years and still be improving. It is also nice to do an activity where there are many levels of competence (white belts through to black belts) in the same class, and you have an opportunity to observe how an instructor makes the class of value to members at different levels.

I have seen trainers undergo tremendous behavioural changes as a result of doing what they have to do to get a *motorcycle licence*, a *pilot's license*, completing a *race car driving course*, getting a *deep water dive ticket* or completing a *skydiving course*. There is just something you have to overcome to do these activities if you have never done them before. The major benefit is their character-building nature. You get to put yourself in a situation in which you do not know anything, where everything is new. You are a true student again. These are the experiences that lead trainers to really know what it is like to be a learner; it changes them in a significant way.

Another great physical activity is *climbing*—indoor or outdoor. Today there is a growing number of indoor sport climbing gyms. Climbing also has many levels of competence. It builds upper body strength and articulated hands unlike any other activity I have seen recently. Indoor climbing is also safe as standards are closely monitored; outdoor courses for those inclined are also available.

Dancing

When trainers feel disconnected from their bodies, or uncoordinated, then dance classes are a wonderful task to tackle. There are many forms of dancing taught here in Australia. For extreme upright posture, and acts comprised of precision, balance, body articulation and elegance, *ballroom dancing* is excellent. This form of dance also provides information about where your body is in space, and pays close attention to fine muscle movements of the head, face and hands.

For women who feel stiff and out of touch with their bodies, *belly-dancing* has been used. In one year, ten female trainers in Adelaide hired a belly-dance teacher to conduct weekly classes for three months during *Training to Train*. These women changed. They became more flexible and fluid in their walk and in their movement on stage. They learned to notice their bodies and to pay attention to what it was doing. Also, the physical strength needed to perform the belly-dancing movements added strength and confidence to their stage performances.

Tap dancing is an aerobic workout and builds tremendous strength. The best thing is that you sweat. Tap requires focus on mastering techniques in slow motion, but then that must be performed without thinking—a sort of unconscious competence. Re-experiencing that process of learning is of great benefit to trainers, teaching them the difference between the value of 'thinking' and the value of performing 'mindlessly'.

You have likely heard of football teams being sent off to *ballet* classes. This is a perfect example of using other life activities to improve performance in another area of expertise. Ballet is about extreme flexibility, strength, balance, control, posture and breathing. Such skills are as useful to the trainer as they are to the footballer.

Singing

I am surprised how many of my students choose singing as an activity, simply because those who choose it seem so afraid of it. Your voice is an instrument that can be trained. If you have never trained your vocal instrument, you likely do not have any idea what is possible. Singing changes the quality of your voice. You learn how and where to get your breath, and to control your breathing. Any time you do any activity that focuses on the use of breath, you will have corresponding changes in posture. Also, singing exercises the facial muscles in new ways and leads to a new range of facial expressions. Many trainers I know use the exercises they learned in singing classes to loosen up their voice and face before they go on stage to speak.

There are several forms of singing activities available. There a *choruses*, where one can hide for a while in the safety of a crowd. Especially good are *a cappella choruses* that use no accompaniment and are happy to take on beginners. You can also take *private lessons* with a coach, but you need to have a personality that can stand to practise daily in your own home. If you are going to be embarrassed about practicing, private tuition is not the best path.

Musical instruments and marching bands

Learning to play a *musical instrument* is a good exercise for learning about the process of learning, simply because it takes a long time to achieve a level of competence. It teaches you about the tolerances needed for frustrating beginnings. Could you play a little every day, not liking how you sound, for the benefit of eventually sounding good in a few months? If the answer is no, then go do it.

Learning to play a musical instrument not only works on your hands (and breathing in some cases), but also requires new technical learning as you approach reading music in different keys. Learning to play an instrument is often a solitary activity at which you work with a private teacher. This can be a downfall for new players. If you can find a class where the teaching is done in a group, you will enjoy a better learning experience.

A great opportunity I discovered in 1995 is available for anyone living in Sydney or Brisbane. This is the opportunity of joining the "Late Starters' Band". I had the chance to meet with the founders of this group, and hear the bands from the two cities play in concert. I have never experienced anything so wonderful for adult learners. To watch these people do something that a year before was impossible was mind-blowing. If I ever run out of things to do, I would go do this.

Acting

In the last section I hopefully made clear the difference between 'acts' and 'acting'. The acts we were referring to are those that comprise our natural behaviour and which influence other people. At no time are we as trainers *acting* on stage in the sense of a stage actor. But taking on the skills of an actor can be a good path for trainers to expand their repertoire of natural expressions and behaviours.

Different types of acting activities produce different results. *Local theatre* presents another opportunity for trainers to extend their range. There is permission to try on new characters—to truly be 'not you' for a short while. *Improvisation classes* teach flexibility, quick thinking, spontaneity and adopting odd characters. It can be a real behavioural stretch. *Clowning* skills teach exaggerated skills—how to communicate just with the face and body, with no words. Imagine how expressive a face needs to be to have an impact through the makeup clowns wear. Clowning schools usually will also teach skills such as juggling and unicycle riding, all of which are challenging and rewarding once you can do them unconsciously. Once you know how to do these skills you will never forget.

Another excellent activity I have seen trainers tackle are *impersonations*. All you do is find a favourite comedian, or monologue from a movie, and work to replicate it. If there is someone who has a vocal quality, or set of gestures, or set of facial expressions you would like to have available to you, then mimicry is a good path. Of course, the goal for the trainer is not to look like or sound like that person when training, but the well-practised impersonator does have more access to behaviours for the experience.

Volunteer work

For some trainers, the acts they want to add are not found by learning physical skills. They want the skills of listening, empathising, staying present or getting out of their own situation. *Volunteering* to do work with different types of people in different situations is another outstanding activity for trainers. If I had my way I would have all trainers go spend a day a week for a few months working in a soup kitchen or halfway house, or staffing a suicide hotline. These situations teach us a lot about ourselves and our values. Many trainers I have worked with do time volunteering for the many organisations that need assistance such as the Meals On Wheels organisation, the Wesley Mission in Sydney's Kings Cross or the Breaking the Cycle group in Melbourne. They also visit kids in various hospitals, planning trips, playing or telling stories.

The library

Some trainers just want to improve their ability to sit still and concentrate. They also have much that they want to learn. And top trainers do not source their information from popular books, magazines or a general encyclopedia. I have tasked many trainers to go to a *university library* twice each week. Libraries are unique environments. They are full of quiet, slow-moving, concentrated people to model. The trainer learns a new way of moving, is focused more finely and learns to slow down their speech. They can choose any material they want to read during their hour or two there, but consistency is the key. This has been another simple activity that has transformed some trainer's performances, and the side benefit is that their students benefit from the rigorous material that the trainer stumbles upon a good library.

Going back to school

Some trainers want to improve their mental prowess and academic credentials. They want to achieve the act of the 'intellectual', the 'academic', of being 'smart'. These trainers *go back to university*. Personally, I think this is a wonderful aspect to a trainer's life. You hang out with other smart people, and read information written by smart people. You are also back in a classroom environment, which is excellent for honing your observation skills of the training and learning process. You also improve your study and writing skills, both of which are essential to the trainer who someday wants to 'go independent' or create their own materials. A doctorate can be a door-opener in some training communities. Even one class each semester will change the trainer forever and, over time, may add up to an advanced degree.

Other activities

In addition to all of those stated above I have had trainers do the following; they may give you some ideas. Consider how *you* might go with:

- sailing;
- horseback riding;
- learning to train dogs;
- doing pushups;
- walking;
- wave skiing and water skiing;
- learning to touch-type;

- taking computer courses;
- sculpting and learning other forms of art;
- photography;
- golf;
- doing standup comedy;
- doing Michael Jackson's "Bad" dance routine;
- writing a book;
- kayaking;
- mastering some video games;
- running marathons.

Some important guidelines for goal pursuits

I think the most important thing about selecting and pursuing these types of goals is to always remember why you are doing it. The activity itself may be fun and enjoyable, but the purpose is to develop new, comfortable, behaviours that would benefit you on stage. The side benefit of all of these activities is that they are learning goals. You get to go into the learning box yourself and re-experience that position first hand.

It is also important that you have some measurable end goal in sight. You do not need to do these activities forever, but picking some achievement that is possible in that activity in, say, a three-month period, is critical. Be specific. You want to know you are going someplace. If your goal is to run, how far will it be? For how long? How fast? If it is to fly a radio-controlled airplane, what type? Do you mean take-offs and landings? After achieving the goal, you can always choose to stay with it and pick a bigger challenge with that activity.

Remember that everything we discussed in Chapter 2 about the attributes of the learner and the experience of learning will also relate to you, the trainer. The more you know about your own idio-syncrasies, the better the odds of achieving the goal. You can always choose an activity simply for the intention of learning these things about yourself.

I would also suggest that you be cautious about who you talk to about your goals, especially at the start. For some people, telling others is a good source of motivation. But many friends, colleagues and family members can make inadvertent comments or ask questions that seem to negatively affect us as we begin. Sometimes I like to hold my new challenges close to my skin until I have had a chance to sort out the details—like why I am doing it—before sharing it with others. At other times, I announce my intentions very publicly, because I know for me it is a way of ensuring it will get done. When a thousand people keep asking, "How's the book going?" I am very compelled to keep working on it.

If you take on physical goals, then you will have to respect your body. Physical changes take time, and injuries do nothing constructive toward reaching the goal. If you have chosen a goal such as running, and you can only realistically do three short sessions each week (to allow time for recovery), you could do other useful things until your body can handle more running time. You could read books about running, or about diet. You could stretch, do some gym work or walk.

Concluding remarks

Unfortunately, you cannot know the benefits of these activities if you never do them. I know that for some readers this may all sound a bit strange. In *Training to Train* I tell my students that the four months of the course are going to pass whether they do anything or not, and really it is up to them. But if they have never tried this approach, they have nothing to lose. At the end of the few months, if it has produced no significant change, they don't ever have to think about it again. As it happens, that has never been the case. Many graduates of the course have gone on to include some new learning activity in their lives regularly, and all have grown measurably in their training and lecturing performances.

USEFUL ACTS FOR TRAINERS — THE RIGHT APPROACH

We cannot really say what are *the* useful acts for trainers. Every individual and circumstance dictates different rules. What I might be able to do congruently might fail miserably if tried by another trainer or in another set of circumstances. I know one trainer who sits on stage in an overstuffed chair (that travels with him) and smokes like a chimney while training. The thousand people in the audience do not mind, or mind much: these behaviours are totally appropriate for this trainer's content, image and character. Another well known lecturer who attracts thousands of students shuffles out on to the stage with uncombed hair, a badly fitting floral frock and massage sandals (you know, the ones with nubbly bits that feel like walking on nails). Her knowledge and credibility are so strong that these parts of her behaviour have become a kind of endearing quality. I once sat in a lecture given by the late Buckminster Fuller. At eighty years old there was nothing odd with his sitting in a straight back chair to lecture. His reputation was such that the audience did not even mind the fact that there were no breaks for the first four hours of the lecture.

The point is that for each of us there is a set of acts that are useful. Our gender, age, credentials, reputation, knowledge base, audience and so on all interact with the acts we adopt.

With that said, however, there are some generalities we can usefully make about acts. I have identified four cardinal outcomes for whatever acts we choose to use. Acts must:

(1) build and sustain rapport with members of the audience for the entire length of the training;

(2) keep the audience focused and interested;

(3) influence the audience to respond—in other words, to do what we ask them to do; and

(4) lead to the perception of *credibility*.

I have found that any acts, or components of those acts, that take away from, or violate, these four effects minimises the trainer's effectiveness, or forces the trainer to compensate for the effects in some way.

Building and maintaining rapport

The behaviours that allow us to build and maintain rapport are those that the audience can relate to as *being like them*, or that *their experience has acknowledged* as true for them and clearly is understood by the trainer. These are the behaviours that make you *likeable* to all of the members of your audience.

Keeping the audience interested and attentive

Second, the acts of the trainers must be *compelling*. Behaviours should make it easy for the audience to *want to listen* and *pay attention*. What the trainer does should keep the audience's focus on what is important to be attended to. These acts must generate a genuine interest in what the trainer is saying, doing and, in some cases, they must generate interest in the trainer themselves.

Creating response potential

Trainers are in the business of *getting other people to do things*, and if the behaviours we have do not build response potential in the audience, we are likely to lose effectiveness. We need to get our audience to do activities, take on challenges, think about information in new ways, try on new behaviours, persist in the face of a difficult learning process, listen to the information, critically evaluate new materials and so on. If our behaviours do not encourage people to do things, or if we leave room for members of the audience to resist our instructions, learning for them is diminished.

Generating credibility

The acts the trainer uses on stage must lead the audience to a perception of credibility—of being competent, and worthy, of being listened to for a period of time. Without a perception of credibility, audiences can minimise the importance and accuracy of the information being presented.

Some acts to consider

In Chapter 1 we re-conceptualised the trainer by looking at the attributes associated with other professions that relate to what it is we do as trainers. The attributes associated with each of these professions—*leading, influencing, facilitating, teaching* and *counselling*— are a good source of information about the kinds of acts that would serve us as trainers in the many diverse ways in which we have to work.

In leadership we find the acts of *visionary, motivator, personal power, risk taker, initiator, principle driven* and *eloquent.* The acts of the leader are especially important to the trainer who wants to work independently. Independent trainers not only need individual audience members to follow their work, they need potential clients as well. These are, of course, nice skills for any trainer to possess, but those hoping to succeed with their own ideas, research and theories must have the ability to access leadership acts.

From the influencers we can appreciate the acts of *rapport builder, credibility, believability, confidence, authoritative, enthusiasm, passion, likeability, inspirational* and *articulate.* What trainer wouldn't want a bucketful of these? Influential people are responsible for many of our own choices and successes. As trainers this is a large part of our responsibility to others.

Facilitators add to our source of acts with *coach, helper, organiser, interactor* and *resourceful.* The facilitator's acts allow the trainer to use many different methods to teach a subject. Facilitators, because of these acts, are particularly good at group work, team building, questioning techniques, creating meaning for the learning experience, allowing the students to learn independently and so on.

The two primary acts of a teacher are *discipline* and *authority*. You can imagine the limitations of a trainer who cannot access these two acts while working with a group of adult learners. By authority and discipline I do not mean to imply carrying the rod and whip to the front of the room. But in this profession we need to have the ability to lead and build response potential in our audiences. Remember, too, that many of our adult students were educated in environments with these attributes, so they will likely quickly respond out of habit to others who use these attributes.

Lastly, the primary acts associated with counsellors are *empathy, compassion, listener* and *non-judger*. In some situations it is precisely these acts that allow the trainer to vicariously enter the experience for the learner in difficult situations. Having a sensitivity to the learner's experience, and not trying to convince the student they are feeling something other than what they are, can be very compelling and highly motivating.

I am constantly observing very competent communicators. I try to identify the acts that they use, and what it is specifically about their behaviours that leads me to label the acts as such. Many times I find that it is something very simple and elegant that they do. These observations guide my choices of what to develop about my acts for the future. Such an approach might help you guide yours.

FACTORS THAT AFFECT THE TRAINER'S ACCESS TO ACTS

The notion of acts, and developing this range of acts, needs to be viewed through four unique lenses in order to view some finer distinctions. We need to focus on:

- personality and values;
- gender;
- age; and
- education and credentials.

These issues are paradoxical: depending on the individual trainer, these factors may be used to advantage or disadvantage, and they can be limitations or sources of enhancement. Again, we can say there are no rules: with enough personal power and the ability to construct meaning (discussed in Chapter 5), any trainer, regardless of age, gender or credentials, can get away with any act. On another level, we must honestly acknowledge that this is not the case for many developing trainers, so these factors will, in fact, play a part in what they can and can not congruently do in their training sessions.

These factors are not being pointed out to form boundaries or set limitations. But they are real issues until the trainer reaches the stage where they have what it takes to break the mould, and hence use, these factors to advantage.

The personality and values of the trainer

It goes without saying that each trainer has their own unique personality, just as do their students. Depending upon how rigid and narrowly focused the trainer is, this can sometimes be a source of conflict. For instance, the students may want it one way, but the trainer may be more comfortable delivering it differently. If they are convinced that their way is the right way, it's a bit like pounding a square peg in a round hole.

Some trainers are shy and introverted, while others are outgoing and extroverted. Some are guided by logic, others by feelings. Some are organised and plan meticulously, others much prefer to 'play it by ear'. The personality of the trainer influences the trainer's choice of methods, their level of interaction with students and the pace of the presentation, and it contributes to their range of acts. Regardless of your own personality, as a trainer you have a special obligation to accommodate, if not appreciate how to work with the diverse personalities in your audiences.

Our personality can place grave limitations on our career as trainers if we do not take on activities to expand our own personal comfort zones. I, by nature, am introverted and not comfortable in most social situations (although I am much better at this now).

Early in my career I was very uncomfortable in social situations where I did not know the people involved, and I much preferred to spend time on my own. This made it very awkward to take piano lessons from a teacher, do classes where I was the student or meet new clients. Over many years I forced myself to take steps toward learning how to be more competent and comfortable in those situations. I still am not an extrovert, but I can access the acts of the extrovert, and relate to them in my trainings. If you take seriously the discussion above about expanding your available acts you will find that a by-product is not a change in personality, but a degree of behavioural flexibility that allows you to act as a different personality type in the training environment.

Moreso than even personality, conflicts with students are often based on a conflict of values. Remember, values are what motivate us to move toward or away from our goals. They are what we use to interpret what is right and wrong, good and bad, normal and not normal. Some trainers will never use simulations and games, because to them they are not normal: "That's not learning, that's playing."

Re-evaluation of your values is hard work, and very confronting. Values drive everything—what you believe in, and the basis of your reality. Who wants to shake that up? Top trainers, for one—and regularly. They do it by being open to diverse experiences with people with different values sets, through books, social situations, volunteer work, whatever. I think the best trainers are those who have found the means to 'get meta', or above, their own values for the sake of understanding that which is true for other people, even if it is not true for them personally. At least they exhibit this trait in the context of training. *The quality of not invalidating students is the hallmark of the best trainers in the business.* We develop this quality only by understanding that values are right for the person holding them, even if they conflict with our own.

Everything you do as a trainer is value-laden. There is no value-free education. The minute you stand on stage and begin to talk, your values are apparent. It is easy to keep values out of strictly factual information. For example, Chapter 2 has very few value-laden statements—it is just data (although it was definitely my values that guided the choice of what to include in that chapter). But Chapter 1 and other chapters are clearly based on my own sense of what is right and wrong, good and bad, normal and not normal about training. It does not make it right, but those values have led me to view training in a way that has proven useful to other trainers.

Issues of gender

Your sex really should not influence you as a trainer in what you think you can do, or what material you teach. But in some trainers' minds, gender counts. I have seen both male and female trainers convincingly play all the major trainer's acts. Remember, we all are up there doing a job, and the acts that work in this job are those that are gender neutral. The acts of 'intelligent', 'funny', 'honest', 'credible' and 'flexible' are easily accessible to men *or* women. Even acts such as 'power', 'influential' and 'authority' can be seen in both men and women.

The acts that we use in some social situations may not be appropriate in the training situation. They may work to get a date, but they do not particularly work to assist someone's learning process. It is when the trainer uses gender-loaded acts in the training context that trouble arises. For example, female trainers oftentimes tell me that their male counterparts do not respect them, demean them in front of others, are afraid of having a woman show them up and so on. But remember the notion of acts. Respect comes to those with the act of being 'respectable' and you have to know how to naturally do behaviours that lead students to perceive that act. I have seen female trainers in a corporate setting using the acts of 'attracting', 'mothering', 'bitchy', 'flirtatious' and so on. I have seen male trainers access the acts of 'macho', 'hunky' and 'warrior'. None of these are highly useful in the trainer's repertoire. Top trainers—men *and* women—instead access acts such as 'intelligent', 'honest', 'funny', 'sincere' and 'well-read'. These are gender-neutral acts. I remind trainers of both sexes to think of why they are there in the training situation.

Issues of age

The age of a trainer actually has more consequences than does gender. It is very hard for a young trainer, or one who looks young, to access the acts of 'power', 'authority', 'credibility' and 'knowledgeable'. And even when they do, it can come across as 'arrogant' or 'know-it-all'. *The older you get the more acts you should convincingly be able to do.* You are simply going to have a hard time doing the act of 'wise' when you are thirty. Maybe the act of 'wise-beyond-your-years' might be more achievable.

The antidote for the young trainer is to learn the trick of adding a few years to their age by changing their dress, style, manner of speaking, and gaining lots of experiences that can be turned into credentials. By the time I was twenty-six years old I could say that I had worked with the US Army, Searle, Tektronix, NASA, every major television network, had owned my own business and so on. It added years to my age in the minds of my students, even though they actually knew my real age. It made me an anomaly, and that is a good act for a young trainer. Other really great acts for young trainers to try to access are those of the 'young eccentric' and the 'young genius'.

Older trainers are only limited by situations they create for themselves. The older trainer can appear out of touch with the current generation if they do not continue to understand the new values of younger people. They can also hinder themselves by losing physical flexibility and strength. As we lose these attributes we lose the stamina to hold an audience's attention. I have found training increasingly easy as I get older. I can do so many more things convincingly with an audience. I do not have to work so hard to be credible on stage, and that is an advantage. When I give a bit of my history now, people actually believe it.

I have found that trainers between the ages of their mid-thirties and their mid-forties have the best of all worlds. They do not have to work so hard to build rapport with a diverse audience, they still have relatively good stamina without having to do much to maintain it and they do not have to work so hard to establish their credibility.

You cannot control your age; the best you can do is analyse what acts are possible for someone of your years and then develop those acts fully. You might also begin observing other successful people within your own age group, and identify the acts that they are able to convincingly use. These insights will provide you with a useful list of acts that you, too, can begin to develop.

113

Issues of education and credentials

The *Macquarie Dictionary* defines "credentials" as: *anything which is the basis for the belief or trust of others in a person's abilities, authority, etc*. Your credentials are the significant artefacts that are accumulated and carried forward from the past; they represent your past accomplishments and achievements and by inference what you are capable of doing. As mentioned above, one benefit of strong, varied credentials is that it can overcome the problems created by youth.

Credentials play two other roles in your career as a trainer. The first is related to getting work, be it a job as a corporate trainer, or new clients if you are working independently. In other careers a person's credentials are likely only to be important at this initial stage. They open the door, help an employer or contractor assess the person's value to the organisation. After that, the person's past plays little or no role. It then shifts to a focus on performance. Yet, for us, our credentials are espoused every time we work with a new group of students. Every time we stand on stage with an audience who is unfamiliar with our past work and experiences, it must be made explicit for the audience. We must answer: Who are you? Why should we listen to you? Credentials relate to selling yourself into the job, or to the audience. Credentials are about *credibility* and *authority*.

Your credentials as a trainer also relate to: what you can ask in terms of your fees or salary; audience sizes you can attract; opportunities that come your way; the size of your client base; your access to the media; and the kinds of acts you will be able to convincingly do. All of these depend upon, and are intertwined with, the active pursuit of experiences, education and challenges—things, incidentally, that then become an artefact to be used at a later time. Everything you do as a trainer, whether directly or indirectly related to training, can be used to benefit your career.

Most people in other careers pay little attention to their credentials. They kind of end up with what came along the way; their university degree, a publication, a certificate. What is different about the life of a trainer is that the trainer pursues activities, adventures, experiences and opportunities expressly for the purpose of enhancing their credibility with clients and the audience. This does not mean that the experiences are not valuable in other developmental ways to the trainer, it is just that they become another scout badge, feather in the cap, or whatever. Experiences that add to one's list of credentials are actively pursued for the sake of being able to work and be accepted as credible by an audience.

CONCLUSION

This whole chapter is about the skills and artistry of the trainer—what we now possess in the way of these skills, and how we might realistically go about adding to our existing range of behaviours. The important notion in this chapter is that training skills are evolutionary; they develop over time through experience. The more experiences and skills we possess, the more we can bring into the training situation. Being a top trainer is rewarding work. We are allowed great flexibility to exercise our skills and improve our knowledge. But the rewards come from very hard, and for some, very risky choices that relate to our personal development. We have to be able to do just about everything we expect of our students. We are better able to convince students to stay involved in difficult learning processes if we ourselves are capable of doing so.

There is a whole world of opportunity available to the expert trainer, whether it be working for an organisation or taking steps to work independently as a training consultant. Any one of us can go just as far as our imaginations take us in this career. Those who have been successful are not different from us or naturally talented, it is simply that they have *done* something: they made choices to continue to learn, to continue to develop.

CHAPTER 4

organisation of knowledge, methods and the training environment

INTRODUCTION

We come now to another factor critical to successful training, namely, a training program's design and the choice of methods for delivery. Many competent trainers lose their effectiveness through incoherence, which leaves students feeling frustrated and confused. So although the student is attentive, participative and in general good rapport with the trainer, all can be lost with a poor structure to the event.

A good trainer with a bad design, or inappropriate choice of methods, will not likely produce the desired training outcomes. The outcome for any design is *coherence*: the content should flow logically from one point to the next, building each new piece of knowledge or skill on the piece before it. This chapter takes you through the stages involved in creating coherence.

The first section of the discussion is dedicated to exploring how to specify a training outcome and determine the starting knowledge and skill level of the students. From there we explore the process of working the content between those points into a logical sequence to achieve that outcome. The goal is to have a design that will lead to the outcome *even if your own training skills are still under development*. This kind of quality design is what allows some companies and organisations to have many trainers, of varying skill levels, producing similar results.

The US military provides an outstanding model of this principle. I found then, and still find to this day, that the attention to detail in the design of their long, technical courses amazing: every hour has its own set of outcomes, and sequence of content or exercises, to achieve that outcome. This is true for every hour in an eight hour day, for courses lasting several months. If the trainer simply ensured that each hour's lesson was delivered and understood by the students, the aggregate knowledge at the end of the course produced competent engineers, tank drivers or whatever. Design at this level is a buffer for the variance in trainer's skills.

This aspect of training is also important for those who are expected to design new courses and then present them to audiences without extensive beta testing. If you face such a task, you will need to better the odds that your course will 'work' the very first time it is delivered. The design process described in the first section of this chapter promotes success on this front.

In the second half of this discussion we introduce the variety of delivery systems used by various trainers. The choice of delivery system—how the content is to be presented—is only made after the design is complete. How can we know what the best method of delivery is without knowing what it is we are trying to achieve? Many trainers have 'pet' methods, those that they are most comfortable with, or those that they simply have a value for. You may have a high value for 'lecture' type methods, or 'process' type methods, but they may be totally inappropriate for the achievement of your outcomes. So you cannot know how to do something until you know what the outcomes and sequence of content indicate.

The design and choice of methods for delivery of the content is guided by your knowledge of individual differences between the learners and the knowledge of your own range of acts. You must be able to evaluate, and make choices, for design and methods based on two factors:

(1) the effects the design and methods will have on different students; and

(2) your own ability to execute the training as designed.

As much attention must be paid to these two components of training as to any of the others we have covered so far.

The second topic in this chapter relates to the many environmental issues that affect your design and choice of methods. The training environment is the place, or space, in which the learning activities are taking place. It may be in a corporate training room, hotel conference centre or someone's backyard. These environments are made up of various elements, and these elements affect both the design and the choice of methods. For example, you may want to use a game to make an important lesson salient, and a game may, in fact, be the most appropriate method. But if it turns out that you end up training in a small, stuffy room, a game may in the end not be possible. You will need to be able to think in alternatives—as I used to say, a hundred ways from Sunday—to get the same outcome.

THE DEVELOPMENT OF CONTENT — SEQUENCE AND DISCOVERY

As important to us as our own range of behaviours, and our knowledge of that which determines the behaviours of different students, is the organisation of the content and skills we intend to teach. It is the design of the training that leads to clarity of the information, the competence with which skills are developed and the ease of the learning process for the student. Design takes care of many of the problems that we confront. A good quality design also buffers any skill that we lack and neutralises much of the diversity in the audience. Design, and design alone, is what allows us to have complete success in achieving outcomes with all members of a highly diverse audience. The consequences of a poor design, regardless of our own training skills, become evident in the reaction of the students: confusion, frustration, avoidance, negative feelings and so on.

A solid design process also allows you to feel confident that the training will produce the desired outcomes the first time that training is conducted. This does not mean that the training will not improve with repeated performances, but the improvements will be more in the nature of achieving elegance in the delivery, and not so much in the flow of the training.

Understanding design processes is even important to those who work exclusively with other designers' material. A designer who lacks real-time training experience cannot know how their sequencing of the content will work in the classroom situation. *What looks good on paper is not always what actually works in the training situation.*

Design relates to three distinct activities:

(1) specifying the outcomes of the training session;

(2) identifying the starting level for the program, based on the existing knowledge or skill level of the students; and

(3) sequencing the content that falls between the outcomes and the starting level.

Creating a good design means thinking about content and skill development from several different perspectives. The content needs to be worked at several different levels. We need processes inherent in which is the drive and motivation to think about the content differently for each distinct stage of the design process.

The six-stage process that follows is one that I have used, and have continued to improve upon, for the past twelve years. It is the process responsible for the creation of all the current work that I conduct publicly—both long-term classes, and short, one-hour lectures. It is a process that needs to be experienced in order to be evaluated. Unless you try it, with actual content, you will have no way of understanding the potency of what the process is driving you to do.

Overview of the six stages of design

On the following pages you will be introduced to a six-stage process of design. Each stage is essential to the process of creating a coherent training with achievable outcomes. Each stage forces us to think about the content from a different perspective, each important in its own way, to ensure that as many potential problems are eliminated before the first run of the event. Additionally, each stage allows us to consider what the impact will be of the training on the future student. A design that works well for the trainer, but that does not work for the learner, should be left on the shelf.

The first stage of this process involves defining the outcomes for the training. You will need to determine in specific terms what the students will know, or be able to do, at the end of the training session—as well as when they return to their work or home environment. The second stage involves determining, or knowing how to elicit, any prior knowledge and skills of the learner. This enables you to know the starting level for the training. The construction of the training's outcomes and the discovery of the starting level of the audience members defines the boundaries of the training's content, and content must fit between these end points. The third and fourth stages of the design process involve building systemas—determining all of the content elements that fall between these two points, and sequencing the content such that each piece builds logically and meaningfully on the preceding piece. When all the content has been sequenced, the fifth step is to evaluate the cohesiveness of that sequence, by running through the content from point to point and locating any gaps in the building toward the end outcome. The sixth, and final, stage of the design process is then to choose the appropriate methods of delivery for that content sequence.

Stage 1: Define outcomes

It should make sense that the first task to be undertaken in any training design would be to do with outcomes. It is *the* reason for training in the first place. How can we know what the elements of a training should be, and how those elements should best be presented if we do not first have a clear sense of what kinds of changes we intend for our students? Defining our training outcomes answers the questions:

- What will the student know, be able to do or feel as a result of having attended the training?
- How will we know if the student has achieved that set of outcomes?

It is common for trainers and designers to think in terms of outcomes, but if these outcomes are not articulated in precise terms, you may not have a way of evaluating whether the outcomes have been achieved.

Students themselves are affected by a lack of specificity in the statement of outcomes. How is that you and your student will know that what was intended to be learned has in fact been adequately learned? The answer to this question must begin with a clear statement of specified outcomes. Competent trainers will tell you that outcomes do not just happen, they need to be precisely designed, and stated in terms that clarifies in our own minds, and in the minds of our students, what they should be able to do, to think or how they should feel at the end of the course.

Another important reason for well-specified outcomes is seen when there is not enough time to construct an adequate design for a training. In that case, if there are well-defined outcomes and the trainer has some content knowledge, it should be possible to make the right methodological choices and sequencing decisions to ensure that the outcomes are met by the end of the training.

Precisely defined outcomes can also assist with the handling of potential problems, especially those problems that relate to the student. The statement of outcomes tells students clearly what to expect of the training, and diminishes problems that arise when they cannot perceive the relevance of elements of the course. It also allows the student to have some tacit prior agreement about why they are attending the course. How many times has a student started a course only to discover that what is being taught is not what they expected? Such problems go away with well-defined outcomes.

Lastly, well-defined outcomes are critical for attracting an audience, especially for the independent trainer. I have always told my students to sell outcomes, not trainings. Sell the potential student on what they will be able to *do* at the end of the course, and sell it specifically and honestly.

Type of outcomes

There are three general categories for the outcomes we are charged with as trainers. The first are outcomes that relate to changing an individual's action, behaviour, performance, competence or skill. These are outcomes that define a change in behaviour, what the individual will learn to *do* or *do better* than they could prior to the training experience: to sell, to design, to write, to create, to convince, to inspire, to type are all outcomes that fall into this category.

The second type of outcomes are to do with changing how an individual thinks—their perceptions, ideas, thoughts, decisions, knowledge. These types of outcomes depend on new information and new ways of perceiving situations. An outcome in this category might state: "The student will be able to empathise, to see new solutions to existing problems, to know, to understand."

The third type of outcomes trainers are responsible for achieving are those related to changing how people *feel*—how they feel about change, about new policies or about others in the organisation.

Of course, many outcomes cross these boundaries and fit into more than one category. They also have multiple effects. Say that an outcome I had was to change how managers *perceive* the behaviours of their young employees. Say that I succeed in achieving the outcome. I am likely to notice that these managers now also exhibit a change in how they *behave* toward, and with, their younger employees, and also how they *feel* about them.

Considerations for the statement of outcomes

I have learned many things from other trainers about setting outcomes; in the process I have identified several considerations that can help us derive clear and achievable outcomes for our trainings. If you have a training manual handy in which outcomes or objectives are written, you might grab it and see to what degree those outcomes have met the following considerations.

The first consideration is whether the outcome statement is saying that the student is moving toward something new, or away from something old. Outcomes stated in the positive—what the student *will* do, *can* happen, *will want* to do, tend to fare better than those stated in the negative—what they *won't* do, *can't* happen and so on.

The second is that the outcome should be conceived of in actual, demonstrable, language. Let's say you have an outcome to make the students happy about the new changes in the organisation. The questions you would put to yourself are: What does "happy" mean? How will I or the students know if they have achieved that outcome?

Outcomes require a statement that is clear and demonstrable: you need to think about what the student will do, see, hear, think, if the outcome has been achieved. The most important questions you want to be able to answer are:

- By what evidence will it be evident that the outcomes of a training session have been achieved?
- How can the outcome be measured?

In the context of training, you cannot know for sure that you have achieved an outcome for which you have no measure, or way of seeing demonstrated. But let me say this: *evaluation forms at the end of the training are not satisfactory as a measurement of outcomes.* Measurements take the form of tests, worksheets, exercises. Outcomes may be measured by new behaviours you observe demonstrated during role-plays or when the student returns to work. They may be measured in quantities or in qualities.

The consequences of not having well-defined and measurable outcomes at the start of the design process should now be evident. You and the student may achieve outcomes other than those intended. You may achieve outcomes and not know it. Different students may come away with different interpretations and levels of competence. *Trainers are paid to get outcomes—everything else is superfluous.* Lack of specificity in outcomes causes everything else to break down—*outcomes are the foundation upon which everything else is built.* If the outcome is for all students to be able to touch-type at sixty words per minute—then everything falls in alignment—I will do whatever it takes to ensure that the students achieve that outcome. It keeps me focused on the task at hand and helps me to mentally avoid distractions and irrelevant tangents.

Stage 2: Determine the starting level

Once you know the ending level, where you want to take your students, you have to define the starting level for the students. More than any other stage in training design, this is the one most likely to be left out or be arbitrarily decided. Too often it is only the educational background and work experience that is considered when thinking about the student. But those factors represent only a very small part of the total picture of what the student brings into the training room.

Not knowing where to start the pitch of the training has two potentially disastrous results, both of which occur at the very start of the training. The first is that if the level is too low, students are inclined to believe they know this material already and tune out before you get to that which is interesting or needed. Students can become bored and argumentative, challenging your opening points. The second danger is that if the level is too high, it can lead to confusion and frustration and a feeling in students of being in the wrong place.

So how do you discover the starting level of an audience? One way is by looking at the common denominators that audience members may share. Perhaps they all belong to the same organisation or club. Perhaps they have a shared experience—like getting a first job, or learning to drive a car. These universals tell us a great deal and can be used.

Another method is to invite the potential attendees to fill in a questionnaire that elicits this information. For any long course I run, such as *Training to Train*, some sort of prior written work or live interview is conducted so that I know this information in advance.

In other situations I will elicit this information at the start of the class by asking why the students are there, what is most important for them to learn and what other experiences have they had that relate to the subject at hand. In such circumstances you will have based the other preparatory stages on an educated guess of the starting level, so after you verify your assumptions, you will need to be flexible about where you actually begin the lesson. Regardless of when you clarify the starting level, you might safely make one assumption: *students will almost always know more than you think*.

But here is the trap. Say you are going to run a course on negotiating skills for young managers who have no formal experience or qualification with negotiating. It is easy then to assume that the students, not being professional negotiators, are bringing nothing into the training situation. But all of us, in other contexts, do negotiate and use skills associated with negotiation: we listen, question, influence. We may use these skills and subskills within our families, for better deals on a car, at auctions and so on. I am always looking at my outcomes and asking: Are there other life experiences from which the student may have gained knowledge about the subject we are going to explore?

Another reason you want to hope that the student does have some associated experience is because in order for them to remember and make sense of what you are teaching, this new information or skill has to be linked to something already known.

Stage 3: Building systemas — identify the content

What the first two stages have done for us in the design process is define the boundaries of the training. They become like big black endposts within which the training now must neatly fit. The more clarity that exists about these two points the easier, and less confusion we will encounter making the next necessary decisions. If these boundary points are fuzzy or vague we will not know precisely what content is absolutely essential and what is merely interesting.

Stages three and four comprise the activities that are called *building a systema*. A systema is a map—a modal map of the training that tells us two things. First, it tells us in detail all of the content that must be covered to train the student from their starting point through to the outcome. Second, it tells us the sequence in which that content needs to be delivered in order to logically build from one point to the next. Everything must connect and make sense. It is this process that *transforms* what trainers know into a viable experience for the learner. *How you organise what you know is not how that information needs to be organised in order for it to make sense to others when you express it verbally.*

This is why experts from various fields do not necessarily make good trainers or teachers. It is not that they are not knowledgeable, it is that their knowledge is not organised in a way that can be coherently expressed to others. Have you not ever wondered why someone, so good at what they do, confuses you when they talk about it? Have you not ever read something that made total sense, but found that as you tried to talk about it to others, they became confused—or you became confused yourself? *Masterful trainers have an amazing ability to translate information from one type of mental organisation to another type of mental organisation.*

Building systemas is a process that helps you *reorganise* existing knowledge and skills, or organise new knowledge and skills you are learning strictly for the purpose of training. *It is a process of ripping information and skills apart and putting them back together in a new way.*

There are five steps in building a systema:

(1) identifying the content;
(2) clustering the content by main topic;
(3) making a decision regarding depth or breadth;
(4) sequencing the content by main topic; and
(5) sequencing the content between topics.

The first three steps are discussed below, the last two steps fall into the area covered by the fourth stage of design: building systemas—sequencing the clusters.

Step 1: Identify the content

At this point I know that many trainers attempt to write an outline of the content between these two end points. But linear outlines only give us our knowledge back in the form in which it is already organised. This misses the point: trainings designed this way are often incoherent from the learner's standpoint.

If the overall outcome is to reorganise existing knowledge or organise new knowledge in such a way that it can be meaningfully communicated to others, the first of our tasks is to get that content out of own minds (or other resources, such as books), and make it devoid of any organisation. It is like taking a completed jigsaw puzzle and breaking it down to the individual pieces again and pretending we do not know what the completed picture looks like.

How we know and use information and skills is not useful to us when deciding how to teach that same material. If I tried to teach you to use a word processor from my knowledge of using a word processor, I am likely going to confuse you—unless I strip apart all the individual components of my knowledge in the hope that, through analysis, I will be able to put them together into a new organisation, one that allows you, the student, to move step by step toward word processing competence.

The single best process I have found for mentally getting into a state for doing this type of activity is known as "brainstorming"—the same process that is used at the start of many new projects, or when looking for new patterns between information, or solving difficult problems. The outcome here, however, is a bit different in that you are not looking for anything new. What you need is a method that lets you dump the information you know about the subject, without evaluating that content's level of abstraction or value to the training. Information is not stored in our brains in a linear fashion, it is random.

If you have tried to create a training in outline form, you will know the difficulties I am speaking of. Until you have sequenced content for the purpose of teaching you will not likely have a linear organisation for the information you know.

In the *Training to Train* program I provide students with a design exercise. They are given the outcome of creating a lecture on any topic familiar to the members of their team—something everyone knows at least a little about. Before beginning they need to establish the boundaries:

- Who is the audience?
- What do they already know about the subject?
- What are the outcomes?

The only boundary I provide is the length of the lecture: one hour.

The students are then divided into teams of five and given butcher's paper and several packets of Post-it notes. After a few minutes together to establish the boundaries of the lecture, they are instructed to all participate in generating as many thoughts and facts about their topic that they know, in a five-minute period. *The single most important outcome for the brainstorming session is to generate the largest quantity of data possible in the time they have.*

All the students are asked to participate by writing their own ideas in a word or phrase, and saying them aloud. This allows the other team members to hear the idea which, in turn, may spark their own next thought. No comments regarding the relevance or quality of the contribution are allowed. Attempting to categorise these thoughts during in the brainstorming session only hinders the process and limits the number of contributions. Time for evaluation will be allowed at a later stage, when that type of thinking is appropriate.

The brainstorming is fast, very loud, and frenetic. The teams generate between eighty and two-hundred separate thoughts about the subject, at all levels of detail, all disjointed, and all disconnected. Various thoughts and ideas are scattered all over the page. Little yellow Post-it notes everywhere. This is raw, dissociated content. It is perfect.

What are the important lessons to learn from this exercise? For starters, ideas spark other ideas. Thoughts are associated, and the minds of the team members, at times, run down the same path. New thoughts produce radical shifts in thinking and spark exploration into new areas or facets of the subject. The oddest thoughts often are followed by important new pathways. And it should be clear that the faster you go, and the less you 'think' about it, the more content is generated. If this process is hard, or takes too much mental effort, it is not being done correctly.

Of course, the brainstorming, being time-limited, does not allow for all the ideas to come to the surface, but enough are generated to begin working with. Other thoughts will emerge during other parts of the process to fill in the gaps.

Building a systema is an evolutionary and iterative process. It is built in layers, and as you move through each of the layers, what is discovered there influences the layer before it. You may find that you are coming up with new and important content elements at each stage of the process. So although the brainstorming phase comes to an end, during other stages of the process you will still be grabbing a Post-it pack to add new thoughts.

You can easily do this content-building process on your own, and as trainers you will likely do this on your own as the norm. The only key is to discipline yourself to set time aside for this kind of activity, and allow yourself to 'go for it' as you would if inspired by a group. If I received a call right now requesting a lecture or training on some subject, I would first work on the starting level and outcomes and then set time aside to brainstorm everything I know about the subject between those points. I would break the content down into its constituent parts.

Step 2: Cluster the content by main topic

The second step in this stage requires a shift in mental gear. We need to evaluate each piece of content and see how it relates to other pieces of content. We will be comparing Post-it notes. The desired outcome is to cluster similar subject pieces together into what are called "domains". It means picking up a Post-it and evaluating the category into which the idea fits, then bringing other Post-its to the same area of the page. The desired outcome is to identify patterns or themes in the data and cluster them by similarity. When the clustering is done you will have anywhere from three to ten little puddles of Post-its.

This process calls for a very different quality of thinking—it requires critical evaluation and analysis. You are asking: What is this? In what category does this idea fit? You are asking your brain to make connections.

There are some special situations that may arise in this process. First, you may find that one idea fits in more than one category. In is case, simply write the idea again on another Post-it and place one in each of the clusters. Second, you may find that you have unnecessarily written the same idea twice. If so, just throw one of the Post-its away. Lastly, you may find that this process generates other thoughts and ideas. Great! Write them down and place them in the appropriate cluster.

You will also notice that different clusters have different numbers of individual pieces of content. Compared to the richness of some other clusters, some clusters may disqualify themselves for lack of content or relevance. Or you may decide to pay attention to the weaker clusters and flesh them out with more facts within that category.

When you finish clustering all the Post-its on the page, write the name of each domain or category in bold letters on large Post-its and place them at the top of each cluster.

Step 3: Decide the depth or breadth

You now have a critical decision to make before proceeding. Looking at the number of clusters, and the amount of content within each cluster, you will likely have more information than it is reasonable to work with. The cleanest way to decide how to cull the information at this level is by making a decision based on whether the lecture or training is to attend to depth of information in a few domains, or go for breadth across all domains. It is unlikely, except in special circumstances (such as long-term skill-based courses) to have, or need, both breadth and depth.

If you go for depth, then the approach calls for you to choose only a few of the many domains of information, keeping all of the detailed Post-its in those clusters. If you favour breadth, then you will keep all of the domains, but throw away all but the two or three most important content pieces in each cluster.

Say that on your paper you have ten main clusters with approximately twenty pieces of information in each. If your decision is for depth you will evaluate which three domains are most important and throw away the remaining Post-its in the remaining seven clusters (but perhaps keeping the cluster labels for future reference). You might imagine in your lecture saying, "Ladies and gentleman, there are ten important themes related to our subject today, and they are blah-blah-blah. Given the time we have, and our outcomes, I have chosen to focus on just three of these domains in depth."

If your decision is to go for breadth you would keep all ten domains and select two or three of the major points about each. In your lecture you might say, "Ladies and gentleman, today we will be discussing blah-blah-blah. There are ten main themes. Each area is very complex and would take more time than we have to treat in any level of detail. What I will be doing is introducing you to all the major themes and some of the major points within those themes. For more detail you can…"

The minute you start thinking about breadth or depth, the job of design simplifies. But this step can only be accomplished after the brainstorming and clustering stages. Imagine, sitting where you are right now, deciding to do an hour lecture on some subject you are familiar with, and at this moment making a decision for depth or breadth. Where do you go from here? Your mind is likely to not generate enough information to adequately fulfil either task.

Stage 4: Building systemas — sequence the clusters

The next stage in our design process calls upon yet another quality and type of analysis. Our job now is to sequence the content in each of the clusters logically, so that each flows one to the next.

Step 4: Sequence the content by main topic

In this step, your Post-its will be transformed from their current formation of puddles, to a linear top-to-bottom row, with perhaps some indentations for minor points you wish express. The easiest way I have found to do this exercise is to talk my way through each of the clusters. "The first main idea I want to discuss is… The most important thing I want you to know is… and that forms our foundation for understanding… and…" The key question is: What does the audience absolutely need to know first?

During this stage you will likely find that there are gaps. You may see no way to get logically from the point you are at, to the next point for which you have a Post-it, without adding some other content. Now is the time to write more Post-its to fill in gaps. You may also find at this stage that some content really is not necessary, so some Post-its will be discarded. At the end of this exercise you will know the proper sequence for teaching each of the topics you have listed by domain.

Unfortunately, in trainings we tend to cross back and forth between domains—a little bit of this, then some of that, then back to the first domain and so on. Before we discuss cross-domain sequencing, however, there is an important tangent we should take. Many trainers write or envision writing about their content expertise. Some thoughts about that process are worth making here.

Sequencing for writers

If you were writing a report, or even a book, on your content expertise, you would stop the design process at this stage. Each domain can constitute a chapter on a particular subject, so you now have the basic sequence of key points to guide your writing efforts. Books are organised differently than verbal lectures; where lectures tend to weave their way across domains at ever-increasing levels of complexity, books do not. This, by the way, is the challenge I face writing this book. The threads of content I have organised for teaching is what I am now trying to gather together by topic into cohesive chapters.

Writers have the opposite problem when they try to lecture. Speaking in depth about each topic one after another does not gel well for a listening audience. If it did, we would just read books aloud to our students.

For writing, this the fastest process I know for converting what we as trainers know how to talk about and reorganising that information in such a way that it plays well in written form. And it's worth practising. Independent trainers, or those who aspire to independence, will especially benefit from authorship.

Stage 5: Sequence the content between topics

The final stage before the selection of methods accomplishes two tasks simultaneously. On the one hand it handles this cross-domain sequencing issue, and on the other it performs an evaluation of our design—specifically, it uncovers whether the sequence flows logically from one piece of content to the next, helping you see if you can verbally make the bridge between the segments. The outcome in this stage is to look for gaps—holes in the content, and incoherence—those times when you just cannot get from where you are to any next Post-it in any domain.

Preparing for stage 5

Before starting this task, there is one thing you can do to make this process easier: sequence the domains from left to right on your chart in the order in which you *think* is most important at this time. Ask yourself: What is the first domain that logically needs to be introduced? What is the second? And the others? After making these decisions you will literally pick up the Post-its and reposition them to the appropriate column. But it is important to recognise that this sequence may change during the evaluation process which follows.

Do a talk-through

The process you will be involved in during this stage is talking your way through the content that sits in front of you on the chart. You start with the first piece of content in the upper left-hand corner, and work your way down. As already mentioned, in a training, it is unrealistic to deliver all of the content in one domain and then skip over to the next. We usually weave between them, and you will do this in your talk-through.

This is doing the training mentally. It allows you to determine how each piece will be talked about (at least in general, off-the-cuff, terms) and how you will make the verbal movement from one concept to the next. If you get stuck and find you cannot logically get from where you are to where you want to go, you should stop and either add another concept you had not previously thought about, or shuffle things around. If all of the content is there, the sequence for the content should be very easy to determine.

Now how are you going to capture these natural movements through all of the content on the chart? The single best way is by audiotaping this session. This audiotape can then be transcribed either in total, or just for the key points, to form the actual teaching guide.

Think also of what this is doing for your rehearsal of the material. This is a very quick way of knowing what you know and in what areas you may be weak. Another advantage is that because you only have one- and two-word short cues for the content, you have to talk extemporaneously about each subject. This will build confidence to work without notes and help you make that breakthrough. You will find it easy to remember the handful of key word cues and begin trusting that you know what to say about those content pieces without referring to your notes.

Remember, you are yet to make any decisions about what actual methods you will be using in the training. At the moment it is as if you will be lecturing for the whole time. At least it is nice to know that you could do that if you had to! But you must accomplish this first task to ensure that the content can be verbally expressed and that it makes sense. Once this is done it is easy to make decisions about the best ways to present that material in the training session.

Summary

You now have a working systema, and have verified its coherence in the talk-through process. You might be wondering if it is worth this effort? From my experience of working with trainers with extensive design experience, they tell me that this process is at least fifty per cent faster than any other process they have used. Another benefit is that this process, given its guided nature, is less frustrating; you always know what needs to be done next. Trainers who use this process tell me they do not get 'lost' in the content as they do when trying to do all of the various forms of thinking at the same time. Lastly, they tell me that it is the only design process they have used that prepares them mentally for actually doing the training—with the added bonus of knowing with confidence that the content will make sense to the audience.

When I teach this process in *Training to Train* I task the students to choose some existing project they are working on, or to just simply pick a one hour piece of content they would like to teach in the future, and experiment with this process. The key is to start simple—I tell them to being with planning just a one-hour lecture. I do not want them to be too ambitious. This process is generative. I ask them to spend just a few minutes each day on some part of the design—ten minutes doing a brainstorm one day, ten minutes clustering the next and so on. They are instructed to put up their work on a blank wall somewhere they are likely to see it throughout the day. Many ideas come to mind while just sitting looking at the chart and thinking of other things, or walking past on the way through the office. This process is evolutionary, and it is very difficult to do all the stages in one session, but gradually, results emerge.

Trainers cannot know the power of this kind of approach without some experience. When *Training to Train* students are debriefed at this point, two other topics naturally emerge. We should discuss these topics before moving on to consider how best to choose the method of delivery for trainings.

Finding and using reference material

Once you have a training designed, one of the best things you can do for yourself, your students and the credibility of the training is to go to the technical literature and support your content with well-referenced academic or scientific research.

Too often, trainers forget, or do not realise how important it is, to cite references that support their content. The questions most asked by students are:

- How do you know what you know?
- What evidence are you using to support your argument, conclusions or claims?

When I sit in a training course, listening to a lecturer espousing some belief, teaching a strategy or giving information, I always want to know the source for that information, and what facts support that information. Unless the trainer is a researcher, I know they are not the source. Remember, unless you are the researcher and originator of some theory, everything you say about it is grounded in someone else's work. You need to contend with the students' constant underlying query: *Who are you that we should listen, let alone believe you?* Audiences want to know that what you are saying is not based simply on your own intuitions or experience, but on some body of research.

Of course, there will be times when what you have to offer *is* based on your own experience. In such a case, it is appropriate to preface your thoughts with, "I am unaware of any research that substantiates these thoughts, but from my experience…"

Citing referenced materials, be it theoretical or experimental evidence, adds credibility to your presentations. It lets the audience know the source of your material, so that they may approach that material themselves. It allows them to question the validity of the material. Where you get your information influences the audience. Citing popular literature, the local newspaper or *What* magazine, is not necessarily bad (okay, it can be real bad), but the point is that by citing where you got your information, students can place the appropriate amount of weight on that information's credibility. A popular 'psychobabble' book may have interesting, even accurate, information, but it may not be perceived as highly credible to your audience. Your best bet is to refer, in all cases possible, to the original scientific or academic researchers in the field. A side benefit is that it will introduce you to, and keep you abreast of, new information and theories in your own field.

Note that any content published in written form is useable in verbal paraphrases so long as you acknowledge the source—not citing the source is plagiarism. Citing references is also a sign of respect for the originator.

Getting through the technical literature

Reading academic literature is an art in itself, and one that I certainly did not possess early in my career. In addition to the fact that trainers often have little time to read, they may find this kind of literature daunting. The consequence is that trainers either have no backing for their content, or the content draws on popular literature that lacks serious credibility. Too many trainers have not had the experience of learning from technical literature, and therefore find studying it an arduous task. If this is the case for you, I would make the following suggestions.

Technical materials or academic papers are not read the way one reads a novel or a newspaper article. There is a difference between 'reading' and 'studying', and technical materials are studied. Take small pieces at a time, and go through several iterations. Read through an article to get a sense of what the author is on about, and discern the key points of the study. Then determine whether or not this information is useful to you. If it is, take more time with it. Perhaps take notes, and paraphrase the key findings.

Most importantly, practise talking about the work. Remember, we are trainers, and how we understand things in our own minds is not the same way we need to organise that information to discuss it with others. Try reading some relevant literature, and prepare short, two-minute presentations that coherently re-present this new knowledge. Knowing something, and knowing how to talk about it, are totally different activities.

Stage 6: Choose the method of delivery

Once you have a working systema, and *only* when you have a working systema, you can begin to think about the methods of delivery that appropriately express your content. In many cases you will not have to think very hard. The many methods that can be used to deliver the information, or develop the necessary skills, is inherent in some content and content sequences.

Types of methods of delivery

Trainers use all types of methods in their practice. Some limit their choice of methods to those they are most comfortable with. Others attempt to use methods they have seen used in other trainings, perhaps without enough flexibility to convincingly manage the reactions they get from students (for example, some trainers, while attempting to utilise a game or activity, fail to get the students to participate). There are many types of delivery systems, or methods, available to the trainer; these are only a few:

- lectures;
- games;
- showing videos;
- computer simulations;
- interactive facilitation;
- group processes;
- role-plays;
- reading assignments;
- worksheets;
- stories and metaphors;
- case studies;
- analysing scenarios or hypotheticals;
- simulations;
- demonstrations;
- question-and-answer sessions;
- brainstorming exercises;

- modelling;
- use of media such as overheads and slides.

Of course these are all major methods, and within each there are many variations. For example, group processes might entail dyads (two participants), triads, small teams of five or the group split in half with a hundred in each team.

Throughout the *Training to Train* program I attempt, at some point, to use most of the major methods to achieve different outcomes. This is predominantly so the students can one day go back to the videotapes of my sessions and, ignoring the content, focus on an analysis of the methods used. For example, during one session on values for money, I use a writing exercise coupled with a group process. This is an appropriate method for the outcome, although there are other methods that could have been used instead. But having used this method for the session, the trainers can now watch that session again and focus on how the method was constructed. What elements were necessary in the set-up? How did I manage to neutralise the potential negative reactions to the use of this method? What is the time frame for the exercise? How did I maintain motivation during the exercise? How did I debrief?

What guides the choice of methods?

There are four factors that will guide your decisions about choice of methods. What is indicated by the systema must be evaluated in reference to these four factors:

(1) time;
(2) audience;
(3) environment; and
(4) the outcomes.

Time

Time is an issue in many facets of the professional trainer's life. In regard to our choice of methods, some simply take more time to execute than you may have, and therefore, no matter how appropriate the method is, or how much you personally want to use it, a second choice will have to made.

A second way time will influence your choice relates to the use of a variety of methods to punctuate a long class session. If you have an eight-hour day with students, an 'all lecture' approach will kill off all but the most resilient students. So even though lecturing may be the most appropriate method, you may need to introduce some others simply to break up the pace.

Audience

Who is attending your course will also bear on your decisions about appropriate methods. The methods must be appropriate, or you must present the rationale to make those methods be perceived as appropriate for the members of your audience. Trainers often misjudge their audiences by believing they are too conservative to try new methods for the sake of learning. My experience has been that this is a misinterpretation. Most people will try new things, so long as they make sense. Oftentimes, it is the trainer who is uncomfortable asking the group to engage in some activity, and if the trainer is uncomfortable, then no doubt the students will feel uncomfortable.

Another consideration is based on the audience's relationship with one another: do they know each other and, if so, what is their relationship? People behave, and are accepting of different behaviours, depending upon whether they are in a group comprised of strangers or familiar people. Within familiar groups the trainer will also have to consider the relationship between the students (for instance, they may have to think carefully when members of the senior management take a course along with their employees).

Environment

The environment, or elements within the environment, may also be factors you need to consider. Room size is a major factor. Will the participants be able to comfortably be active in the class? Also, different venues will have different guidelines and rules. Some will not allow the use of music, some will not allow students to do exercise anywhere but in the conference room.

The outcomes

The following are some guidelines I follow when making my decisions about delivery systems that relate to my outcomes of the course I am designing. They are not rules and they are not right in every situation, but they do provide a framework for me to think about what is, and what may not be, appropriate to do within any given training situation.

(1) The methods chosen should not be chosen because they are fun. Fun is not a criterion for learning. That 'it is fun' is also not compelling, nor convincing, to many who are there to 'learn'. No matter what choice you eventually make, you must feel certain that you can make that choice relevant and rational to the audience. They need to agree that it is the most appropriate way to get the outcome.

(2) The methods chosen should have no other purpose than to operate as an educational tool. The choice must have been made because it is the best method for achieving the given outcome.

(3) If more than one method will get the outcome, the easiest, most elegant, means must be chosen—the one with the fewest movements, fewest components and shortest time frame.

(4) You must feel confident that you have the skills to execute the method you have chosen.

MORE SPECIFICS ON ENVIRONMENTAL FACTORS

You, as the trainer, are the single most significant part of the training environment—and truly masterful trainers can produce results regardless of all the other elements combined. A good trainer will be able to build and sustain motivation toward the outcomes in 40-degree heat, on cement floors and with bad lighting. Fortunately, most of us do not very often have to contend with such extremes. Some trainers have the good fortune of having a great deal of control over the environment for their trainings. Equally, some have the good fortune of either having enough clout or enough financial resources to pay close attention to the environment they create. Yet this is not the case for all trainers and, unfortunately, not all trainers have yet learned to manage their students' attention such that poor environmental features are not a distraction.

Elements of the environment — its impact, your control and some cautions

The training environment consists of many elements. There are two broad categories of environmental elements to consider. There are those *inherent in the space* itself: exit signs, airconditioner noises, uncovered windows, floor coverings, wall coverings, tables and chairs, outside noises, room entrances and lighting—to name a few. Then there are those *introduced by the trainer*: staging, spot lighting, microphones, music, student handouts and materials, flipcharts or overhead projectors and the like.

Before we address some specific thoughts about some of these elements, there are two general themes that relate to any of these elements existing within that environment. The effect of these elements on the student, and the amount of control the trainer has over the elements, warrants mention, as do a couple of cautions about relying on the environment to help achieve outcomes.

The impact and suggestiveness of the environment

We need to consider environmental elements because of their capacity to be noticed by students. What all environmental elements have in common is a sensory-based *impact* on the participant; they reach the students through their five senses. Therefore, they have the capacity to capture attention. If elements in the room that play no part in achieving the training outcomes capture a student's attention, there is distraction—distraction away from you and the tasks you set.

There are many potential elements that have the capacity to distract attention. For example, a loud airconditioner might keep kicking on and off, poor lighting might make reading difficult or melt you into the shadows, there might be glare from uncovered windows, the chairs might be uncomfortable. Such elements lead the student to 'feel' something—if that feeling is unpleasant, they will act to change their relationship to the environment—perhaps by leaving it. Whatever they do they will in some way act out—and that acting out may not be in the best interest of their own learning process, or may affect the learning process of others.

In addition to having some impact on the students, these elements may be *suggestive*. They may influence how the student perceives the training and its content, or may influence how the student perceives you personally. This, in turn, affects whether you will achieve your outcomes. This suggestiveness predominantly relates to the environmental elements that you, as the trainer, introduce into the environment for the purpose of managing the classroom and achieving outcomes. Outside noises may annoy students, but students are not likely to look poorly upon you because of it. But items you are perceived as controlling will impact their feelings and thoughts about you and your content. For example, in recent years some trainers have begun using background music in their classrooms for the purpose of enhancing their students' learning. To some participants this may suggest a sense of fun and relaxation, to others it may suggest that you are a new-age fluff-bucket. Tidying up the participants' notebooks, pens and other supplies while they are on breaks will suggest to some students professionalism, while to others it will suggest that you are nosy. Keeping the room very cool will suggest nothing to those not bothered by it, but may suggest a lack of sensitivity to those who are freezing.

So the first level of analysis regarding your training environment is led by these two questions:

(1) How will different types of students interpret an environmental element?

(2) What impact will that element have on different types of students?

Environmental control

Once you address those two questions, you need to address the issue of *control*—how much control you actually have over the elements within the environment.

Not all of the elements in the first category can be controlled: it will not be possible, for instance, to move structural posts that block the view to the stage, or cover exit signs, or move power points. But there will be some measure of control over many of these elements: windows can be covered, seating arrangements can be such that windows are at the back of the room, scratched tables can be covered with cloths, more comfortable chairs can be hired, mints and candies placed on each table by the hotel can be removed by the trainer, squeaky stages can be made not to squeak and so on.

All the elements in the second category are obviously controlled by the trainer, although the quality of these elements may not be within the trainer's control. For example, the trainer may decide that a sound system is needed, but may not have any control over the quality of that sound system. However, the trainer does ultimately have control over these elements: that control is either to use them, or not. If the frequency of the microphone happens to be the same as that of the passing taxis, and radio calls keep coming through the system, the trainer does have a choice to teach without the microphone.

For me, before the event begins, I minimise the impact of any elements in the environment that I can control. First, if it is not needed, it is not in the room. There are no extra chairs, or tables, or coat racks or whatever. Second, I go for consistency whenever possible. I use the same sound system and microphones supplied by the same audiovisual organisation, I have spotlight trees on hand to brighten a dull room, all signs and pictures are either removed from the walls or covered and so on.

The problem with relying on the environment

In recent years there has been much emphasis placed on environmental support in trainings. Every effort is put into ensuring that the students have a comfortable environment. This is a good thing. However, I have a word of caution. Beware of convincing your students that some environmental factor or factors are responsible for their outcomes and performance. Additionally, be careful about working in training environments that are far removed from the actual environment in which the student will need to use the skills you have taught.

Let's take a ridiculous example to demonstrate both of these problems. Say a trainer believes that if the students sit facing north, they will learn more easily, and furthermore, sitting in a north-facing position is the best way to perform. So during the class the trainer convinces the students of this principle, and they do sit facing north for the training, and get an excellent result. Now what happens when they return to their own work environments, where they sit facing south? This is likely to affect their feelings and thoughts about, and use of, what they learned. Or worse, they may try to convince their co-workers, who didn't have the same experience, to turn their chairs to face the north. These co-workers are likely to think their colleagues have gone off their rockers or, worse, have been manipulated by a weird training guru.

I apologise for the silly example, but others that come to mind are real situations that may offend. I only caution for the possible negative effects on the use of what you teach when students return to their own environments.

The problem here is one of transference. Of course, we want our environments to be comfortable and conducive to learning, but we also should be aware of the environment to which our students will return. The features you add to the process of learning need to be contextualised in just that way, and the students need to be given strategies to still utilise what you have taught them when they apply them in their own special circumstances. What you make safe to do in your classroom may be socially inappropriate back in their own environment.

The questions to keep present in the back of your mind are: What is the environment in which these students operate? How is what I teach going to play out in that environment? *Training is not just about a student's success in your classroom, it is actually more about their ability to transfer what they have learned back to their own.* And a rule I try to follow is this: if the student cannot, or likely will not, do something in their own environment, attempt at all costs to have them learn without that in the training environment. Hugs and warm fuzzies may feel good to some students, but they are not essential to learning effectively, nor to working effectively. If they are not essential, cut them out.

Specific issues

Now to some specifics. In the opening chapter we introduced the diversity different trainers work with. Therefore, so much of what follows will depend on your specific environment. You may not have options to do much about any of this, but to the degree that you can, you should. If you cannot control the feature, don't worry; the next chapter will teach you strategies for minimising or neutralising the effects.

Room set-ups

There are many different types of room set-ups, and each one serves a slightly different purpose and encourages a different type of interaction. How your training room is set up will depend on a few things:

(1) the activities the students will be doing in the session;

(2) the profile of the students;

(3) the amount of space you have; and

(4) whether you have staff to make changes to the room set-up on breaks.

The number one question you want to be able to answer is this: For what purpose does the room need to be set up in this way? If there is no real outcome-oriented purpose, then stick with the expected norm—theatre or classroom style.

The two most acceptable and least threatening room set-ups are theatre style, and classroom style. I say most acceptable and least threatening because these are the models that most adult students have of what a classroom or lecture should look like. Anything different will have an impact and needs to be dealt with before they enter the room. When I start a new class, without any previously built rapport with the group, I want the room set up in such a way that the students do not have to figure out why I am doing what I am doing. Opening a new lecture with the seats set in a circle, or no seats and just pillows on the floor, is going to suggest unuseful things to many students. If the major outcomes at the start of your training are rapport, safety and comfort, the room should suggest nothing but the expected norms.

If the students need to do coursework and take notes, seat them at tables; writing on one's lap for any length of time is uncomfortable, and therefore most students will stop taking notes. Also, sitting for any length of time can be uncomfortable, and leaning on the table can relieve some of that stress.

You might also consider keeping the tables clear of anything not necessary for achieving your outcomes. Personally, I do not have mints or water and glasses or hotel pens and pads on the tables. If it is a long class and I am providing materials, then only a notebook with paper and a good quality pen will be on their tables. They will get frequent breaks to refresh themselves, and the sugar from the mints has a real adverse effect on the students' energy over time. They will need to keep eating mints to stay awake!

If you either have a short lecture, or a large audience, the best arrangement is still going to be theatre style. If the chairs are moveable, you might want to ensure that the room is not set perfectly parallel to the stage; it will be hard for those on the end to stay focused on you. If you curve the ends of the room so all the chairs have some forward facing direction, you'll alleviate this problem.

Remember, too, that people will need to move around, even if just to go out on a break. Therefore, try not make the rows too long. You might put in two aisles instead of one centre aisle if needed.

Alternative set-ups may be appropriate for some classroom activities. But these need to be introduced once you have rapport with the group, and they need to be explained so the students are not shocked. If I am going to change the room on a break—say to a large circle of chairs—I will tell the students before they leave on the break, and explain the reason for the change. When they come back into the room they are prepared and they know the rationale for the change. I have seen trainers do room changes, and when the students come back into the room, they do not know what to do, so they just stand by the walls looking for clues from the behaviour of other students. For each moment they lack clues for the appropriate behaviour, they will feel uncomfortable.

Room temperature and airconditioning

Room temperature will absolutely depend on the activities of the group. The appropriate room temperature for students sitting and listening to a lecture for an hour is not appropriate for a group moving about and engaged in some activity. There is a notion that the room should be kept cool, but I would change that to say *comfortable* temperature. Remember, students have different body types and metabolism and each individual will experience the room's 21 degrees differently. For some it may be comfortable; for me it would be uncomfortably cold. I observe my audience all of the time for clues as to how they are feeling. What I try to achieve is that no student is beating their arms for warmth, and no student is dripping sweat from their face. I aim for somewhere in between. No matter what temperature you set for the room, some will wish it to be a bit cooler, and others will prefer it to be a bit warmer. So find a middle ground and tell them that.

The bigger problem with airconditioners and heating systems is noise. Some have a low-frequency hum that drowns out all of the variation you are trying to create with your voice, if not making you hard to hear altogether. This noise distraction is often worse than the effects of having too warm or too cool a room. When I have been in this situation I have said to the students, "Listen, I know it is a bit warm in here, but you will find the noise of the airconditioner is very distracting. What I will do is turn on the air during the breaks to cool things down, and give you a few more breaks throughout the day."

Breaks

Breaks you provide for the students are not just for fun, or ritual. They serve a purpose toward the end goal of getting your outcomes. They provide the students time to refuel. Learning, and the concentration it takes to learn, burn essential fuels in the body such as glucose and water. Also, students have a capacity for one type of concentration and will need to break that state periodically to shift gears. If a session has been highly stimulating, students may need to time to stop and reflect on the experience. If a session has been of very low energy, they may need to take a walk to get some blood-flow to keep from falling asleep.

I do not have any set rituals for breaks. I may know that there will be two breaks sometime in the morning, but the timing for those breaks will vary depending on the activity level of the group and their own state. It does not serve a group to break at the height of some learning experience. They may have trouble re-engaging in the experience when they return. It also does not serve a group to continue with something when they are clearly not 'present'. Breaks also serve the purpose of punctuating your class—it signifies a completion or mini-completion of one piece, and when they return they will expect to move on.

A big problem can be created with too few breaks. No matter how interesting the content, the trainer who has personally experienced a two-hour lecture will know the value of frequent breaks. It allows the students to refresh themselves—and stay awake. Also, if students know that there are frequent breaks they will resist leaving in the middle of sessions to go to the toilet, get a glass of water, take a walk or have a smoke. Too many breaks can also mean problems. Students will wonder when they are going to get on with it. I design for short, very intense sessions, with frequent breaks.

Lighting

Lighting is another critical element the impact of which is often lost in most trainings. There are two types of lighting to be considered—stage lighting and classroom lighting. When lights are dim in a classroom, students may drift off, reading can be difficult and they can get annoyed. This is the problem with the use of overhead projectors: dimming the lights to view an overhead is fine for a brief moment, but continuing to lecture with those lights dim can drive students to distraction.

Whenever possible, the stage should be the brightest spot in the room. It will attract the students' attention forward. Professional trainers will have spotlight trees positioned on the sides and back of the room to lighten up the stage area and defeat any shadows. Unless the room is no larger than a small room that would seat about twenty people at tables, I will attend to this detail. Remember, you need to stand out.

Staging

Staging has two advantages: the trainer can see the face and upper body of all of the students in the class; likewise, all the students can see the trainer, regardless of their position, without craning their neck. Staging is easy to hire and install (typically it comes in one metre square segments) and can be moved to whatever end of the room suits the set-up.

It is important that the stage be covered with some soundproofing material like carpet. This keeps the creaks to a minimum. Without soundproofing you will likely find that you instinctively stop moving on the stage, or do as I have done, and asked the class for permission to kick off my shoes and walk around in my socks!

151

SUMMARY

This chapter addressed the third essential quality of the top professional trainer. We discovered the importance of creating a coherent sequence to the content you teach, and looked at how to ensure that the choice of methods and use of environmental factors are considered from the design and learner's perspective. We did all this by working through a six-stage design process, inherent in which is the type and quality of thinking we need when attempting to translate information from one form to the form required in order to present that information verbally.

The ease of the process should in no way mask the complex task it allows us to perform. I would wish that some time soon you make an appointment with yourself to test this process for yourself.

CHAPTER **5**

the construction of meaning in real-time training situations

INTRODUCTION

The preceding three chapters have taken a static and separatist view of the components of the training situation: they looked at the learner and their experience; the trainer; and issues of coherence, design and environmental factors. The discussions treated these features as if they were frozen in a slice of time. Yet, as we all know, training is a dynamic real-time process. This presents one of the difficulties in writing about these processes—we lack real-time situations to analyse. But we can begin to put movement into these features, and this chapter begins that process.

To do it, we are going to explore training from a new perspective and view these components in interaction—how they play against one another and how a competent trainer *manages* this interactivity.

153

In every minute of the training session, components of the training situation act upon one another. They share a reciprocal relationship: you do, or say, something and it triggers an internal or external reaction in the student; something unexpectedly occurs within the environment to distract the students and your next action is affected. In real-time most of this reciprocal interaction occurs outside the conscious awareness of both you and your students. But in the next two chapters we are going to address the question: *By what means does the trainer control this dynamic process?*

A close analysis of select trainers shows that there is one particular skill used in a wide variety of ways to maintain control. This is the skill of constructing meaning for events and experiences for the student. This chapter will explore how we create meaning, and in some cases, how we change it.

THE CONSTRUCTION OF
MEANING AND RELEVANCE

Trainers, when they stand to talk to an audience, have very specific meanings in mind for the information and experiences in which they engage their students: in other words, *this* means *that*. Unlike an artist's canvas, where each viewer creates their own special meaning for the work, a trainer usually needs all members of the audience to have the same precise meaning for their work. The specific meaning the trainer has in mind for any particular thing they say or do *does not just happen*, it must be explicitly constructed for the student. Meaning must be controlled by the trainer.

There are three distinct uses for this skill for the trainer. First, *everything* the trainer does and says will suggest something to the student. What we do as trainers is filtered through the student's own past experiences, personality and values. If you neglect to control the meaning of events by making things explicit, the students will make up their own meaning—and that meaning may be counter-productive to their learning process. This is the single most significant cause of problems in training situations.

Second, students enter our environment as complex entities with rich histories. Sometimes the meanings they have attached to past experiences may affect how they behave in your classroom. The meanings and interpretations they have attached to these past experiences may need to be re-evaluated by the student and, ultimately, changed. You will need to know how to do this.

Third, you will need to be able to create meaning for the experiences the students have in the exercises and class activities of the course. For example, if a student should fail a test in class, it will be your responsibility to create meaning for that experience such that the student continues to perform.

The scope for controlling the meaning

Top trainers succeed for one simple reason: *they control the meaning of everything that the student sees, hears, feels and experiences during the course of the program.* Specifically, the trainer controls those interpretations that lead to negative mental and emotional reactions: perceptions of threat, embarrassment, silliness, controversy, discomfort, confusion, difficulty, ambiguity and so on.

So what is meant by "controlling the meaning"? Trainers know that students process every nuance of the information presented, the objects in the environment and the trainer's behaviour through their own filters, and proceed to make sense of things in their own unique way. What the competent trainer does is *tell* the student, either overtly or covertly, what that stimulus means in a particular situation or context. For example, when a professional trainer announces a test, he or she will know that the activity and notion of tests have very different meanings for different students. Those different interpretations will lead each student to their own unique internal processes—such as self-talk and the accessing of memories, external behaviours (like changes in posture or eye movements) or visceral arousal (like a change in heart rate, or sweat gland and gastric activity). These different responses will affect the student during the test. A good trainer knows this in advance and creates a meaning for the "taking a test" activity that is consistent for the entire audience.

Controlling the meaning of objects and events serves two functions. First, it constructs one meaning for all students in that context (for instance, the meaning of "test" that the trainer wants them to hold). Second, the trainer has anticipated the likely reactions of the diverse group and used that information to *tell* the students how to interpret their own reactions. The trainer creates meaning for both the activity and the student's reaction. And trainers do this for *everything*.

Why the trainer should determine the meaning for the activities and events

The appropriate meaning for all that occurs in the training situation stems from the rationale for why the trainer chooses to do an activity in the first place. This is why it was so strongly emphasised in the last chapter that the careful choice of methods is for the express purpose of selecting the best one for achieving the outcome. You have to know why you are doing and saying everything. If you do not know the rationale, or if that rationale is not realistic, how will the students know the importance of your choices? *You* have to know and then you have to *tell them*.

Some student meanings are just not based on fact

Why can't we just allow the students to utilise their own meanings and interpretations while in the training situation? We cannot allow this for the simple fact that we do not know, nor can we guarantee, that the meanings our students have for, say, a group activity, or a piece of controversial information, will be accurate or useful. They may have meanings and interpretations that lead them to inhibiting behaviours which adversely affect their own learning process. The meanings that students have affect their behaviours, and their behaviours affect their learning achievements. For example, if a student has a set of negative feelings and thoughts triggered by my American accent, my ability to work effectively with that student may be limited. It is my job as the trainer (given I haven't been able to change my accent) to give my accent a meaning that allows the student to remain receptive to me. They may still quickly judge and turn off from other American-accented people, but my goal is to neutralise these effects when they think about or work with me.

Constructing meaning is the way to manage the feelings and emotions of the students

As we now know, the environment, methods and trainer's behaviours trigger emotional and physiological changes in the student. By managing the meaning of environmental factors, your choice of methods and your behaviours, you in turn manage the learner's emotional responses to these factors. Students who become anxious about taking tests may still feel anxious, but much less so, if they understand the purpose of the test, your intention, what they can do if they feel uncomfortable while taking the test and what they can do if they fail the test. This helps students understand their own reactions and provides them with a means by which they can internally process those reactions in a more useful way. It is as if they can say to themselves, "Oh, this is what this feeling is, he said this might happen. I just need to relax and keep going."

Predicting student responses becomes possible, with experience

How does the trainer know how the student will react? The simple answer is through experience. A trainer on stage is also learning. They are listening and observing their students. In the early days of a new training, we do not really know how the students are feeling or thinking. We do not know how they are interpreting the messages and activities. When a training is new, the trainer spends a lot of time exploring these facets with the students during debriefs. With repetition the trainer eventually collects enough knowledge to know what is going on for most students in most activities. He or she can see the signs of it from the stage. The trainer knows what they need to say to the students before doing whatever is next because their experience tells them the likely problems that some students will confront.

Of course, anomalies will also stand out. For example, if a student starts crying during the telling of a story—a story that no one has ever responded to with tears before—the trainer will have to discover what happened so that it might be anticipated in the future. It might be that the next time the trainer is ready to tell the story they might say, "Before I tell you this next anecdote, I must tell you that for some reason it has evoked some sad memories for some people. If that should for any reason happen, then… [tells them how to feel about that and what to do]." The trainer might also feel that the one teary student was just a fluke and choose not do anything unless it should happen again.

Think about this scenario. You have a whole class of students who have been studying for an exam. You know everyone has done the best they can in their preparations, but you also know from experience that some people will not pass the exam: it might be that they freeze up while taking tests, or they may need another pass at the material before it will truly make sense for them. What do you do, knowing that, for some students, failing will likely create a meaning for that experience that leads them from ever trying again?

You might say that you will meet with those who fail the test and offer to tutor them for their next attempt, or you might try to console them in some way. Trainers need to know how to construct a new meaning for students when there is some unanticipated negative reaction. Yet, reconstructing a meaning for an experience after the student has had their own interpretations working on it is very difficult. The best approach, if you can foresee difficulty, is to handle it up front. Short-circuit a student's interpretations *before* the event. The following strategies are some of the ways you might do this.

Two methods for the construction of meaning

Tell them directly

As has already been stressed, if you can anticipate the variety of negative reactions students are likely to have to some object or event in a training, you will want to handle it up front. Information is the great leveller in a diverse audience. The time for this construction of meaning is during what are called set-ups—the introduction to new activities or changes in direction of the information delivered in the course.

Set-ups are the time in which the trainer creates a context and meaning for what is about to happen, for what they are about to do or for what the students are about to be asked to do. When the trainer does this they are telling the student *how* to react, or how to interpret their reactions, during the next piece. It is the time for anticipating and directing students toward the best set of mental and physical behaviours to get the most out of what is going to happen.

Conducting good set-ups is a hallmark of excellent trainers. Nothing is left to chance or the imagination, and therefore many potential student problems are handled right there at the start. Put the other way, so many problems that are encountered by students (and reciprocally by the trainer) are caused by the lack of, or poor quality of, the set-ups. Set-ups are so important that they are one part of the training that I mentally rehearse, and for which I will even use notes. Forgetting things at this stage can lead to mass confusion in the students, which harms the whole of what is to come.

Not only is the set-up used to neutralise anticipated negative reactions, it is also the time for creating relevance—relevance for the information, for the activity, for methods, for everything that student might question (and in questioning, thereby lose the benefit of the lesson). Without relevance, people will not participate, or will not take the information or the trainer seriously.

A third use for set-ups is to handle another kind of 'how to' question: how to participate in the up-and-coming activity. It might be related to the mechanics of how to do an exercise, how and what to notice in an exercise, how best to participate to learn, alternative ways to participate, the consequence of not participating and so on. Essentially, the trainer is telling students how to behave, how best to learn, how to get the most out of the session.

There are many negative consequences to a poor set-up—as you will see in the final chapter when we address situation-specific questions and problems that confront trainers today. In that chapter we will also discuss the finer points of determining how much the students need to know, from nothing to full disclosure.

Tell stories

Story-telling is another way that top trainers construct meaning and manage the reactions of their students. When a trainer knows from experience that certain reactions may occur, then telling a story so that students come to a way of perceiving the situation before the event is an elegant way of dealing with these likely situations.

When I was the trainer for the *Learning to Learn* program, the improvement of students' reading speeds and comprehension skills were a major outcome of the course. On the final day of the training, after having gone through all of the exercises, the students were post-tested to see how much their reading skills had improved. One time a student came to me in tears at the end of the session, being very disappointed with his test results. As I explored what the actual results were, I discovered that he had actually improved his reading speed by eighty per cent and his comprehension had jumped from seventy per cent to ninety per cent. His disappointment stemmed from the fact that he did not do as well as he had hoped and that so many other students had even better results. The experience with this student taught me to anticipate that some students, even after a successful result, will still feel bad because either their own expectations had been set too high, or they had compared themselves to others. So I began to tell the story of this student before post-testing other classes. After telling this story I would ask the class a series of questions: Who was the only person they could realistically compare themselves to? Of course, they replied, "Ourselves." I would then ask what they should be comparing themselves to? "Our own past performance." How many times have they tried to use these new skills? "Never, this would be the first time." Would any step in a positive direction be a good sign? "Yes."

With these understandings now in the students' minds, there were never again people who cried after a positive result. There still were occasions when a student would express disappointment in not having done better, but this disappointment was coupled with a neutral emotional response and an understanding that the skill would improve further with practise.

Remember, too, that stories trigger students' memories from their past. I am always looking for ways to have my students remember past successes, or past struggles they overcame, or experiences with other people who had good strategies for surviving difficult situations or whatever. These memories create a way of making a useful meaning for what they are experiencing now in the training session.

Debriefs and the construction of meaning

The construction of meaning in a set-up is meant to assist the student in getting the most out of a session or activity and handle any likely derailments that might otherwise occur. Debriefs are what the trainer does at the end of an activity, or the completion of some block of content. The construction of meaning in a debrief is to ensure that everyone in the class has learned what it was intended for them to learn, and that the meaning the student attaches to the experience is positive and useful. Lastly, debriefs are the time for reconstructing the meaning for any problem or situation that occurred that was not anticipated in advance.

Methods for debriefs

There are several different ways to conduct a debrief, and most are addressed in the final chapter. But two of these methods are important to this discussion. Inevitably, the method you choose will depend on the amount of time you have, your relationship with the students and your outcomes for the session.

Questions

Questions are one of the most common methods used for debriefing a class. Students can simply be asked to share their experience with you and the rest of the class. You might ask, "What did you learn about _____?" or "What did you notice about _____?" Note that these are not couched as open-ended questions. I have found that open ended-questions can lead to useless tangents. Students will in fact learn many things in any exercise or class session, but usually we are only interested that they learned specific things. These are what we want to explore with them in the debrief. As the students respond, you can use their comments to reiterate some important points to ensure they are salient for everyone in the group. You might simply repeat the student's response, modify it, add to it or tell a story to make the point truly significant. You can also use rhetorical questions such as, "Did you find that _____?" or, "Wouldn't it be nice if _____?" These bring the salient points of the lesson to mind without having to take the time to elicit responses from the group.

Tell them what they learned

Another debriefing method is simply to tell students what they learned in the lesson, perhaps punctuating that with stories of your observations of the group while they were engaged in the activity. This method can realistically only be done after many repetitions of the training and many question-based debriefs. With that experience, you will, for the most part, know what the student has experienced and learned. When this method can be used, it saves a great deal of time.

You might also put the class into small groups to explore specific things they learned in an exercise before you debrief the whole group. I do this when there have been many individual insights in a given activity and an open class debrief would take a long time. In small groups they are able to share all of the diverse experiences, which benefits the members of the group; I then might ask for any common or unusual experiences to be shared with the whole group.

CONCLUSION

Understanding this principle of constructing meaning for the choice of methods, behaviours and the anticipated reactions from students has illuminated, for me personally, the single most significant factor that allows some trainers to produce such consistent and profound results. For you, the first step I would suggest is simply to observe the ways you are already using this strategy in your own work. Second, I would suggest you observe the kinds of problems you currently encounter in your communication experiences, and think of how you might use the strategy outlined in this chapter to deal with problems before they even begin. Mastering this skill is quintessential to becoming an artful trainer.

controlling chaos — spontaneity and the unexpected

INTRODUCTION

In this chapter we are going to apply to actual training situations the skill of constructing meaning and the insights formulated in all the preceding chapters. We are going to start with the most complex situations we face as trainers—the training situations that are most daunting and most demanding of us—namely, chaotic situations that arise unexpectedly through the training day. My belief is that a trainer who can handle the unexpected elegantly can easily handle any part of the training that is going according to plan. This chapter will prepare us to make more sense of the more ordinary real-time events that confront trainers (events which we will discuss in Chapter 7).

Most professional trainers spend a great deal of time preparing for their classes and work with meticulously planned course outlines and well-designed materials. With a good understanding of the learner's process, and a good range of appropriate behaviours, doing what is planned is easy. However, as anyone who has had the experience of conducting even one day of training knows, no matter how well the material is rehearsed, and how well potential trouble spots are thought through, unexpected events happen. The real demonstration of the skills and artistry of the masterful trainer lies in their ability to deal with the unexpected and chaotic nature of training. In the world of training, unexpected events are the norm, not the exception. There are times in a training day when what is happening is not in the plan, when the trainer does not know what just happened and certainly does not know what exactly is going to happen next.

There are two kinds of unexpected events that dominate trainings. The first are based on the mere fact that students exist—where there is interaction and response between people, the unknown is more pervasive than the known. The second source of unexpected events is quite simply the nature of training environments. Murphy's Law is alive and well in the trainer's world: if something can go wrong, it will.

Before we begin, for the first time in this book we need to distinguish between 'training' and 'lecturing' activities and environments. In general, trainers and lecturers have enough common threads to benefit from all of the preceding discussions. However, unexpected events are more pervasively a part of the nature of trainings than of presentations and lectures.

A couple of metaphors may help make the distinction clear. The art of lecturing or presenting is much like the performance of a dance routine or a stage play. Everything is rehearsed and planned— movements, gestures and timing. It is a performance done *to* the audience, not particularly *with* the audience. There is little room for the audience's reactions and responses to change the performance— those responses are typically calculated in the design and preparation and are not surprising to the actor or dancer. Training, on the other hand, is like playing a sport in which there are two teams. Your team has developed a range of skills—hitting, catching, throwing or whatever. Your team also has developed strategies to deal with the various contingencies the other team may throw at you during the course of the game. But what will actually happen in the moment of play depends on the interaction between your team and the other team. What your team does in any given moment has everything to do with where the other team is and what they are doing. What your team will do next depends on how the other team responded to your last move. In a training situation, the trainer is on one team and students are on the other. Trainers, therefore, need to have a game plan, a set of skills, quick thinking and reaction times, and the flexibility to change their tactics depending on the reaction and responses of the students. What actually happens in the moment of interaction with the students changes everything—student responses determine precisely what the trainer does or says next.

It is rare that we are called on to deliver spontaneous, off-the-cuff presentations, but trainers, more so than lecturers, do need the skills of the masterful, extemporaneous speaker to deal effectively with the unexpected events that happen in the course of a training day. We need the ability to maintain control in the face of the hundreds of things that can cause chaos, the ability to think on our feet and the ability to turn unexpected events into valuable lessons in the learning process.

In this section we are going to discuss the common sources for these unexpected events, how we can best be prepared to deal with them and in what way we might (if necessary) minimise their occurrence and effects.

AN EXERCISE IN UNEXPECTED EVENTS

In my courses for trainers I use an exercise to introduce the topic of dealing with unexpected training events. All the elements of the topic are embedded within it, and emerge as a result of this exercise. The exercise also allows the participants to observe the management of chaos. I actually do not have any idea what is going to emerge, or how what emerges will manifest itself in the exercise. I do know the key points of the lesson that I want to see made explicit. Yet, how they emerge is left for the process itself. Here's the set-up.

The set-up

The students are told that they will be engaged in an exercise that will highlight all of the important points about the kinds of things that can throw our well-designed, prepared-for presentations into disarray. They are told they are about to experience the little jolts that force them to think on their feet.

In the exercise they will have an opportunity to see how they respond to those situations and also how other members of the class deal with similar situations. I inform them that the exercise will require working in teams of five people, and with their team they will design a short presentation. The presentation can be on any subject that has been covered in the course that they and their team-mates feel comfortable enough to talk about for a minute or two with little preparation. The only rule is that all five members of the team do a segment of the presentation, one after the other. So one team member will begin, followed by another, then another and so on until all five have made a contribution. Their outcome is to pass their segment of the presentation to the next person in line in a 'seamless' fashion, so that by the end of the talk, the audience has the feeling that they have heard one contiguous presentation. They are instructed that the length of each person's segment will be approximately forty-five seconds to a minute in length.

Before I send them off with their classmates to design their presentation, I do let them know that I am withholding one piece of information about the presentation—reminding them that the exercise is designed to give them the experience of dealing with unexpected events. Clearly, the unexpected event they have to deal with is being withheld for the moment. This makes them appropriately nervous.

The unexpected event

Ten minutes later the class is brought back together to give their presentations. They know which team member is presenting first and second and last and have some idea of what they are going to say. I ask for a volunteer team. I want a team whose members feel confident enough to go first, as they will be the only team who has no idea, or time to think, about how to deal with the unexpected event programmed into the exercise. There is always one team willing to have that experience.

The team comes to the stage and stands in a line, one next to the other, ready to begin. I stand in front, pull a box of matches from my pocket and hand them to the first speaker, and announce that the variable being added to their presentation is the variable of time. They are told that the length of each person's segment of the presentation can be as long as, but not exceeding, the time it takes for one match to burn. The rule is simple: light the match before you begin to speak and when it goes out, for whatever reason, stop talking. The next person will then light their match and pick up the presentation at that point.

What happens

With the first team anything can happen. They have had no time to plan at all for this contingency. A person with no match-lighting skills may either not get the match lit at all, strip the head off the match when trying to strike it, or see it flaring out of their hands into the audience. Another person may light their match and begin their presentation, but make a big gesture and accidentally extinguish the match. Another person lights their match and stares at it for the entire length of the presentation—looking as if they have put themselves and everyone else into a deep trance. Some match-holder presenters go all the way to complete their part of the presentation, but the match is still burning, so they fumble to add some extra bit that was never planned for and step on the toes of the next presenter's piece. Another presenter finishes their presentation just as the match goes out, but in their relief they forget to pass on the matches to the next presenter and no one seems to be able to get their attention—they forgot that they are part of a team. Some people actually just keep talking if the match goes out before they finish. This makes everyone jumpy and nervous.

If the unexpected can happen with a match, it has happened to this first team, burnt fingers and all. At the end of this presentation, the first team is acknowledged and thanked and sent to their seats.

Back to the drawing board

Now that the remaining teams know what they will have to contend with they are given five minutes with their team to discuss any changes they want to make to their presentation, or to create a new strategy or whatever. Some teams do major work in this five minutes in an attempt to control this now-known variable. Other teams go for coffee and do virtually nothing—they figure they'll take it as it comes. When their planning time is complete, I reiterate the instructions: one person after another, seamless presentation, no talking by the presenter once their match has extinguished. You might think that planning would help. Well, it does a little (for some), but matches are a very consistent source of continued chaos, no matter how much planning the team does.

The remaining presentations

The entire class is asked to notice the various ways that groups attempt to manage the chaos-inducing matches. They are also asked to write down any thoughts that come to mind regarding what the matches metaphorically represent in training sessions.

With this last set of instructions the teams come to the stage one after another. Some teams do seem to manage the matches. They have planned how to pass the box of matches after striking the match, they have learned to keep an eye on the match without losing their focus on the audience, they have learned not to use big gestures, they use the matches to punctuate their lesson and so on. Some teams, or team members, are still flustered: the burning matches seem to melt their brains into puddles of incoherence. Some apologise to the audience, some get really goofy, some try to remain rigidly professional.

WHAT DO THE MATCHES REPRESENT?

There are three basic categories for the 'matches' that frequently flare up in training sessions. There are environmental, student and trainer matches. Each category has its own type of effect on the training process, and each has a different level that can be controlled by the trainer. First, let's list just a few of the hundreds of types of matches that can occur in each of these categories.

Environmental matches

Environmental matches are any unexpected event that occurs as a result of something in the training environment. For example:

- you show up at the venue and discover the hotel hasn't set up the room;
- there is faulty equipment and technical glitches:
  - the sound system blares music in the middle of your talk;
  - the bulb in an overhead projector burns out;
  - your microphone fails;
  - the paper falls off the flipchart in the middle of a session;

— your pens run dry;

— there is a power failure;

- the fire alarms are set off;
- there is a lack of flexibility in the venue:

    — there are rigid timetables for breaks and lunch;

    — there is an unwillingness to move the stage spots to kill the shadows that are making you 'disappear' occasionally (and look ten years older);

    — hotel staff enter the room to replace empty water jugs on the students' tables—while you are lecturing;

- lunch is lousy;
- posts in the middle of the room obstruct a student's view;
- the stage is squeaky;
- lighting is poor;
- construction work is going on next door;
- taxi radios interfere with your microphone or sound system;
- the stage or room set-up restricts your movement;
- room set-ups restrict participants' movements, so you cannot easily do any activities, and they have to climb over one another to get into their seats;
- the tables and chairs are of poor quality or are dirty;
- there's no parking.

Participant matches — when they trip us up

Students themselves are a huge source of matches that can flare up in a training session. For example:

- they show up late for the start of class or after breaks;
- they don't turn off pagers and mobile phones—in fact, they answer them while you are teaching;
- they walk out in the middle of a session without you knowing why;
- they announce special needs, like diet, seating, lighting;
- physical disabilities suddenly need to be accommodated;

- they ask questions without raising a hand, and whenever the mood strikes them;
- they're cynical before you've even said anything;
- they take control of the room through humour, questions or appearance;
- they spread rumours, or generally influence other members of the group in a less than supportive way;
- they forget assignments;
- they don't do assignments;
- they refuse to participate in activities;
- they get sick during class;
- they're annoying to the students sitting next to them;
- they drink too much alcohol at lunch;
- they question your material in inappropriate ways or at inappropriate times;
- they turn out to be in the wrong training—what you are teaching is not what they expected.

Trainer's matches—when we trip ourselves up

Of course, as trainers we are responsible for lighting many of the matches that flare up in trainings. For example:

- we time or construct questions poorly;
- we side with some students against others;
- we invalidate students by either ignoring them totally or putting them down in front of the others;
- we don't listen to what is being said or asked;
- our pacing is poor, which either bores the students or does not allow them time to express their own thoughts and opinions;
- our acts are arrogant, or 'preachy';
- we run out of time and fail to achieve a clear conclusion to the course;
- we tell students what they should do or feel;
- we forget what we were about to say;

- we cling to a sinking agenda;
- we yell at a participant (or anyone for that matter) in sight of other students;
- we tell bad jokes—racist, sexist, nationalist, or otherwise—but not funny;
- we suffer unexpected physical disabilities—headaches, broken legs, colds and flu, allergy attacks, toothaches;
- we forget to follow-up on something we had said we would do;
- we miss our flight;
- we lose our luggage or notes;
- we oversleep;
- we abuse someone on the road on the way to the event, only to find them sitting in class;
- we spill something on ourself, break a zipper, or nick ourself with a razor;
- we misspell words, quote an incorrect source or use outdated references;
- we've been seen or caught in some compromising situation.

GENERAL PROPERTIES REPRESENTED BY THE MATCHES

The general properties of all the events that the matches represent are their unpredictable, uncertain and unknown qualities. These are events that create tension and pressure that either knock us off the path we are on, or present us with opportunities to be creative. Either way, they interrupt the trainer and student, and distract attention away from the planned process.

The matches may also represent simple distractions. They may be things that distract you, although they are outside the awareness of the students. However, this distracting situation, if mismanaged by the trainer, can become a distraction to the students. Likewise, some events may distract the students, although they are outside of your awareness. There may be distractions to only one or two students. These events also have a time frame—they last for some period of time. Some unexpected events can last for a brief few seconds from onset to conclusion, while others can affect the flow of the entire training event. The final general feature of unexpected events is the amount of control the trainer has regarding the event. In some cases, the trainer will have a lot of control, in others, little or none.

173

What's the likelihood of matches occurring?

The likelihood of having to deal with one or more of these types of events in any given training is very high. Remember, matches are naturally occurring phenomena in the training environment. I recall very few days in which absolutely nothing unexpected or chaotic happened. Remember that trainings are complex interactions between people and their environment and that the purpose for the gathering is to accomplish something specific. It is an event which has high expectations, and where there are expectations and plans, any variation will stand out against that backdrop.

Minimising unexpected events that really serve no purpose

Of course, you can control some of these events. By control I mean prevent, or at least minimise, the likelihood of the event occurring. Your past experiences are a good source of thoughts about what could go wrong. Anticipation is the key to controlling many of these events. If they can be anticipated (based on prior training experiences), then planning is possible—you might check equipment, fly in the day before an event, leave an hour earlier than usual if driving, hand-carry one suit (including an extra shirt), bring training notes and so on.

You do not have to be the one doing all these checks and double-checks. If you can, delegate the tasks to someone else, such as a personal assistant. This person can liaise with the venue staff, arrive early to supervise the room set-up, and be available to handle things that show up unexpectedly—like late students. Sometimes it is hard enough just to do the training itself, and these extra tasks can be quite a burden. If you work for a company with other trainers, you might consider providing this service for each other. It is important to remember, however, that you, the trainer, will ultimately be responsible for what happens in the training room.

You can also assist students to anticipate, and be prepared for, likely distractions. You might find yourself needing to say, "I've been told that the hotel will be running fire drills later in the day. I'll try to find out when, and if possible we'll take a break, otherwise we'll just have to do the best we can to get our work done." You could also request that the students turn off mobile phones or pagers, or switch them to silent mode. I'd add the caveat that if turning off a phone is not appropriate for any members of the class that they be encouraged to sit near the door and leave quietly before answering the call. Anything that helps you manage possible distractions and stay focused on getting your outcomes should be considered.

THE BEST PLANNING
STILL WILL NOT
CATCH EVERYTHING

Of course, the best planning isn't going to eliminate all these events. You can count on spilling something on yourself on a day you don't have a spare shirt. So what are your options when such an unexpected event happens? There are three things you can do. You can ignore it, use it or neutralise its effect. Only one of the options, however, will be appropriate for any given situation. Let's look at the rules to determine which of these options is the most appropriate for each situation, and the options for resolution.

Ignore it

You can ignore these events if, and only if, you are the only one who has noticed it. The students do not need to know everything that is going on, especially if it does not affect them. If they did not know in advance what was being served for lunch, then it is not important to tell them that the menu has been changed from steak to meat loaf. If they are not aware that your microphone is acting up, don't bring it to their attention. If they seem not to be distracted by the squeaking on the stage, then leave it alone. If you look normal to them even though you have a cramp in your foot, just keep going.

What is the purpose for ignoring these events? It is twofold. The first is that the minute you make the student aware of the situation, they will have a greater sensitivity to it, so it is now likely to capture their attention. It is *not* where you want their attention to be. The second is that many of these unexpected events have nothing to do with the outcomes of your training. If you can still get the outcome without the overheads that you left back at home, the audience does not need to know that something is missing. If you make it a problem, it will be a problem.

Problems should not, unless they involve everyone, be dealt with in front of the whole class. Even individual student problems should be dealt with elsewhere. The problems or situation of one student can soon grow like a weed and take over the minds of many other students. Explication of the problem publicly makes other students think about things they otherwise might never have thought about, or would have solved on their own. For this reason, I ask students at the start of every course to see me or an assistant on a break with any problems they may be having or special needs that have to be addressed. It minimises the number of matches that flare up in the classroom.

I mentioned above that these events can only be ignored if you are the only one who is aware that they are happening, and there is no benefit for the students to be involved. But in many cases, the students are well aware of something going on. If that is the case, ignoring a problem is not the right approach. There are two strategies you can use once the situation has entered the students' awareness—use it, or neutralise it.

Use it

The rule is: if the group has been interrupted or distracted, you must do something. One of the things you may be able to do with the unexpected event is to use it to punctuate a lesson. Such situations can bring bright sparks to otherwise dull content. They can generate spontaneous humour. They can create a whole lesson for the group. They can spark creative solutions to problems you might not have thought about before. They can even be used to change the mood of the room. They can spark interest, curiosity, excitement, a sense of anticipation, a real demonstration of your skills and flexibility. They can break the rigid pace of a lecture and allow it to be a bit more fun for the student—and you.

I am fortunate in that I teach trainers, so there is very little that happens in the course of a training day that cannot be used as a useful lesson, or as a demonstration of some principle the class has been working on. During the "matches" exercise, which focuses on this very subject of unexpected events, I can use anything that happens to emphasise the points of the lesson.

Once, I was teaching a class about memory strategies, and in the middle of my lecture someone raised their hand and yelled something out, distracting me. As a result I totally lost my train of thought (a common occurrence for trainers). You know those times when you absolutely do not have any idea what you are supposed to say next. Well, this stumbling was clearly noticed by the students, but it provided a great opportunity to reiterate the part of the lesson about the effects of distraction on memory. I view these kinds of unexpected events as blessings in disguise, and where possible I will try to actually manufacture them in the future.

Neutralise it

There will be times when things happen that one or more students notice but which has absolutely no value to the training outcomes. If the situation only involves one student I try my best to deal with that student directly and outside the awareness of the other students. For this reason I always request that if students should have any problems or have any special requests that they see me or an assistant on one of the breaks. Unfortunately, this doesn't always work.

Vegetarianism did this to me a few years ago. As I just said, I normally instruct students to see me or my assistant (or if in the absence of an assistant, to write me a note and leave it on my desk) during a break for any personal questions or needs—I know the potential problems that can be created if I don't do this. A few years ago, I either did not do this, or I did and the student ignored it. Just before the first break, a hand went up in the room and I took the question, "I'm a vegetarian and I was wondering if the hotel could serve a vegetarian lunch?" I answered, "See me on the break and I'll see what we can do." Before I could dismiss the class, someone else yelled out, "Me too!" Suddenly, I had a situation. I could not now ignore the fact that there were likely to be others. So, now, I had to ask, "How many others in the class are vegetarians?" Four other hands went up. Someone else said, "I eat meat, but not red meat, do you know what they are serving for lunch?" I didn't, but now I had to find out. All I could say in the moment was that I would do some research with the hotel and see what could be done. This whole thing from start to finish would have taken ten minutes of class time and all of my break time to resolve. Do you know what it is like trying to get a hotel to add different kinds of meals to the menu, when they have had no warning?

There were four things to learn from this situation. First, had the individual who started all of this come to me on the break, it would have been easy to take care of it for her. I would have had lots of options: eat what you can of what you are served, it is not that long till dinner; I will have someone on the staff organise a separate

177

lunch from a local restaurant; here is where you can go for a vegetarian meal in the neighbourhood; and more. Second, given that it now was a public situation, something had to be done for the group, otherwise you know—and they know that you know—that half-a-dozen students are not going to get what they want. Third, it begs the question: what would have happened to other people on special diets if this issue did not come up in the class? They would have done something to solve it on their own—they always do. Fourth, it has an implication for those who did not care what they ate for lunch—if poorly managed, they will get upset because the situation does not relate to them, and they can perceive your dealing with it as a waste of their time.

When I am in front of a group of students, I just want to do my job. I do not want to deal with these issues, but once they *are* issues, you have a whole new job—as manager.

Of course, many of these events will be in the awareness of the whole group from the start. If it is a little weird thing that happens, the antidote is to acknowledge that you know that they know whatever just happened, and move on. This takes authority. Your job is to pull their attention back to the task at hand. If it is something that is going to be a problem for an hour or a day, you will have to stop and actually talk about it with the group. Your purpose for this talk is to give meaning to the situation or event so the students have a way of interpreting it. You tell them what it means and what response you want them to have.

During a program I was conducting at a ski resort in Northern California I got up in the middle of the night in a pitch-black unfamiliar room and tripped over something. I fell face first into a rough wood bookcase. What a mess. By morning I had a black eye, a long gash on my cheek and a big swollen gob. Otherwise, I was fine. It was not an option to not teach, and there was no way my students were not going to notice and probably be concerned about me through the day. So the only thing I could do was to talk to them in the morning. I told them what happened (if I didn't, I am sure they would have made up their own story, and likely not in the most useful way), how I was feeling and that my sense was I would make it through the day. I did say that I had enough energy to do the day, but I did not think I had the energy to manage too many disruptions, so if they could just stay focused on getting the outcomes and manage themselves, it would be appreciated. It probably was the easiest day of teaching I have ever done. They were little angels.

The key here is to create meaning for the situation or event for the students. If you do not do this, they will make up their own meaning, and that interpretation will likely distract them from the outcomes of the course.

The meaning students attach to these events can also affect your credibility with the group. Some training manuals and books suggest that if you talk about these things then you create a problem. I have seen, in writing, a suggestion for trainers that goes something like this: If you spill coffee on your shirt, you don't have to say anything about it; no one will care, so just keep teaching. I think just the opposite. If you have spilled coffee on your shirt and you know they can see it, your only way to avoid a potentially negative impact is to create the meaning you want for it. If you just leave it unspoken some people will for sure think you are a slob, and that will affect what they learn from you. But if you said, "Listen, I know that you all are likely to notice this coffee stain. I just hope you can remember a time when you've spilled something while rushing around in the morning, blah, blah, blah." Then just get on with what you are there to do. Neutralising an event means taking the wind out of its sails.

Preparing yourself for unwanted matches

There is no one right answer for how to prepare yourself for the unwanted matches that occur in trainings, but I have some thoughts that may help. Obviously, the first thing you can do is review your personal past experiences in training situations. It is likely that you confront the same distracting and interrupting factors repeatedly, especially if you teach the same content, in similar environments, repeatedly. You should know by now your own vulnerable spots.

Your review should provide you with your own personal hot spots, and therefore, you have the opportunity to double-check these items beforehand. For instance, I have never been plagued with missed flights like some of my trainer friends, because I always leave the day before the event. But for a long time I was plagued by pens that didn't work. So I pay extra attention to that fact. I have extra sets and they are tested and refilled throughout the day.

Another healthy thing you may consider is to change the meaning of these unwanted intrusions so that problems become opportunities. I have a hundred ways now of neutralising and creating humour for pens that do not work. I learned to use that chronic problem as a way of teaching.

Mental run-throughs of your event can catch a lot of potential problems. For instance, I walked into an event recently in Melbourne. There were two-hundred participants expected. A break was scheduled for a mid-point in the lecture. I had only scheduled ten minutes for the break. Doing a mental run-through, I could see I was going to have a problem even getting these people out to the breaks area in ten minutes, let alone giving them a chance to have coffee and get back into the room. A quick room-change to make exiting easier, a second coffee station and a slight change in my lecture made this potential problem invisible to the participants.

The courage to stop and tell the truth to a student is a quality that should be sought by every trainer. There will be times and situations when you are out of your league. I've seen trainers try to muscle through these awkward moments; their cover-up serves no one's interests.

There are times for stopping and talking with your audience about what is happening. Nearing the end of an event a few years ago, my personal assistant was mysteriously absent from the room. When I inquired after her I was told that she was in another room having a bad asthma attack. By the time I got there, it was to see her being taken to the hospital. My problem was that I still had sixty or more people waiting in the classroom for the end of the program. I was very distracted. This was a time when I had to just stop, sit the class down, say what was going on and ask them to work with me to finish the program without disruption so I could get out of there quickly at the end. This approach, when warranted, builds incredible rapport with people.

This leads to the notion that as trainers we might think honestly about our abilities and our limitations—knowing what we can do, and what we can't do, what we do know, and what we don't know— and letting those limitations be known when appropriate. Somehow trainers have developed the notion that they are expected to know and do everything, but it is a great source of problems in trainings. Trainers do all sorts of weird things to avoid exposing their weaknesses to students. Do what you can do, and be really clear with your students about what you cannot do or do not know.

One of the problems trainers cite most often is the fear of not knowing the answer to questions asked by the students; therefore, they avoid taking questions from the audience. Know this: not knowing the answer to a question is not a problem perceived in you by your audience, it is only a problem in your own mind, your own meaning attached to not knowing. To some trainers it means not being smart, not being as smart as their students, looking silly, being shown up, being attacked. It really doesn't mean any of that, nor is that an accurate representation of the students' perceptions. You cannot know everything. While reviewing some videotapes of past trainings, here are some lines I found myself using when I did not have an answer to students' questions:

"That's a great question, but I don't have a clue."

"I've never really thought about that. Let me think about that for awhile and see what comes to mind."

"I am not aware of any substantiated research on that, but my experience has been..."

"I read recently that... I don't know that I agree with it, but to be honest it is not my field and it wouldn't be appropriate for me to make any comments."

"I don't know, but I know who I can call. Leave it with me until tomorrow."

"I don't know, but you might call the university librarian and see if they can help."

These are not bad answers, nor are they cause for embarrassment. What is more embarrassing is making up an answer that misleads your students. Even worse is deterring students from asking any questions—when you know you could probably help out many students—just because there might be the odd question you cannot answer.

You can also prepare your students in such a way that matches are minimised. Trainers do this by telling their students what is expected. People do not resist, knowing that in terms of producing results there are some ways of behaving that are better than others. It is just that the reasons need to make sense. For example, many people who attend my courses attend other courses. In these other courses they are allowed to bring coffee and snacks into the room. For me, that is a source of unexpected events, spills and other distractions. So I ask my students to be willing to finish their coffee and food on the breaks and not bring it into the room—and I tell them honestly why this works, not only for me, but for them. In this way I have eliminated one source of potential problems.

SOME MATCHES ARE WORTH LIGHTING

If it were possible to eliminate all of the odd events that can occur, I believe training would have the potential to be boring and under-stimulating. Students might not be bored by a well-constructed, never-varying event, but as trainers we would. There is some value in allowing a bit of chaos to exist in your trainings—keep in mind that it is likely to be an impossible task to eliminate them all anyway.

The unexpected can be exciting

It can be a lot more fun when you do not know in advance everything that is going to happen in a day. Boredom is a killer of good trainers. Unexpected events can create significant moments in a training that you could not have calculated. By allowing students a fair bit of expression, it is true you will never know what they will say or what they will do, but these are opportunities—for the students to learn and, more importantly, for you to learn. These are the opportunities when you find yourself making new connections, gaining new insights, hearing new stories to use in future trainings and saying things in a new way.

Thinking on your feet is good for you

Allowing a number of 'out of control' situations to emerge in your trainings is great stimulation. It makes you think, and discover. It makes you stop and breathe, and sometimes ask the students to work with you to find your way out of a knot that has been created. Of course, you are never really out of control, but it can look that way, so everyone has a chance to learn a bit more.

The unexpected helps turn content into a professional presentation

I have found that my best material, my best presentations and my best metaphors and stories were not actually created at my desk during the design phase or preparation phase of my trainings. They were created spontaneously in the moment as a reaction to some unexpected situation in the class itself. I am careful to remember these new creations and then actively construct and use them in future classes. In the design and preparation phase I may learn the course content and have the sequence and methods well thought through, but the actual expression—the words, intonation, humour and so forth—show up while conducting the course itself.

Manufacturing matches

Unexpected glitches are never really fun, but there are ways that trainers loosen the grip or add dynamics to training situations in order to seek the benefits of the unexpected. Good matches provide opportunities. The following ideas create response potential: a heightened responsiveness of your students to your training.

Ask open-ended questions

One way you can introduce a bit of flexibility into trainings is to use open-ended questions. If an exercise has been run well, and you know the students have received the desired benefit, then questions allow those lessons to be expressed by the students, rather than you telling them what they have learned. Of course, we can never know exactly what they will say, in what way they will say what they say, or what experiences they will share; therefore, these can be wonderful opportunities for you to be spontaneous. The first opportunity with questioning like this is that you can take what the student has shared and make that comment meaningful to the rest of the group. The second opportunity arises in the nature of memory—their responses can be great memory triggers for you, reminding you of experiences that have a direct bearing on the lesson that you can now share. A third opportunity is that the student's responses can suggest important metaphors and stories that you might never have thought of before. These can then be packaged for retelling in your next class.

But what about the risk of losing control by asking questions? It is true, you can create a problem out of anything. Even a well-run exercise can be lost if the question you ask is: "Did anyone have a problem with that?" All of a sudden students find problems—and then you have a real problem. If you are going to use open-ended questions like, "What did you just learn?" it is wise to have done a little boundary-setting before asking the question. For example, you might need to say, "I know many of you enjoyed that, but some might have found it quite difficult—that might be simply because you are tired, or were distracted, or just needed a bit more time. If that is true for anyone I would like to ask that you hold that experience for the moment and listen to the experience of the others who 'got it'. Their experience may help you see where you might make corrections." This kind of statement tells the group the kind of feedback I am looking for and will acknowledge.

Tell stories

Another way to introduce flexibility is to allow ourselves to use personal stories to punctuate our deliveries. These experiences will often come to mind while we are talking, and rather than resisting them, they might serve the audience well if shared. What is good about personal stories that relate to, or punctuate, our lessons is that they make the students think of their own experiences or how they relate to the one you are sharing. In this way different students can learn different things from the same lesson. They can learn what is personally important for them. Your stories also tend to support the students telling some of their own stories, and again, these can add a nice unknown, but relevant, dynamic element to the training session.

Create curiosity

Creating curiosity is a third intention we can have that will add flexibility and spark to the trainings. Curiosity can be designed into a course in many ways; its benefit is the high response potential that is built up in the room. Students' attention is heightened as they look in anticipation for answers to that which they are curious about. Students' curiosity can be directed at you, or at aspects of the training—either way, they wonder what's next.

What creates curiosity is the anticipated, yet unknown. If I see a prop, like an arrow, sitting on your table on stage, but you never say anything about it, I'm going to get curious about what the arrow is for, and a part of me will be waiting for you to tell me—of course, in the meantime I'll be listening to everything else you tell me. If you on occasion pick up the arrow and play with it, but still don't say anything, I will be even more curious. Students are curious about everything—who they see you speaking with on breaks, what you eat (or don't), how you're dressed, where you come from, other activities you have. This is natural; if they like you, they will want to know more.

Be unpredictable

Another way to create both curiosity and flexibility in your training day is to be unpredictable. What we can predict and accurately anticipate bores us after a while. Taking on a different character or act is healthy. It changes and adds to the student's relationship with you. You get to be multi-dimensional and will be able to impact on the students in more ways.

Periodically changing the set-up of the room helps break up the rigidity of trainings as well, especially if the class meets in the same room over a long period of time. If you are doing a residential program you can do all sorts of things even outside the classroom. In one seven-day course I conducted in 1994, students would wake up and find notes and other equipment outside their hotel room doors. They might be instructions for an assignment to complete before breakfast, or a topic of conversation to engage in with other students before class, or a new meeting location. I could have prepared them for this in class the day before, but surprises do wonders for response potential and increase the odds of flexibility in the day. They are even curious and anticipative when they go to sleep, wondering what, if anything, they will find tomorrow outside their door. In this business, a little mystery goes a long way.

CHAPTER **7**

going real-time — responses to frequently asked questions and solutions to common problems

INTRODUCTION

Finally we have reached the stage where we can explore possible solutions to the specific questions and problems we most frequently encounter in the training environment. We have knowledge of the factors that contribute to the idiosyncrasies of the learner, information related to the experience of learning, an understanding of the effects of the trainer's behaviours, factors related to design, methods and environmental issues, and an understanding of the two key strategies trainers use to manage their students' learning process. We can begin to apply this knowledge to real-life training situations and to ground that knowledge in experience.

The questions and problems are organised into five categories. The source of these questions and problems were the 120 trainers who attended the 1995 *Training to Train* program. Added to this, I have included common problems and questions I have been asked most often by trainers and presenters over the past few years. Some sections contain more questions, because of the general nature of the category.

Given the diversity of the participants who attend my courses, these questions cover a large territory. Some questions relate to problems with particular types of students in classroom situations, while other questions relate to personal issues we, as trainers, have to contend with. Other questions relate to design issues and the setting of clear outcomes.

I have tried my best to capture the same style of voice in writing that I would use if these questions had been asked of me in a live-audience situation. Two goals guided me in this writing process. The first was to write in a natural, 'spoken' language that links the content of the preceding chapters with how that content is applied in real-time training situations. The second goal was to use this mode of expression to introduce other concepts and thoughts—that which would naturally come to mind when exploring a problem in real-time. Overall, I have tried to create a 'training session' atmosphere and move away from the more calculated methods used in rest of the book.

My responses to these questions are by no means 'techniques'. They are just thoughts, considerations, and possible approaches that can be taken. Nor do these responses constitute the 'right' answer.

They are simply approaches that have worked for me or other trainers who have confronted similar situations. Consider them as suggestions for something new to try based on the information presented in this book.

This chapter shares a difficulty of the preceding chapters: on the one hand, there are so many factors interacting in each moment of a training, or at each specific time period in a trainer's life. No two students are the same, no two environments are the same, and no two trainers can execute the same skills. On the other hand, there are some reliable ways of dealing with most problems confronted by trainers: the construction of meaning and the use of influence. In every case possible I have attempted to put you, the trainer, in the position of power—I suggest that *you* decide what you can do about a situation, or think about what you might have done (or not done) towards creating a situation. If we look at the student as the problem, our options are limited. If we look at our own behaviours as having contributed to the problem, we have more possible solutions, because it puts us in a position of control. I always try to make whatever happens in the classroom a problem with me: the situation always derives from *my* lack of skill or competence. Likewise, the solution is something that *I* must work out.

I have placed the questions or problems that allow the most coverage of thoughts related to the issue up front. Following that are other versions of the question or problem allowing for finer points to be made. At this stage of the book you are (finally!) free to skip about. There is no particular sequence, nor value, in approaching this chapter sequentially. Regardless of the type of trainings you conduct, the audiences you attract or your personal aspirations, I believe you will find many of the problems and questions relate to most types of training situations. Please note that you are free to utilise these approaches in your own training sessions. They work. I would, however, suggest personalising them to suit your own audiences and your own training styles.

PROBLEMS WITH
STUDENT PARTICIPATION

Everything would be so easy if we didn't have to have students in training sessions!

The number one question I am asked relates to one, or more, participants who are resistant to doing activities. I have included several versions of this type of problem as there are many ways that trainers and presenters experience lack of participation in their programs. But first, it's worth making a couple of general observations.

Sometimes lack of participation is limited to individuals within a group, while other times there is universal resistance. When the resistance is limited to individuals, the participants can sometimes be grouped into a class (that is, younger participants, women, analytical thinkers, whatever).

Problems with student participation may also relate to the trainer's methods. For example, reluctance to participate may be to do with:

(1) when questions are asked;
(2) when experiential exercises are conducted;
(3) when group work is required; or
(4) when outside assignments are given.

Now, to the questions.

**How do I get maximum participation in class
activities? Some students are very resistant.**

One thing needs to be made clear. Participation has almost everything to do with the personality traits and dispositions, values and preferences, past experience and feelings of the individual student. However, although the issue arises based on a student's idiosyncrasies, you, as the trainer, are responsible for what happens—not the student. They are just responding, and will continue to respond, in the way that is most appropriate for them.

I can speak personally about this, because as a student I do not like participating in activities, especially if they are group activities. This is not because I don't like the trainer or I don't understand the value of activities; it is because I just don't like to *do* things in unfamiliar situations. If you tell me we are going to do an exercise, I am likely to get nervous. If you announce it in such a way that I don't feel I have a choice about participating, I may leave, or I may participate but gain little from the exercise because I am uncomfortable. If you tell me I am going to *have fun*, as a mismatcher, I will get very resistant. So what can you do?

If we view participation from the student's perspective, the problems that arise are easier to solve. If you want maximum participation, you need to be sensitive, aware, and anticipatory of the student's experience in the activity.

For a student to participate in an activity:

- it must make sense;
- it must be relevant;
- there must be some choice about participating, or there must be different ways of participating; and
- it must be non-threatening.

'Because you say so' does not satisfy the criterion of relevance. Telling a green-vegetable hater that green vegetables are good for them is not going to convince the green-vegetable hater to dive in and eat green vegies. People need to know why the activity is important, what can be gained by participating (although some will be more motivated by knowing the consequence of not participating) and what other choices they have for learning if they do not want to do the activity.

Too often, trainers believe that the activity they devise is 'good' and 'fun'. They remain blind to the fact that some participants may not find the activity fun at all. For some students, some activities are embarrassing, stressful, confusing, over-stimulating and so forth.

In my own courses I do a set-up for activities that include the following components, and I don't ever forget to do these steps:

(1) I introduce the activity as an opportunity.

(2) I tell the students directly, and honestly, what it is designed to accomplish.

(3) I acknowledge, up front, any negative reactions that some students may have while engaged in the activity. This step is *critical*. If I know the activity will be anxiety-provoking for some types of students, I tell them so, and explain the meaning in this context, of feelings they experience. I also tell them what they can do if the activity is too uncomfortable. Contrary to popular belief, this will *not* create more anxiety or make the students more resistant. It will let them know that *you* know that some will feel this way, that it's okay, and that they will survive.

(4) I give the students whatever realistic choices there are about either not participating or participating in different ways to get the same outcome. But I also let them know the consequences of not participating.

(5) If a student chooses not to participate, I tell them their other options—what they can do instead. For example I might say, "If you choose not to participate in the activity, that's fine, but I'd ask that you leave the room and take an extended break." Now, it is important that students opting out of an activity have a reason for, and an understanding of, the consequence of making this choice. So I explain, "I'm asking you to do this because people doing the exercise might feel awkward with others just looking on," or "I'm asking you to do this because you might want to do the activity later and it will be important that you have not seen it done." The consequence I outline might be: "For those of you who choose not to do the exercise, again that's okay, but it may mean that some of this afternoon's content may be a bit confusing. You'll survive, but it may be a bit more difficult." These reasons and consequences need to be truthful and sincere.

The outcome is to provide a choice that makes everyone feel safe to do whatever they are going to do anyway. Your job is to make the learning available regardless of that choice. And remember, you are not their mother or father. You can't get your own children to do everything you want, and these people are far less obligated. You do have a responsibility, but it's important to keep it in perspective—it is a limited responsibility. Remember, these people are adults, they will not die or be particularly affected by not participating in a class activity.

If you do these things, two other things will likely happen. First, because people now have an honest choice to not participate, they will usually join in. Second, if they don't, and you demonstrate that it's not your practice to invalidate their choice, they will be more likely to participate in subsequent exercises. In short, they will learn to trust you.

An aside. A valuable strategy I learned from a book centring on the techniques of the late Milton Erikson, a renowned therapist, involves offering what he called a "worse case choice"—a choice that will be even less comfortable than the choice you want them to make.

When I was teaching at a residential camp for teenagers, not only was participation a challenge, even being there was undesirable for some of these students. In the first hour, that problem was addressed. I said to them, "Clearly some of you do not want to be here. I know some of you have been forced here by your parents, who probably unsuccessfully tried to convince you that this was a good idea. I can imagine not wanting to be here myself. The truth is you *are* here, and what we're going to be doing here is… I am not in a position to just let you run off for a week, but what I can do is offer you the following. We legally have to have you supervised while you are here. If you don't want to be here in the classroom, now, or at any time, that's fine. Our staff working in the kitchen offered to supervise you. So if you'd rather be there, that's fine."

The result from this offer of a *worse case choice* was as follows: Out of 800 students, only one student ever chose to go to the kitchen. She spent the whole first day there, bored out of her tree, while she could hear music and other teens in the classroom. On the second day, she came in to ask if she could come back into the class. Nonchalantly, I said, "Sure, join in." That was the end of it.

You are offering a viable choice—but it's one that happens to *feel worse* than the choice you really want the student to make.

194

I have a problem getting participation in class activities from some trainees, specifically from trainees who are long-term unemployed in job search programs.

The first comment I would venture to make is that the problem of getting participation in activities likely has little to do with the participant being long-termed unemployed, even though this may be a type of group with whom you experience the problem. Level of education, job titles and other generalised factors such as these are rarely attributes contributing to the problem.

What if, after I have done everything I know how to do, there is still one person who won't participate?

It can happen. And the truth is, you really should not do much of anything about it. Not directly anyway. The first step is to make the individual feel absolutely safe with their choice. Slowly, as opportunities present themselves, you may have some openings to intervene.

Here is an example. I was teaching juggling to a group of fifty or so people. It was a mixed audience of men and women, and everyone in the group was participating in the first exercise—all but one guy. He took himself off to the side of the room while everyone else was throwing a ball up in the air, counting aloud, tapping their feet to some sixties rock'n'roll tune. I noticed him—and he noticed that I noticed him—but I didn't do anything. I didn't approach him, I just did my job. He knew that I knew that he wasn't participating, and he also knew, or was testing, whether that was okay with me. What mattered to me was that he was still in the room, observing. At the end of the exercise, the students sat on the floor for the debrief, and he joined them and was talking easily to people on either side of him. In the next few class sessions, which were conducted back at tables and chairs, he seemed fine, and participated in the class. When the next juggling segment came up, he once again walked to the side of the room to watch. Once again, I figured he was fine; he was there, and I chose not to do anything about it. What I was not going to do was make any assumptions about why he wasn't participating. If the opportunity presented itself I might do something, but there was nothing to do for the moment.

On the next break, this gentleman approached me. He said that he wanted to explain why he wasn't participating in the juggling so that I didn't think it was about me. His reasons aren't important here, but what I said was that not every exercise is right for every person, and I was happy for him to do whatever he felt was best. I acknowledged him for staying in the room and participating in the debriefs. I also told him, should anything change, I'd be happy to have him participate in the third and final juggling segment, or if he felt more comfortable, he was welcome to come into the room on breaks and ask one of the staff to work with him, and if not, that was okay too.

In the third juggling segment, he once again moved to the side of the room. But I noticed he had one juggling ball and was tossing it in the air. The most important thing I did was to not pay any real attention, not make it a big deal. I just remained neutral. This allowed him to not feel uncomfortable about making these small steps. It made it possible for him to change his behaviour.

So here are the pointers. Don't make assumptions about why any one participant is doing what they are doing. You cannot know unless they tell you. Trust that no one will die or be dramatically less successful if they don't participate in an activity.

I have had a whole class mutiny at the suggestion of an exercise. Did I do something wrong? What's the solution?

That a whole class banded together to *not* do something a trainer requests is highly unusual, and I cannot think of any one thing that would lead to this group behaviour, unless it had been building over time, unnoticed. So I can't say much about the potential causes, but

I have a few thoughts about what to do in that situation. First, there is a 'good thing' happening in this situation; the class is bonded, even if it is through controversy. I'd stop the class. I'd change my position on the stage, perhaps sit on the steps, or sit on a low stool, and simply ask what's going on. I would tell them what I notice, and what I'm trying to do, and acknowledge that I'm aware of the resistance. Again, I would not be inclined to make up what they are experiencing—I have no way of knowing it. So I'd open it up. For this I need a different kind of skill. I need to *manage* a situation. I need to tell the truth. I may need to change my approach.

I am a trainer in a company and my manager has a rule: every student has to participate in every exercise. What do I do if someone doesn't want to play along? They don't have the option to leave.

For me, if I didn't have someone looking over my shoulder, I'd probably still run my class in a way that makes it safe for everyone to learn in their own best way. But say you do have your training manager checking in to see that you are getting everyone to do these exercises. Then what I would do is tell the students exactly that. And I would then give them an even stronger set-up: explain what the exercise is about, what they will have to do, how to get the best out of it. I would tell them, if they are uncomfortable, how to handle and stick with the process. I would also give them a time frame. "For thirty minutes, this is what we're going to be doing, then we'll get back to our desks." Time frames work wonders in assisting people who are uncomfortable with exercises. Sometimes the source of the discomfort is not knowing for how long they will need to be active.

How do I get left-brain oriented people to 'loosen up' and participate in activities?

Why do you think they need to 'loosen up'? Some personality types are just 'up-tight' when they have to do things, and they are likely to stay that way. I would be more inclined to consider that they can be up-tight, and participate and learn. Trying to get people to behave in ways that are not natural is an uphill battle you are likely to lose. Besides, people do tend to relax over time if the exercises are set up in such a way that they feel better doing the exercise than not doing it. Remember the discussion in Chapter 2 about emotions and feelings. It takes an unusual person to be willing to stand out from the crowd. Everyone else participating is a compelling feature for those resisting if you let it work for you naturally.

What do I do when one of the participants clearly does not want to be there, or isn't getting what they thought they would out of the course?

An important lesson for all of us to learn as trainers is that we cannot serve everyone. When a student wants to leave a course, there can be many reasons: the content may be different to what they expected, or not relevant to them, they may have other problems outside the training or they may simply not feel comfortable with what you are doing. It's okay. If you can, you might try to make the course more relevant to them—if that is the problem—perhaps in some way they haven't thought about before. If that is not possible, let them go. Don't argue with them. Just demonstrate that you are hearing them, and let them follow their own course without embarrassment. You can let them know that the door is always open should they wish to return. I have always had a money-back guarantee—no questions asked—in my classes for just this situation.

I get many students who say they want to learn. They start the program but always find reasons to miss sessions, or stop attending altogether halfway through the program. Am I doing something to cause this, or is something happening with them that I don't understand?

Motivating people over time is always tricky. There has to be something about attending the sessions that feels better than *not* attending the sessions. You might have the students do some writing on the first night about their goals for attending, or have them stand up and state why they are there and what they intend to get out of the course, thereby evoking some sort of internal commitment. You might also, in the first session, set up a buddy system, so that each person has someone to rely on to help them get to class. Also, make it okay, if they do miss a session, to return. People have competing priorities. You might request that they call you if they are going to miss the class. Most will find that more discomforting than attending.

PROBLEMS WITH PARTICIPANTS' BEHAVIOURS

Student participation is not the only problematic student behaviour. Problems can exist because of the different types of needs that students bring into the training, or be generally based on how they interact naturally with others. In this section we continue with questions and problems posed by trainers that relate to behaviours of our students.

How do I get my students to experience learning as fun?

My counter-question is: Why? Why is that important? Most learning activities and situations are not fun. What they are is: difficult, challenging, confusing, arduous, boring, repetitive and so on. Fun is not an attribute of most learning situations, it is an attribute of activities that we know how to do. For example, learning to touch-type is definitely not fun; for the most part it is repetitive and boring. It only becomes 'fun' after you can do it. As a trainer, one of your biggest jobs is to help people extend their tolerance for difficult situations; extend it long enough for them to learn enough to begin to enjoy the new skill.

I teach adults who are attending a program by their own choice. The problem I have is they don't do the exercises and readings, which, although 'optional' are central and

critical to making the desired progress. Some participants start and fade off. Some reject from the start and never get into it. What should I do?

First, if the exercises and readings are central and critical to the student's success, they should not be optional. *Macquarie Dictionary* defines the word "option" as: *left to one's choice*. This is likely the reason some are never getting started. Many learning activities, such as reading assignments, may lead the student to feel bored or confused. For such people, it is an activity that is easy to abandon if there are more pleasant things to do.

You run the risk of making people feel invalidated if, as a result of not doing an 'optional' assignment, you treat them as if they should have done it. If it truly is an option that you think will benefit some people, then state as such, make a good case for what they'll get for their efforts, and then leave it.

This brings another thought to mind. Activities and information essential to a student's success should, at all costs, be encountered in the classroom and not be left to outside work. You cannot control students once they leave. If it's an essential piece of knowledge or skill, teach it to them in the classroom.

I used to teach guitar classes to beginners—lots of beginners: fifty at a time. What I knew about adults learning to play guitar through private tuition classes was that they usually quit after just a few weeks. The thirty-minute lesson was usually used by the teacher to listen to the student—a daunting process for the beginner—and then to assign the next week's assignment. This left the student to figure these things out for themselves. It is a rare individual who will stick with a practise session that is hard and confusing, and then get up and do it again tomorrow. What I did differently was to run my classes for two hours. In those two hours, everything that was essential for them to know, or that required a lot of repetition, I had them do in the class. Then practise at home could be optional. The only thing I asked them to agree to do was to unpack their guitars the minute they got home from the lesson and place the guitar near where they relax—near the bed if it happened that they read every night before sleeping, by the lounge if they watched television at night, whatever. If they did practise, it was simply to reinforce what they had already learned in the class; anything new would be done during the next class. I knew in my heart of hearts that some people would just not ever practise, but I didn't want them to use that as an excuse for quitting. I also knew that after six months they would know enough and play well enough to begin to enjoy their own sound, and that that might better the odds that they would stick with playing and even survive the private lessons that followed.

How do I handle a student who, in the process of not 'buying in' to the training process, not only becomes non-participative but becomes destructive to the group?

It depends here what is meant by "destructive". If they throw a chair at you, call the police. But more seriously, I would remind you that you are the one who is in charge, and behaviours that don't work should be addressed. I tend to handle it covertly while teaching, or overtly in a side bar during class or during a break.

By covertly handling the problem I mean managing the problem from the front while continuing to lecture. For example, if the destructive student is talking, I might continue lecturing to the class, but focus my gaze upon them. It's hard for anyone to keep up a conversation while being stared at. I might also move into their space, sit on their desk or just stand behind them and continue to lecture—it unnerves them. What I don't do is the 'technique' of asking them to share their comments with the rest of the group. They are likely to be of little value, and anyway, why implicate the rest of class? That technique also tends to be seen as aggressive and that isn't the relationship you want with a student. You want to keep your rapport, and just guide them back into focusing on the lesson.

If a destructive student raises a hand at a time I don't want to be interrupted, I'll put my hand out like a stop sign and look at them, and might say, "Hold that for a moment, I'll take questions at the end." It's just good classroom management.

By a 'side bar' I mean I would tell the rest of the class to keep busy for a moment, and go over to the student, get down on their level and have a chat. I might offer them the opportunity to leave the room and handle whatever they need to handle. Again, I can't know what they're on about, so I don't make it up. I just give them the benefit of the doubt, and another choice—like the choice to leave the class until they can be there, fully present. If all else fails I will meet, or have one of my staff meet, with the student on a break. I might instigate a bit of research to find out what's going on for them, and then offer some way for them to get it handled. I do not ever involve the other class members in situations that relate to only one student.

How do you deal with the varying expectations between the members of the group? For example, some have an expectation of, and need for, very detailed and specific class instructions, while others see that as a waste of time. Could I perhaps do something different in my presentation either verbally or in printed form?

The appropriate way to deal with this will be twofold. First, you need to decide whether or not detailed and specific class instructions are necessary. Making that decision will then isolate the group who is going to be problematic (either the 'needy' or 'not needy'). From here, it is the same solution for both groups, just with an appropriate twist.

If you decide that detailed instructions are in fact not necessary, then the 'needy' groups' behaviours will need to be anticipated and handled. For example, you might have to say, "I know some of you may have a high need for lots of detailed class instructions. What I have found from my experience, however, is that it can get in the way of the learning we are about to engage in. So I'm going to ask you to suspend that need for awhile and see how you go. Then, should you have any difficulties, please feel free to see me on the break."

It is just the opposite with the 'not needy' group. You say to them, "I know some of you find detailed class instructions a bit of a drag and a waste of time. Sometimes they certainly can be, but in this case, for these reasons..., it will be important. If you want to move a bit faster, then see me on a break and I'll give you a way to up the ante on the processes while you are here in the class."

Remember, it is always about anticipation, and addressing these likely scenarios *before* they take hold in the student and start affecting their behaviours. You have to know why you are doing what you are doing—if you do, then you have some rationale. You also know that if you don't tell the students that rationale some are going to make it up, and if they do so inaccurately they will be right to feel or think or behave the way they do. Your job is to make everything meaningful ahead of time.

Many of my students crave the security of extensive, step-by-step instructions of the entire course for their reference. Usually this means they rote-learn the material, so they are only ever able to use the data in identical situations. Are there some good strategies to encourage participants to let go a little in this area?

There are three steps to any problem like this. First, remember that anything you are going to do in the class—and that includes deciding whether detailed instructions are necessary or not—will be based on your outcomes, your experience and the previous experience of the learner. So the first step is that *you* have to decide whether or not step-by-steps are necessary. Once you've made that decision, you have to follow it through regardless of how individual students respond. So step two is to anticipate how the group will respond. Your experience may tell you that some will be happy, some not. Isolate the problem reactions. The third step is to address the potential negative response you feel some will have, and give them your rationale for doing what you are doing. If it makes sense, it will override their negative reaction when it comes or, at least, neutralise it to some degree.

For example, you might say, "I know that some of you have a preference from past learning experiences to want step-by-step instructions as a reference while you are here in the class. That makes sense because it does make succeeding in the class more assured. However, the problem with that can be that you will find it difficult to use these skills when you leave here..."

203

I would also do something else. If I know that transference is an outcome, and that the method of giving detailed instructions may prevent achieving that outcome, I would program into my design a weaning of the students off the detailed instructions with each exercise (as opposed to having them go cold turkey, get really nervous and then not perform well in the class anyway). If this can work for you, then you need also to tell them this at the end of the above communication: "What I've decided to do to assist you in being better able to transfer this knowledge to new situations outside of the classroom is... here is what I know prevents that..., and here is what I'm going to do differently..." Again, give them the option of meeting with you on a break if there is any problem.

By the way, the reason I keep suggesting that you offer students the chance to meet with you on a break is that, although you may need to handle things, it sets up a choice while at the same time establishing how you want it done (that is, not in the class where it distracts others). Plus many people do not feel comfortable coming up to you on the break and it may force them to figure things out on their own or ask other students.

Many of my clients sending staff for training are rigid about outcomes of expectations. They resist completing registration forms or answering any questions regarding outcomes. In some cases this is clearly because they don't know—they are training staff because that's what modern managers do! In other cases they have different agendas. Is there a simple, effective and non-confrontational way to

better set up the participants who need clarity in the area of outcomes to best utilise the training experience?

This can be hard, and you are right—many clients who contract training do not have a clear set of outcomes or perhaps lack the means to express those outcomes in a way that makes sense. If I have enough rapport with the client, and they are interested, I will usually offer to spend an hour or so with them to help them sort out the specific outcomes they are looking for. I try to get them grounded by using very specific questions. For example I might ask, "If this training were successful, how would you notice the changes in the people who had attended?"

If the outcomes are unachievable, or cannot be stated in any specific set of terms, you might consider turning down the request for your services. Unachievable outcomes are an easy way to lose, and thereby lose a bit of your reputation.

If you do choose to take on a training job in which the management isn't clear on the outcomes, I would most definitely let the students know that. You might say, "Here's what I've been told is required in these sessions, and what I think that means [or what I've taken that to mean is…]. So how I've approached this training is… To measure whether we've gotten that outcome I intend to… If you have any finer distinctions about this as we progress, would you please make some time to see me later in the day."

What can I do when I'm presenting to people with blank looks on their faces?

I suppose it depends on the reason for the blank looks. I can think of four interpretations for the blank look; whichever interpretation is true for you will determine what you do.

The blank look may simply be a sign of boredom due to content that you've not made interesting, or a presentation that lacks variety. If so, change your pace, or your tactics. The second reason for the blank look may be that the student(s) may be tired. If so, send them on a break or do some sort of interactive, blood-moving activity. Even a small group discussion will facilitate this, especially if you make students choose classmates from the other side of the room—that way, they have to move around. Third, the blank look may signal confusion. Stop and do something to verify that students are understanding what is going on. Lastly, the blank look may also be a sign of absorption! Students may be so absorbed in your presentation or content that they almost look as if in a trance. If this is the case, keep going.

So how can you tell the difference? Test the water and eliminate the potential causes. You might start by first acknowledging the blank look. "I notice some of you look a bit tranced-out; can I get a sense of what that indicates? Is this material confusing?" No. "Do you find it fascinating?" No. "Is this a good time for a break to re-energise?" If the answer again is no, you'll know they're bored, and it's best you get on to doing something, anything, different.

There are times when I get asked a question by a student, then when I answer that question, they don't accept it. They keep pushing, and I don't have anything else to offer them. What approaches are available to me in that situation?

If you are answering a question accurately and then that answer is challenged—wow. Two thoughts. First, make sure that you are citing your reference—from what credible source did you get your information? If it's from your own experience, you might need to tell your questioner how you came to your conclusion. If you do not have a source for your information, you might think of going off and finding that support. You may also need to learn how to structure a convincing argument. If your information is well-substantiated and argued logically this situation should resolve itself, and not occur again.

How do I get participants to be willing to consider a new way of looking at things long enough for me to make complete the argument?

Just tell them that this is what you need from them. Say: "I'm going to create an argument that supports a new way of seeing a situation.

I'm going to ask you, for a short while, to suspend any rush to judgment until I've made the points and tied them together. At that time, if necessary, we can critically evaluate the merits of this new perspective." Now, if anyone violates this by attacking prematurely, just remind them of your request and ask them to give you a break until you finish.

How do I manage a loud, overbearing and dominant participant?

Who is in control? If this were me, I'd be asking in what way *I* was giving the aggressor an opportunity to express themselves the way that they are, and then change what I was doing.

What do I do about participants who turn off and ridicule any in-service sessions, even sessions with well-known, excellent speakers? In my case, these are overworked teachers who have to be there.

Clearly, teachers, as well as many other professionals, have had many bad experiences with in-service trainings, and this supports an initial negative reaction to another one. It is not their fault that other trainers have let them down; they might be rightly sceptical of further trainers. The only thing you can do is to ensure that those who you bring in for these sessions are, in fact, excellent. They are then the ones who have to deal with the group's disillusion with being there.

Don't take it personally. I have entered many lectures with teachers who have been talked to death by supposed experts who have no idea, nor do they acknowledge, that teachers already know a lot about what they are doing. My own framework for lectures is that I am simply there to share some thoughts with them which they may find useful. It is evident that I am not there trying to tell them how to do their jobs, what they should be experiencing and so on.

How do I handle someone who takes my power away with one question or statement?

Ridicule works really well here! Just joking, but you may have to learn to do quippy things that don't invalidate the student, but put them in their place so you can do your job. I've had people in classes who were really bright and oftentimes one step ahead of where I was heading. They usually sit in the front row and shoot one-liners at me. I tend to just laugh with them, or nod an acknowledgment of their cleverness, but I stay in control. If it gets out of hand, I'll usually have enough rapport to have a chat with them on a break, or go sit with them at lunch and drop a few hints.

I would question the assumption that they are trying to take your power away by their behaviour. It may not be the case at all—they may just enjoy what you're doing and want some way to interact with you.

I confront a lot of participants who act as if they know it all and seem intent on putting me, the presenter, down. Specifically, they ask questions, setting me up, as if I won't know the answer. It wastes time and causes problems. What can I do?

Why are they being allowed to exhibit this behaviour in the first place? I think some trainers need to learn to have a strong opening and a fast pace that doesn't allow room for some students to intervene so easily. Once they have a sense of what you're on about and you've established some honest credibility, I think you'll find these situations disappear.

Participants continually question what I say, disagree and disrupt group dynamics. What can I do?

See the above response. But this question's phrasing brings up a few other thoughts. There is some room to think that the students may know more than you do, or have a different experience, and therefore be right. You may learn something from them. I always assume I have people in my audience who know more about a given subject than I do; therefore, I am rarely dogmatic or rigid.

If I am teaching something based solely on my experience and not grounded in the technical literature, then my languaging will indicate it: "Some thoughts I have…" In this way there is room for someone else, who in fact knows more, to contribute. I don't assume that someone interjecting is intent on being disruptive, just intent on being heard.

A second thought is that some individuals in a training need time to express themselves. You may not be providing enough opportunities, so their urge gets hold of them and they behave accordingly.

Perhaps you sound a little righteous. Many respond argumentatively to this style of delivery, just out of habit. But remember, the bottom line is that you are in control of whether and how questions get asked in the classroom.

How do I get people to believe that they can learn?

First, acknowledge that their belief that they can't is probably true for them. This belief has likely been built up over time through experiences of failure (or, more probably, they have interpreted learning events as failures). It matters not whether these interpretations are accurate or inaccurate—the student is going to respond as if they are true anyway.

To change this belief it will take lots of new experiences in which it is made explicit what it is they have learned, and meaning is given for their experiences. We can have these uncertain students re-evaluate those situations in which they thought they couldn't learn, but did. We can also use our own experiences as metaphors. Share recollections of when you didn't think you could learn, and then through perseverance or whatever, you did.

How can I get my students to understand that it is okay to laugh in a training?

Humour is an interesting topic. Laughing is rarely an outcome for professional trainings; however, it can be an expression that students use for responding.

Laughter in trainings springs from insights, not particularly from a 'funny' trainer. By insights I mean that the trainer takes the students down a path of thought, but the conclusion that the student comes to is unusual or not anticipated. This is what causes natural laughter. It can even occur in serious sessions with serious content. There isn't anything I know of that you can do that will make it 'okay to laugh', but there are ways of constructing your content such that students will laugh simply because it is the most natural expression for them to make in response to your communication.

PROBLEMS WITH DESIGN AND OUTCOMES

In my own career, and it appears in the careers of many trainers, problems can be encountered that focus on the design processes itself. Sometimes these problems are due to lack of specificity surrounding the outcomes, sometimes they are to do with the methods we choose to use in the classroom.

Of course, there can also be difficulties or questions that relate to specific features of the design, such as the use of simulations or assigning homework. I receive many questions addressing problems with the design and outcomes aspects of training, and my thoughts about these follow.

Trainers are sometimes involved in assisting with significant change processes within a company, such as corporate restructuring, in which employees who choose not to take redundancies will in fact be working in very new and different ways. I'm in that situation, and I will need to change people's beliefs and move them out of their comfort zone—what do I need to know about achieving this type of outcome?

You need to know that this process is based more on therapeutic skills than training skills. You will need to think about the experience of those who are 'changing skins'. I have found that people highly resent being told what they feel, what they should feel, what they will feel. They just want to be heard and agreed with. From there, you have an opportunity to help.

My experience has been that these processes are very difficult for people. Our job is not to try to get them to believe that it isn't going to be difficult, but to agree that it is hard. Then, we need to give them options for coping with that change process. I would recommend you spend some time reading the extensive literature on change through the lifespan—find out what this process is like and what people can do better in order to cope. The point is that people don't want to be convinced of something that for them isn't true. They want to be heard, and they want to know how to survive.

What is the value of simulated exercises, such as role-playing and 'table-top' exercises in a short, one-week course?

Simulations and role-playing can be an excellent method, so long as two criteria are met. The first is that the simulation closely matches the actual experience in real-work situations. They have to be believable, or students will not be able to transfer the lessons from the simulation to actual experience. The second criteria is that the exercise must be repeated. I have found that a one time experience is not enough. If I am trying, say, to teach some new communication skill, I keep in mind that communication patterns are habituated, so students will need many, many repetitions before this new skill will take hold.

You may not have time to do a lot of role-plays, but you *can* have every student do one or two repetitions with different partners, and then ask the students to incorporate that new technique in all their other interactions through the course (be that on a break, with their spouse at home or when speaking with you). Give them lots of opportunities to build some comfort with the new pattern.

How do I gauge how much 'homework' is appropriate to set for my participants, and how do I convince them of the importance of getting it done? What can I do about those who fail to do their homework?

I personally try to set as little homework as possible, only because I cannot control whether or not they do that homework. If I do assign it I try to focus the homework more on reinforcing the concepts I taught than on learning new material. This way if they don't do the homework, what they've missed is reinforcement, not some key concept.

Your situation might be different—students might need to do some learning on their own through homework. I think the best thing you can do for them is to be honest about the consequences of not doing it, and provide some different ways that they might approach accomplishing the task. But don't lie. If you say that not doing the homework will lead to confusion in the next day's session, then that has to be true. Because if they don't do the homework and then easily survive the next day they won't trust you and they won't ever do the homework.

I actually try to make homework more of an additional benefit to the student rather than a negative consequence. For me, this has worked well. I really don't want someone to quit the course just because they can't get to their homework.

One last thought on what has been effective: you might suggest that if doing homework in the evenings is likely to be difficult that they consider doing it over lunch or coming in early for class and doing it there. The student may not have thought of these options—whenever I suggested this strategy, I've always been surprised how many of my students show up an hour early to sit and study before class.

What do I do when students are communicating well, and learning a great deal, but because of all of the interaction the program falls behind its planned time?

You have to make a choice. If you don't mind that the course falls behind, and the students don't mind either, then keep it the way it is. If, however, it bothers either you or them, then it is a matter of tightening up the reigns. Acknowledge to the students their interest in continuing to explore the current issue but tell them that they will need to find a way to do it in their own time, because it is time for the class to move on.

I've far too much material to cover in the time I am allocated for the course. I try to cram it all in, but the lesson feels rushed and I'm concerned about overloading the students. What can I do?

First I think you need to assess if all of the information is in fact critical to the students. If not, I would start subtracting some of the deeper levels of detail. If the information is in fact critical, you might make the details available in the form of worksheets and articles that the students can take away with them. You no doubt realise that, although you are covering all of the material, it is unlikely the students will remember that information for very long. It's just too much. You could verify this by testing them three to five days after they have completed the course. You might be shocked at how little information really has stayed with them. It doesn't make any sense to train to an overload point, but if you have no choice in the matter, enlist the students in the situation—let them know what is required of you, and therefore how they might best support an otherwise-difficult process of learning.

When I am learning and researching for specific programs I find it a challenge to keep the facts and statistics in the foreground—in other words, to be able to let them roll off the tip

of my tongue. How can I assist myself to store these facts and statistics and make better use of research material?

It is very difficult to learn new and complex material in such a way that we can talk about it almost as if we were giving an extemporaneous talk. Nevertheless, I do believe if you use the systema-building process we discussed in Chapter 4 that fact-recalling will be much easier. Sometimes it just takes teaching that new material a good number of times. But I have designed very technical and detailed courses using the techniques we talked about and, because the structure of the process, the quality and type of thinking and the repetition involved, I have been quite successful standing up and finding those facts not only available but sequenced properly.

When I write content for a new or revised program I don't know how much time to allot for delivery of set-ups and debriefs. It seems like I include too much content — the result is that certain material is rushed and ultimately not effectively used by participants. How do I plan the percentage of content per minutes or hours? Is there a formula?

There isn't so much a formula, but there are some steps you can take. Set-ups are easier than debriefs because you have a specified outcome when you are designing. You will know in advance what it is the students need to know in order to do the exercise or whatever. Once you know the components, you can then talk your way through it as if you were on stage, so you can time yourself. Add five minutes to that time and you'll likely be in good shape.

Debriefs are a little harder to calculate and will depend on the method you choose. If you use questions for the debrief then its duration will depend on what questions you ask and how many students have something to say. I think the best strategy is to write very clearly the key points that you want to ensure are made in the debrief, then make a good guess at the time frame you want to allow those to surface. In the debrief, if you are way over time you can take over and simply give students the key points. If it goes more quickly, extend the debrief by asking more open-ended questions such as,

"To what other areas in life might this relate?" or, "What other examples of this concept have you seen in your work?"

How can I create a training module which can be successfully facilitated by different presenters?

There are two keys to successful replication of a course by other trainers. The first is ritual: design your course with strong and frequent signposts for the new trainer to achieve (first you do this, next you do that). The second is by making the program as *material-dependent* as possible. This means that the program has many pre-fabricated exercises, handouts, games, models and so on. Done well, an exercise, game or model does the teaching—the trainer is simply there facilitating those processes.

All the critical learnings in the course should not be dependent on the skill of the trainer to produce—this is where the variance in outcomes emerges from different trainers of different skill levels. It's like McDonald's. There are a million ways to make a hamburger, and every cook would do it slightly differently. But McDonald's has taken this variable of cook-skills out of the equation by ritualising exactly how to cook a McDonald's hamburger—you use this tool, on this grill, at this temperature, for this length of time, flipping at this point in time and so forth. The cook has much less discretion. If you have a successful training that you want others to replicate, then create a formula that others can follow.

I am presenting basically the same information, to basically the same people, year after year. How do I do it differently or freshen it up?

I have this very same problem. The antidote for me has been to allow myself to continually refine my understanding and learning about the subject matter. I study new literature, I experiment and I talk to others in the field. And I make sure that every year I apply what I teach to new situations in my own life. This allows me to have new stories and anecdotes and insights to share with the new group. This keeps my energy up and allows me to feel that I am in touch with the latest thinking along these content lines.

For example, *Training to Train* students are taught about developing behavioural flexibility by taking on other life projects in the ways we discussed in Chapter 3. Every year I, too, take on some new learning project. This experience allows me to relate to the current year's students and have new insights and stories for next year.

What is the best way to deliver a lot of dry data in a short time?

The first key is to let your audience know that you will be delivering dry data—because that's what's required. But I would then emphasise that you are going to work very hard to get through the material quickly and efficiently. I would ask the students to do whatever it takes to stay present and alert; that way, they support getting through the material as fast as possible. You might create a series of worksheets or information sheets so that you can break up the pace of the session. You might start by delivering some of the content, and then sending students off for twenty minutes or so to have a break and read on their own, or work with a small group to learn the next piece from the handout. When they come back to class you can use question-and-answer methods to reinforce that material and ensure everyone has interpreted the material correctly. A few cycles like this, with a few pace changes, will get you through a tremendous amount of material and yet keep the audience alive in the meantime.

What are the strategies for reducing the amount of material delivered without losing the main point?

I suppose it's by simply focusing all of your content on the *main point*. But I would be clear with the students that you are simply working with the main point—which is likely at a fairly high logic level—and that they will not have the entire picture in depth. I have covered an amazing number of concepts in a short one-hour lecture, but to do that it has meant simply providing one or two main pieces of information for each concept, without any depth at all. This is fine for some types of outcomes, but you want to make sure that your students are not fooled into believing that they have a solid understanding of the subject.

216

I have a problem designing my speeches so that they are relevant to the audience. How do I pick the relevant points for the audience?

I haven't personally had this problem as I usually am told by the client what is important for the student to know. In the times when I am designing a course I think is important, then the information itself tells me what the relevant points are—these are the pieces of information that are necessary to understand the subject. If I have an audience who already has a good knowledge base in the subject area—like my trainers—then I start my day by eliciting from them what would be most important for them regarding the subject I am going to teach. I then pitch the content toward those issues, concerns and needs of the students.

I want to use other people's material—material I haven't developed myself. What do I need to know about ethical use of other people's material and licensing rights?

Researchers and writers produce their work in the hope that others will find value in that work and use it to their best advantage. If something is in print, it is part of the public domain and you have all rights to cite that work. But that is the key: you are not teaching someone else's content as if it were your own, you are citing someone else's work. That is the responsibility you have, otherwise you can be accused of plagiarising.

In my own work, only some things I teach are based on my own research and theorising. The rest is based on information that has been developed by other academics and scientists. When I teach those concepts I inform the students of the source of that information and how they can pursue that research further on their own. Oftentimes I just want my students to know that some particular concept exists for them to follow up if it is relevant to them.

If you choose to reproduce any printed material from another source—graphs, charts, quotes—beware of the governing laws. If you are quoting a paragraph, then a reference is adequate. If, however, you want to reproduce and give to your students (say) the chapter of a book or a few pages from an article, you should contact the author or their representative and seek permission to do so. When you choose someday to write your own book or articles, other trainers will need to seek your permission.

I find it difficult to differentiate between 'training', which is interactive, and 'presentations', which are directed at an audience. In the latter case, how do you judge during the presentation if you are getting your message across and that the audience is enjoying the experience?

Probably the most obvious way is to observe your audience. It doesn't take much to notice when students are agreeing or disagreeing, attentive or distracted and so on. Audiences are responsive; a trained eye can spot the clues which reveal what is happening for the various members of the audience.

The second way to test audience response is by periodically asking them about their response to the delivery, perhaps opening up the class to comments or questions. This can be quite appropriate even in a short presentation. If it is a longer presentation I tend to mingle with the group—or have a staff member mingle with the group—when they are on a break or out to lunch. I learn a lot about my presentation by overhearing the comments of students when they are in a more relaxed environment.

How do I motivate people to take information away and apply it? I find that despite their best intentions they generally do not do this. Urgent work on the job seems to take priority over practising these new skills.

This can be a bit of wishful thinking. There is no real way of guaranteeing that students will use what you teach unless you have some mechanism in place for you to continue to influence them after the course is over. If you believe what you are teaching is important and throughout the program you are continuously ensuring that the students see concrete demonstrations of the effectiveness of using what you teach, then this is probably not that big a problem. But in most cases your influence over students' behaviour stops at the door. You can only hope that at some time in the future what they learned from you will find its way into their daily behaviours and thought processes.

What are some methods for evaluating the effectiveness of a training course? Examination? Critique?

You first must decide who you need to convince of the effectiveness or value of the training. Are you trying to convince yourself, the client or the participant? Not that that will affect the method you use for evaluation, but it will affect how the information is represented. Will it just be a mental note, a description of the changes presented to the class in the closing or a formal report? The question you are trying to answer is: By what evidence is change apparent in the students' knowledge or performance? Or, How do you, your students and your client know that you achieved your stated outcomes?

There are several effective methods for evaluation; which you use depends upon the content and skills you are developing. Obviously, tests of all types are a good way to measure new knowledge or new skills—you get to find out what the student now knows, or can do as a result of your course.

To make tests useful for evaluation it is always best to pre-test your students on the same material at the start of the course. This provides a quick way to perceive the actual learnings that went on in the course. This can be very important to the students, and to the client. It is amazing how many students, if tested only at the end of the course will believe that they would have already known that information if they had been tested at the beginning. Of course, this is rarely true—and a pre-test/post-test will demonstrate this to them. It allows a way for the student to say, "Oh, I really did learn something."

Another good way to evaluate a course is to invite a critique from another industry professional. Someone who, based on their knowledge and expertise, observes the changes in your students. I have oftentimes asked other professionals to monitor my courses and provide an evaluation in written form that I can provide to both the students and to the client.

I have also used videotape extensively as a way to capture students' skill levels at the start of course. At the end of the course, their skills can be compared to those they began with. If you are teaching telephone skills and using role-plays as a teaching method, then video is excellent. You can have the students perform for the camera in a role-play situation at the very start of the course, and again at the end. These videotapes then can be compared. You can even have the students do the analysis of these tapes to come to their own conclusion. They become not only a means of testing the changes, but they are also a good teaching tool.

The one method of evaluation I have found has little value is the end-of-course evaluation sheet in which the student rates the course, the instructor, the content and so on. These forms really only tell us how the student *feels* at the end of the program—and my experience is that students don't really provide very useful or accurate information at that point in time (they may be tired, they are ready to go home, they may be on a high from the final exercises, whatever). When I *do* use evaluation forms is several weeks following the course. I mail the evaluation forms to each student and ask them to assess *how they are using the information or skills back in their work environment.* I ask questions such as: How easy or difficult was it to apply the knew knowledge? Or, Based on your experience in attempting to apply it, what might be added to the course to make that process more efficient? Remember, the reason for training is really not about how they perform in the classroom, it is about how they perform outside it. At the end of the class day they cannot assess that aspect of the training. They cannot honestly tell you if they learned anything—they simply haven't used it.

FREQUENTLY ASKED QUESTIONS ABOUT THE USE OF HANDOUTS AND MEDIA

There are many 'handy hints' written in training technique books; however, in the real-time world of the classroom, many experienced trainers still encounter difficulties. In this section I have isolated questions relating to this specific feature of training events.

What are the important things to think about when deciding whether to use handout materials?

As with everything else we do, the key question is: For what purpose are the handouts relevant to your program? There are three basic reasons for using handouts. The first is to provide instructions or set-ups for some activity. The second is to deliver information, such as articles or exercises to be completed in the students' own time. Third, handouts are used as reinforcement material for the content of the course. The student can use the handouts for review purposes once the course is completed.

What is important to think about ahead of time is why you have this handout and how the student should use those materials for their own benefit. When you do hand out the material, it should be accompanied by clear instructions from you as to how the student might use them to their own best benefit.

When do you pass out handout material?

This is an excellent question. I have gone to courses where all the handouts—usually reprints of the overheads—were in a binder on my table at the start of the course. Remember that students make up meanings for what they see in your training. Oftentimes, when they see these materials in advance, they make judgments that might not be useful to you when you are trying to teach. For this reason, *my* students enter a course to find a binder with notepaper and a pen, but no course material. They will receive their material on an *as-needed basis* throughout the course. If the materials take the form of notes to reinforce some content piece, they are handed out at the end of the session—perhaps passed out at the door as they leave. If it is a handout or exercise sheet that they will need sometime in the middle of a session, then I have these handouts placed face down on their desk during the preceding break. The student then has easy access to the handout, without disrupting the class waiting for them to be passed out.

Is there any research on the best fonts, line lengths and graphics used in computer-based education packages? Is there any research on the appeal and comprehension based on these choices?

I have seen research on these factors, and these issues are no doubt critical to designers of computer-based products, as well as to those who create printed materials for training. Unfortunately I don't have access to any of the latest work that has been done in that area. I think a few phone calls would net you good results. Desktop publishers and designers of interactive computer packages would be the place to start.

I want to use overheads, but as a presenter, I find that using them distracts me from the flow of the presentation. Any suggestions?

Overheads are one of those support materials that can be used very effectively to punctuate a lecture, but if they are used inappropriately, they can also destroy a lecture. I avoid using overheads for the same reason stated above: they disrupt the flow of the lecture. Also, in order for the overhead to be seen clearly, the room lights have to be dimmed. If the lights are left low for any length of time, students start to drift off—they can't see you clearly enough to stay focused.

If you think of the purpose of overheads—to highlight the key points to a talk—you might start to think of alternatives. In my case I have handouts printed with the key points, and they are passed out at the completion of each lecture segment as a way for the student to review those points in the future. If you do decide to continue using overheads you might think to have an assistant, or assign a student to actually place the overheads on the projector and to handle the lights. This frees you up to stay in contact with the audience.

If I use automated activities, like videos and interactive computer programs, will anything be lost in my courses due to the isolation of the students, and if so what can I do to counter the effects?

The use of various forms of media, including interactive media, is becoming more and more prevalent in trainings these days. And you can expect even more in the future. I think it is a good idea to set up some means of live interaction with students to supplement these materials. Perhaps the answer is to do set-ups and debriefing sessions regularly. This time can be used to assist with any problems that arise because of the content but, more importantly, this can be your time to manage how the students are *feeling* about their progress. Left to their own devices, students often have no way of coping with the unpleasant feelings that come with studying and learning new material. Without your interaction they may quit the course, or perform poorly.

FREQUENTLY ASKED QUESTIONS ABOUT PERSONAL ISSUES OF THE TRAINER

Another category of question I am asked to address frequently relates to the kinds of personal issues that we confront in our training career. These questions centre around the personal factors of gender, age, stamina and health, and our relationship with the members of our audience. Again, these are not to be construed as 'right' answers, perhaps just useful ways of looking at a situation that suggest a different approach to whatever might previously have been considered.

The majority of my past students see me as a 'personal friend' and I am concerned that this takes away my credibility, authority and acceptability as a trainer. They don't see me as their teacher, they see me as their friend. Is this a good thing?

This shouldn't be a problem unless you make it one, by having a problem with it yourself. If you are a professional trainer, then when you are acting in that capacity, people will usually shift gears and respond to you appropriately. It should in no way negatively affect your credibility, authority or acceptability; it may actually enhance it, especially if these people see that in your own life you do what you teach others to do.

You could also choose to pay attention to the level of friendship you allow between yourself and your potential students. I walk a cautious line with people for whom I will be in this situation. It is rare that a student who attends a class I teach is likely to be interested in the same hobbies and activities I'm engaged in in my regular living time, so friendships among students are rare, and when they do occur, crossing boundaries is not usually a problem.

Now I do have some thoughts about those social events we sometimes need to do with students—like going to the pub after a session, or taking a class on some sort of field trip. In these situations you really are not a peer, nor a friend; you are the trainer, and this social time should be paid attention to in the same way you pay attention to students' perceptions of you on stage. A lot can be lost.

How do I solve the conflict between me being an individualist, loving to work independently, and fulfilling the need for a peer group, a network that gives me opportunity for exchange support, learning and so on?

I face this conflict myself. I do spend most of my time studying independently, yet I benefit greatly from interactions with others in my field. I think the solution is to make the value of the interaction more important than the discomfort of engaging in that interaction. I would also recommend that you be very selective about the groups you choose to network with—they do not all carry the same benefits, and some take more than they give. I always remind myself that these external events are time-bound: I only have to interact for a short while to receive a large long-term benefit.

Is there a network for trainers? Are there regular gatherings?

There are some very good networks for trainers around Australia, probably more than I am actually aware of. Two that I have found very responsible for supporting the continuing development of trainers and lecturers are the AITD (Australian Institute of Training and Development), and the NSAA (National Speakers Association of Australia). Both of these groups have chapters throughout the country and do meet regularly for functions.

I need a strategy for using a microphone—I find I speak too close and it comes across as too loud. How do I learn to use it properly?

This is really a matter of practise—it sounds like you already know the problem. If you can switch from a hand-held microphone to a lapel microphone you can set the microphone position appropriately when you are setting up and then not think about it again. If you are using a hand-held microphone be sure to test the microphone levels before you begin your talk. You can adjust the volume and gains such that if you do bring it close to mouth you won't generate that blaring sound.

I usually have my microphone levels set low because I want to be able to still use my own vocal control. I don't want to have to speak differently—such as softly—to compensate for the microphone levels.

Why do I find it so comfortable at question times in front of a group compared with when I deliver a straight data presentation? I find that when answering questions I can be totally focused, congruent and unaware of being on stage.

Different trainers certainly do have different strengths and different ways of feeling comfortable on stage. Unfortunately, students do need for us to deliver content—they are there to learn new information. I would venture to say that you feel comfortable in the questioning interaction for two, maybe three, reasons.

First, I would imagine you use this technique often, and through repetition it has become a neutral experience for you. Second, I would imagine you have good success with this method which has led you to strong beliefs about your competence with the technique—and that too contributes to your comfort. Third, you use your brain differently when addressing questions, and you have no doubt developed a strong skill in using this form of 'thinking on your feet'.

I think it may be time now to devote some energy to developing other aspects of your training skills, perhaps increasing the amount of time you spend doing straight presentations—they *will* become more comfortable with practise!

How do I handle the boredom of repeated trainings?

It is very hard when our trainings become so familiar that we are bored presenting them. This was my experience with the *Learning to Learn* program for the last few years I taught it. I was doing some sixty repetitions of the program each year. There were times when I would be backstage on a break wondering how I was going to get out there and *say those words again*. I think this is the experience of some stage actors, like those who did eight shows of *Evita* every week for ten years. How do you make it look like it's the first time you've ever done it when you yourself are bored out of your mind? You cannot change the show or your training when it's working just because you are bored with it. That might be good for you, but you're destroying a working formula and introducing risks that don't need to be there. For me, I had to continually make the audience more important than my own feelings. I would force myself to do this material as if I'd never done it before and enjoy the audience reactions as if I had never seen those reactions before.

Now to answer this question. Although the actual training time may be boring, you can acknowledge that you no longer have to spend any time preparing for the class. This other time now can be used for other important and interesting things. When I no longer had to spend any preparation time beforehand or on breaks, I started bringing in other work that interested me. While the class was doing an activity or taking a test, I would be in the back of the room reading, writing or doing some other project. Because my trainings were settled (albeit boring) the rest of my life was able to benefit from the extra time. Of course, you could begin looking to exit that particular training. In my case I did do this eventually, and sometimes now I actually miss that well-constructed course when everything was so easy and predictable.

My planning is very global and therefore I find that at the end of a segment I may have omitted some detail. How can I ensure that all detail is covered without losing the spontaneity with which I present my courses?

If certain details are important to the 'image' you are building for the student, their inclusion really shouldn't be left to chance. If omitting details is a chronic problem in your presentations, there are three things you might think to do. The first is to write a list of key notes for the detail that is essential. It shouldn't be something you have to focus on to see or read, just write a few big words on the side of the stage that you can glance at periodically to ensure that you don't miss important details. You can also prepare a handout for the students, so you can give them all the detailed material at the end of your talk. Reviewing this with them allows you to fill in any gaps that you inadvertently missed along the way. The third thing you can do is rehearse your lecture to include the essential details. You can practise introducing the structure of these details into the talk at the appropriate time, which will leave room for you to be as spontaneous as you want in between those points. But always remember, the desire to be spontaneous should never be more important than the students' need for precise information.

I had a situation where I responded inappropriately to a group member. The student was sharing some very personal information, telling the group how she felt deskilled because of the work she was doing. She was saying that she was not contributing her potential and felt as though she was not appreciated. I thanked her for the comments, and started to say that I felt her presence was very valuable and that my experience with her as a trainer gave me insights — but she pushed my assurance away. This was devastating for me! How do I know when not to go into 'fix it' mode?

I know that for some trainers, in some contexts, it is a habit to want to jump in and make everyone feel good and smart and appreciated, thinking that if we could just get them to see it differently, or feel better about themselves, then all would be right with the world. But there are many times when a student just wants to share their experience or feelings *without receiving a response*. They are not looking for 'help'.

In this case, trying to 'fix it' by telling the student that her presence was valuable actually invalidated her. She just told you how it was for her, in her experience. Your response was like, "No, you're wrong." In her mind she feels that she is not appreciated, so that is what is true for her. In the moment, the best response is simply to agree that that is how she feels. You do not have to do anything with that. You can do more later covertly to demonstrate your appreciation of her contribution without ever having to challenge her own feelings and beliefs.

My problem is that I have no time for further study. I am in demanding paid employment where extra jobs are thrown my way which are difficult to avoid and take all of my working week. What are my options?

I do get how hard this is, but there has to be a point of making this critically important. That there is some time set aside, every day, for your own development. Perhaps you might think of furthering your studies through a formal academic course. You may find it easier to say to others, "I can't, I have class tonight" than simply saying you want 'free' time to study. Also know that time will pass whether you do anything about this or not. That means that ten years will go by. A little work, even one university class a year, may eventually add up to a degree. Try changing your thinking from the short term (which of course traps you into the feelings of the pressure and lack of time *today*), to the long term. Is there a few hours a week? How many hours does that give you to further your studies over the next few years? What is important is to do something, no matter how small, to get this process going. Once it's part of your life, you may find that everything else just finds a way to fit around it.

I am constantly being asked to have input on many issues. Often I do have some important perspectives to add, but my workload is growing ridiculously so that I work late most nights. I have salaried employment and get no overtime pay, I have restricted promotion prospects and therefore this extra work is a cost to me with little benefit. Help.

This is the dilemma of anyone who is good at what they do. But it is important that we are the ones who set up this dynamic where others see us as a resource to be used for everything. In our desire to help we become depended on. There is great wisdom in knowing how to say "No" to requests for these extra tasks. Think of what you are losing in time to develop yourself: the more it is lost, the less valuable you will be to people in the future.

I feel as though I am in a training rut, and that I'm providing less variety and flexibility than I am able. How can I re-energise myself and my presentations?

This can happen to anyone. If leaving training for a while isn't an option, then I know what I would be doing. I would take on some of my own personal challenges and go have a few adventures. I'd do something that shifts my thinking and wakes me up a bit. I find if I can shift my own level of excitement about some other aspect of my life, that excitement will oftentimes follow me into the classroom. Also, every new adventure or skill I tackle vicariously affects my range of behaviours and hence my variety and flexibility. So go get certified in skydiving, or get your dive ticket, or go learn to race a Formula Ford car, or go climb a mountain.

How do I maintain high energy throughout the training? I get tired and my energy gets flattened.

Training is always going to be a demanding task. It asks not only a lot of your brain, but also a lot of your body. But you can only maintain the energy if you have it to begin with.

The energy we use in training is very similar to that of an endurance athlete. We need to sustain momentum over an extended period of time. Losing energy before the end of training is typically a sign of lacking fitness and perhaps even an improper diet. I have found in my own career that my energy levels during training varies depending on how much exercise I'm getting and what I am doing with my diet. I know it can seem like an impossible task to find even more energy to manage those factors, but the price for not doing so is dear. Although I haven't always been good about doing so, I do for the most part try to stay physically strong and active— be that via gym work, running, training for triathlons or whatever. I also notice that during a training I lose my appetite—as if my body is already working too hard to want to add the task of digesting food—so I can end up running on my nerves. So now I try to eat well and load up on fuels for a few days before the event. The model I have found most appropriate is the diet of athletes who engage in endurance events. I then maintain my energy during trainings with food that is simple to digest—such as rice, pasta, soups and the like. I try to avoid sugars and red meat during the training itself; they tend to make me tired for the next few hours.

Another thought relates to what you do after the training event to recover for the next day. I know that at the end of the day we can be pretty 'hyper'—almost over-tired and wired for sound. I try to do whatever it takes to come down quickly—be it by taking a bath, eating a big meal, getting a massage or having a beer. I do whatever it takes to settle me down enough to sleep well. I rarely plan for social events while I'm training. I find the extra effort to continue to communicate takes its toll on my work the next day.

I hardly ever feel nervous anymore. Should I be concerned?

I would not be concerned unless you are finding that your performance is lacking punch. Sometimes it is nervous energy that gets us up with enough energy to really perform well. Without it many trainers are flat and uninspiring. But if you are finding that you can 'get up' without using the adrenaline from being nervous to do that—good on you. Personally, I still have a good case of nerves before beginning my presentations. Not so bad that they are debilitating, but enough to get my blood pumping. On the occasions when that is not the case I tend to stretch and do a little jog or something to get my heart rate up before I go on stage; it has a similar effect to the nervousness.

I run classes once a week at a health club—ongoing over two years now. I now run 'series' of six- to eight-week classes with titles such as, "Handling stress", "Improving running" and so on. Despite having a course title and providing a clear outcome, I still have some new people coming every week and others dropping out. My goal is to have everyone who attends to have such a powerful, valuable experience that they 'get it' and return. How do I do that?

I think this is the hardest thing for a trainer to do—get people to show up continuously for classes when they don't *have* to be there. It really isn't about how powerful or valuable you make the experience—that still may not be enough to get them there. Even if the class content is really important to them, they may not show up. Just before coming to class they are likely to be comfortable doing something else, so they have to shift gears and put in effort to get to your class. In that moment, they likely *don't feel like going*. And you are not there to influence that. I'm thinking now of what gets me to my classes and you might analyse your own process to see what you discover. I attend some classes in a couple of subjects every week. When I think about these activities, they are very important to me and I enjoy myself when I'm there. But every week when it's time to get ready to go I have this fight with myself. Here I am at home, it's getting dark, I really just want to sit down and relax, but I have to get up, get ready, get in the car and drive where I have to go—*I don't ever feel like doing that*. The keys I know that get me where I'm going are the following. I have to consciously remember that I always feel this way before class, but that five minutes after I arrive,

I don't want to be anywhere else. I also consciously think about how *bad* I'm going to feel in a couple of hours if I don't go. Another important thing for me that I incorporate is having someone else to go with who depends on me to go. And lastly I have to really have a liking and respect for the instructor, someone in whose presence I looking forward to being.

When I am teaching classes, like the guitar course that required people to show up one night a week after work, I would talk to them about all of this. How they are likely to feel before class and that those feelings can lead them to deciding to stay home. I offer them as many strategies as I know to help them simply get there. Once they are there I know they will feel differently and, if they show up often enough, this will get to be a part of their routine. This is also why I had to make the class possible even if they never practised during the week—knowing this was the number one reason they would give themselves for not coming to class. And I knew that many would not practise initially. Have a chat to your next class about this and see what they come up with to support themselves to get to class for the next six weeks.

In my group workshops I would like to bring in more of the 'non-physical'. In other words, I want to give people some of what I used to call the 'wanky stuff', like extrapolating the lessons to other areas of life and learning. I am a bit anxious that I may lose people if they feel threatened by this type of content. How can I present this material without losing people?

The first question you need to ask yourself is: Why is this important? Ask the question from the students' standpoint. If there is relevance from their perspective, you should have no problems convincing your audience.

People will only feel threatened by that which they don't understand or cannot make sense of. They may be uncomfortable for a while—these may be new behaviours—but that will change with experience. The point is that if you cannot make a cohesive argument that makes sense for adding these components *from the students' perspective*, don't do it. Remember, just because we as trainers think something is neat or important doesn't necessarily mean it is for our students. Just make sure that this isn't something you want to do for just your own sake.

I conduct a training program that involves the participants in having to make a presentation that is videotaped at the end of the two days of theory work. They are informed on the morning of the first day about this presentation, however, it does create a fair bit of tension. How can I introduce this without stressing out the participants?

The simple answer is that you can't. Some people will be stressed no matter when you introduce this kind of exercise—truth is, I'd be nervous too. This is exactly the kind of activity that causes stress naturally in many people. So you can't stop that, but you can explain that the stress is natural, and that it doesn't need to interfere with their learning and eventual performance.

The question you want to seriously ask is: What is the benefit to the outcomes of your course for telling students about the activity so soon in the course? If there isn't a good reason, I'd actually wait until I had more rapport and the students were more trusting of the process—probably after they've had a few successes with you. If there is a reason, then you need to tell them this and apologise for the effect this knowledge is going to have on them in the meantime. For example, you might say, "We are here to do... Part of knowing if we have accomplished our task will be to observe our own performances. How we're going to do that in this course is to videotape these performances at the end of the day tomorrow. I know that for some of you this may be daunting, but by the time we are ready to do the exercise you'll be well prepared for it, so there really isn't any benefit to you to spend time being nervous about that now. The reason I am giving you this information now is... And if any of you are really concerned about it, please come and see me and we'll see what alternatives we might have. But first give me today to see if I can't convince you of the value and ease of the exercise. If at the end of today you're still a bit worried, just see me."

How do I quickly identify people's personality styles so that everybody can be catered to, to enhance their learning rather than have them sit there for a day or two feeling uncomfortable about what they are doing?

There isn't really a quick way of determining any one individual's personality during the course. (Actually, you can, but it's too late and that isn't really what you need.) All trainers and designers should assume that the training will contain the various personality profiles. The best thing you can do is to design your training such that all of the reactions of the various personality profiles are thought about ahead of time.

For example, it doesn't matter particularly that I know who is an introvert or extrovert in my classes—given enough time, I'll know this just through interaction—but that information isn't really meaningful. What is important is that I assume, before the training, while I'm preparing, that I will have some introverts and some extroverts. I have to know in advance that I can't satisfy them both in the methods I choose—I can only do one thing. I can know that some group members will feel good and some group members will feel not so good. The value of knowing that some students won't particularly like the methods is that you can use your set-up to manage their responses in advance, thereby creating relevance and meaning for your choice of methods. Also, you may find that by thinking about this ahead of time you can offer the students a few variations on the exercises.

How do I get my message clear in my mind so that it comes out of my mouth exactly how I think it, and so that the participants 'get it'?

Remember that how information is stored in our minds needs to be converted to a structure that makes it make sense when it is spoken

verbally. This is an active restructuring process. I would highly recommend that you construct a systema for your material and then
do many, many talk-throughs until you learn how to talk about it,
and not simply know it. When you've done that, you can either
audiotape yourself doing this talk or present the material to a few
friends. It is amazing that you can listen to your own lecture on an
audiotape and hear where you are clear and where you have lost the
plot. It is an easy path to making corrections.

**It seems that I am clear with my outcomes when I begin
presenting, but as I start speaking I find that my outcomes
become 'should do's' to the participants rather than
possibilities. My passion and (my judgments) then take
over, putting me into a 'blamer' mode to get the participants
to take action. What other strategies are there for speaking
powerfully as a facilitator?**

There are many other strategies, but for those who identify with this
case, I think it has a lot to do with the habitual way of communicating that has been learned. Changing that will be more than a matter
of a new strategy. This form of communication has likely served you
in other areas of your life, which is why it is pervasive and why you
fall back on it in this situation. But clearly, it isn't very effective in
your training role. People do not respond well to being told what is
'right', what they 'should do'. It makes many personality types argumentative—and this is hardly your outcome. I would begin to think
about role models who communicate as you would wish to do yourself in these circumstances and go learn to do what they do. I
wonder in your case what the effect of doing some volunteer work
with the elderly, or AIDS patients, or street-kid programs would
have on this behaviour?

**I think my students notice my nervousness and my lack
of knowledge. This makes me afraid of speaking out and**

speaking up. I have a strong critical internal voice accent-uating my self-doubts. How do I gain more confidence?

Is there a way you could verify if your perceptions of the student's observation is accurate? You may discover that this is not true for them at all and, if it's not, there is nothing you really need to do other than convince yourself. You might want to ask yourself: By what evidence do I know that I am smart and knowledgeable? Determine what it would take to convince yourself—and then go and do it.

I think the best presenters work with minimal notes. How is time managed effectively when most of the content is delivered without a written script?

Some trainers have a really good internal sense of time, or like myself, a habit of glancing at my watch. I also like to have a clock at the back of the room (out of the view of the students) but where I can see it easily for a reference point.

Of course, repetition and practise also helps in this area. Once the training has been repeated a number of times, notes are not needed, and you are basically doing the same thing over and over again and should take about the same amount of time. The less experience I have with the material the more attention I will pay to the clock.

I need to know exactly what I am going to say on stage in order to feel confident. Therefore, I take a long time to prepare a speech, and I am not flexible on stage. Should I change this?

I would change this, but only because of the limitations it presents. It is hard to be flexible when you are over-prepared, and it no doubt creates a lot of stress for you. But at the same time it is important that you feel confident. Therefore, I would start very small. Perhaps choose a small ten-minute section of an hour-long session. Learn the key point you want to make and then spontaneously deliver that content. You may have to do this a few times with the same piece until you become more confident with this approach. Slowly over time you can do this with other segments and, eventually, with longer segments, until it becomes the 'natural' way for you to train.

I am not comfortable when audience members ask me questions which I cannot answer, or questions I do not understand. This affects how open I am when presenting. What can I do to overcome this discomfort so I am open to being asked questions?

It's so true; you never know what you'll be asked if you open up the class to questions. And students can come up with some doozies. You may need to start small, but this really is an important dilemma to overcome. It is affecting your behaviours adversely, and that means your students are missing out as well. One of the biggest things you personally lose by avoiding questions is the chance to grow and learn. Questions you cannot answer are a great source of motivation to continue to study the material related to your field. I know as much as I know thanks to the questions I could not answer earlier in my career.

The only questions you should feel uncomfortable about not being able to answer are those for which you should know the answers—those that you are counted on knowing. Beyond that, it's good to create comfort and ease while saying the words, "I don't know." For example, I am often asked questions by parents and teachers about working with young children. I don't have any experience with this subject, but at the same time I don't want to curtail the questions I can answer that naturally arise in my courses, so I know in advance that I will have questions asked that I can't answer.

I have two choices in this situation, and so will you. The first is to gain some expertise in the subject area so you can answer those kinds of questions. The second is to find someone else who is an expert in the particular area. The latter is the choice I made and now as I receive these kinds of questions I refer them to this other resource.

I worry about questions I cannot answer, thinking that it reflects on my ability as trainer and subject matter expert. What do audiences really think when you cannot answer a question?

I say "I don't know" a lot, but I have never had a student express disappointment in the fact that I don't know everything. I would worry more about what the audience will think when I give them a poorly constructed or misguiding answer than what they will think if they know that I don't know the answer to the question. The only time not knowing the answer to a question will reflect poorly on your expertise is if you *should* know the answer. You should at least know where to get the answer to questions within your own field of expertise. But students make all kinds of connections between what you are teaching and other domains. These are the questions that can frighten us most. We have to learn to say, "That's a great question, I never considered that before." Admit that it's literally something you've never thought. Perhaps now you will think about it, and it will add something to your future presentations.

In my present work I often feel I have to give all the time. This results in me running out of ideas and creativity, leaving me feeling dull and boring. How do I encourage my students to come up with their own ideas, skills, etc?

If you set up precedents with your classes that you will answer all questions, do all the research, essentially do all of their thinking for them, then your students will come to expect it—and you will be trapped by your own behaviours. If it is important that your students learn to think for themselves, or rely on themselves, it should be structured into your design, and the earlier the better. Students should be given small tasks to complete on their own or with other classmates. As the class progresses and the students become more comfortable and competent relying on themselves, they can be given more and more responsibility for their own learning.

I also learned very quickly in my career the value of asking questions of my students. I would ask, "What would you do?" or "What would you have done in this situation in the past?" or "Why don't you spend a few hours thinking about that and if it's still a question come and see me later?" People naturally take the path of least resistance, so if a student knows that you will give them an answer and they don't have to think so hard, they will take advantage of that—I would, too, if you were my instructor!

I find the preparation for workshops or seminars is difficult sometimes, because during the process of the workshop I take the direction that presents itself during the discussions, such as issues brought up by the participants. What's the resolution?

This is a good technique and one that is quite appropriate for many types of trainings. The way to prepare for this type of workshop is to set boundaries around the key content areas that are critical to discuss during the course. If you do this, you can ensure that you are comfortable with the content between those boundaries regardless of how it unfolds with the actual group.

You will need to use your set-ups to focus the class on a particular issue so the class doesn't take you off on undesired tangents. You may find that it is helpful to learn how to say, "That's an interesting point, but that is not a direction we want to head in for the moment," and then reiterate the kinds of content and experiences that are appropriate to that discussion.

During a week of training my life seems to get a bit beyond my control, like the housework, food and relaxation. How do I train and still keep up with life demands?

The key is organisation and prioritising. When I am not training I am quite happy to handle life demands in a flexible way. I'm also happy to be nitpicky about the details—everything has to be hung up, socks must be folded and so on. But when I am training, that is not the case. During those times I have to decide that some things I'd like to see done, or done a certain way, are just not going to get

240

done by me—or maybe not done at all. For example, I may like to have well-prepared, home-cooked meals—but during training cycles that isn't realistic. But you don't have to sacrifice good food. In the past I have had someone come in once a week to make what I like to eat and freeze it. Also in those days I knew every good restaurant that home delivered.

So I guess it's a choice of letting things go, having them done by someone else or sacrificing yourself and your time. If you do decide to just let the laundry pile up for a week, don't worry about it— remind yourself it is just temporary—it's not a sign of a new habit.

If you still want the same quality of life during these times, then know that there are people out there who provide these services. There are people who will wash your car, come to your house and wash your dog, buy your groceries, iron your clothes, clean your house, mow your lawn, take out your rubbish, everything. You may think you can't afford it, but think for a moment of the value of your time. As a trainer you will progress and receive financial and other professional benefits based on your continued involvement in your industry and development of yourself. If doing the laundry takes a couple of hours of your time that you could have spent studying or meeting with other professionals, I can promise you that the value of using your time to improve yourself will more than pay for someone to do your laundry.

How do I get centred and in the 'flow' all the time, not just most of the time?

This is another good question. I don't know that I've found a way to do that in every circumstance myself. There are these odd times when we seem to struggle to find our pace. I can certainly have this problem if I have not been teaching for a few months—it's like the timing between my brain and mouth are skewed.

I think one of the keys has to do with understanding what interferes with that flow process in our own training life. Over the years, I have been able to observe certain things that tend to have a big effect on whether or not I am 'on' when I take the stage. One thing that interrupts this flow for me is if I allow myself to be interrupted with conversation just before I go on. Usually at that time I am very introspective; I am already 'talking' to the audience in my mind. I find it really hard to recover if I am interrupted at that point. For this reason I am usually not accessible to the audience just before going on, or going on after a break. Another thing I have discovered that can interrupt my flow while on stage is having to read anything aloud. I just do not do this well—I tend to stutter and my hands shake. And the effect of doing that is still present long after I've completed reading.

The point here is to perhaps begin to look at your own rituals. Identify what do you do on most occasions that gets you into the flow—and what if not done interferes with that. Then get a system going that minimises those interfering features.

How do I find time to prepare and continually learn new material of my own design?

Slowly and persistently. So many times we are frustrated because we lack the time to do what matters most to us. I have found that doing a little bit regularly over a long period of time adds up to new knowledge and new skills. I may never find a year to stop and study, but I can find an hour or two a week, even if it's over a morning coffee. Studying and learning has to become a habit—something without which would make you feel less complete. You can become very knowledgeable about any subject given a little daily attention over a long period of time.

I'm not preparing well enough for sessions—it feels like I haven't enough time (I'm training thirty hours a week). Are there any short cuts?

You may find that for a while you will need to work a good sixty- or seventy-hour week to accomplish this, but the outcome is to get to the stage where all you have to do is get yourself to the classroom on time. Remember that preparation is a time-bound activity, so you should have to prepare less and less the longer you are working with the material. What happens is not that you remember the material more easily but that you find ways to ritualise the training so you have less and less to do before you enter the room.

I can recall the early days of teaching *Learning to Learn* which was a thirty-two-hour course conducted between 7 pm Friday and 11 pm Sunday. I would spend every day of the preceding week preparing. Even then, during the course I was still doing final preparations for each segment during breaks and overnight. This was what I had to do in order to ensure the quality of the training. Within a year though, having ritualised the stories and metaphors and exercises and content and everything else, I had only a little preparation to do on the Friday. After eight years I could virtually walk in the room at 6 pm on Friday and just check that everything was set properly. The point is that the time you spend now preparing, if done with the thought in mind to minimise preparation in the future, is worth the effort. Then you are in a position to have time to pre-prepare for future events without so much stress.

How do I develop a different style of presenting? I have a strong 'teacher' style that directs and dictates. I want to be more of a facilitator who works with what the group wants to learn, despite the program!

Don't knock your direct teaching style; there will be many times that it is exactly what you will need. One strange thing you can do to break this habit of dictating is to videotape yourself and then force yourself to watch it as a student. I would venture to say that if you teach in a dictatorial style, you probably don't like to be dictated to. Watching yourself will probably annoy you but it will also set up some move away from doing those behaviours again.

But that of course won't give you anything to fall back on, so you'll need to begin taking on some activities to develop the facilitating skills. I think that the best sources for that skill development is working in special situation programs—programs for the homeless, for single parents, for teens in trouble, for the aged, for the infirm. You will learn to listen—these people know their own situation so much more intimately than you—they will give you the content that you can't know and you can learn to mould the lessons.

I have the problem of being perceived as 'the little girl'. People know I am knowledgeable and competent in what I am doing, however, when speaking to others I am sometimes referred to as their 'little helper'. I work in an all-male environment. How can I change their perceptions of me, or at least their behaviours?

Well this can be a touchy situation! And there may be many solutions depending on the specific situation—but I hesitate here because I don't want to make this into a problem when there may not be one. I'm probably going to annoy someone here, so be nice!

The outcome here is, at all cost, to maintain the respect they clearly are projecting in their perceptions of you as knowledgeable and competent. You don't want to destroy what you have; you need to be effective. You also wouldn't benefit from a change from being seen as their 'little helper' to 'the bitch'; that's equally deadly. I would first suggest that you are doing the right thing already by looking to yourself for the solution. It can be a mess trying to change other people. So anyway, here are a few thoughts that come to my mind (recognising that I really do not know your situation).

First, if it's not a really big deal and you know in your heart that there is no malice intended—that your male counterparts see their comments in their own unique way as some form of endearment—you might just leave it alone. I have had situations where I have worked in all-male environments, where the men were also twenty to forty years older than I. In their eyes, I was smart and respected, but I was also like one of their children. It didn't bother me. There was no harm.

If the difficulty lies with just one individual, or several who are your age, it might be different. I think there are a couple of things you might be able to do without disrupting the other perceptions they have of you. First you might question yourself: What is it about your behaviours that lead these men to have this perception? Knowing this, work to change it. Ask in what way, honestly, are you behaving that leads others to perceive you as the 'little helper'. Perhaps *how* you are being helpful is what leads them to think of you as always willing to be helpful. The next time they make a request of you, you might store that away in your memory and, sometime in the next week, make the exact same request of one of them—"Oh Joe, seeing you're heading over for coffee, will you pick one up for me?" All they can do is say no. And if they say yes, you get to thank them.

Second, you can behaviourally discourage the use of an offensive turn of phrase. A good curled lip in response to its use will usually be enough, but is not so confrontational as to invite its further use. You just want to create a situation where use of that term becomes linked to something uncomfortable—not terribly uncomfortable, but just enough.

Third, you could say something to them. Nothing threatening, because they likely aren't even aware their behaviour bothers you. They might even be surprised to find out that it does. It can be as simple as saying, "When you do this… I feel this. I don't think that's your intention, and although I'm working hard to not inter-pret it that way rationally, it's how I feel." That too will probably just handle it—allowing you to then get on with just being your knowledgeable and competent self.

Without using gimmicks, how do I develop a powerful opening that gets attention quickly and arouses interest?

Step one: Become someone whose appearance, posture, move-ments, gestures and voice are captivating. That's no gimmick. *You* become someone who gets attention quickly and arouses interest. Everything that you need to do is available in the world to you. You might think of spending a few weeks just walking around town and being in restaurants and noticing those people who seem to get your attention without really doing anything overt to do it—notice how they dress, how they walk, how they gesture—these are all learnable skills.

Step two: When you open your mouth to speak, ensure that what comes out is something of interest to your audience.

How do I move into the corporate training sphere when my background is in school education?

So long as your content is of interest to the corporate market, your background should be no hindrance. You might, depending upon your current style, find it useful to hang out in the corporate sector a bit; they have their own language and style of dress and way of representing themselves that is different from many schoolteachers. You might find you need to think about some sort of transition in that context, but again, if your content is solid, then I can't imagine there will be any problem.

I do not know how to gain experience to become more of a motivational speaker; presently I am quiet. I do not know where to go—what is the first step?

First recognise that there are some very inspirational speakers who are very quiet—but their story carries a big wallop. You may not need to change this style depending upon who and what you plan to teach. However, if what you want is a bigger, more gregarious or evangelistic style, this is a modelling exercise. Find other trainers, entertainers, ministers and so on that you can model until these new forms of behaviour become part of you. You probably would also greatly benefit from vocal and acting coaches—people who can teach you to use differently the instruments that are your body and voice.

I want to become a legitimate mentor and role model such that others will want to follow. Should I improve my educational qualifications? Move away from teaching, becoming more of

a change agent (consultant) for adult education? Teach my skills to others to improve their lot? What should I do?

If you go out in the world and continue to do interesting and valuable things, you may find one day that others come to you wanting to learn. In my own life I am guided by my interests and curiosity, quite selfishly. I do and learn about those things that interest me, whether they have value to others or not. If you choose to go back to school, do it because it is what *you* want to do. Having a goal of inspiring or mentoring others is a very hard one to achieve by overt actions. I don't know that those who inspire us are motivated to do what they do for the sake of providing inspiration—they just do what they do because it's what interests them—their influence on us is simply a by-product.

How do I get comfortable with, and deal with, 'adoration'? How do I live up to the expectations others begin to have of me?

Adoration from students is a part of a good trainer's life. If you do a good job, people will want to do and learn more from you. They may even think they want to hang out with you. That is a fact of life in this business. I think the key is simply to accept that this is what is true in the students' perception of you, but there really isn't anything you need to do about it or with it. It shouldn't inherently change you or change what you do.

As far as increasing expectations goes, I think we bring a bit of that on ourselves—students I find are actually pretty cooled out about our limitations—it's just that we might begin to think that we can't show any weaknesses. My students always know my limitations, and this keeps their expectations in check. You just can't do everything. If what you have been doing in life is leading others to admire you, then just keep doing what you are doing—it's working. Adoration from students only becomes a problem if you start using that in some way—it can turn into a nice little power trip that has a big dead end down the track.

In my own life I have found two things that balance all of this out. The first was learning how simply to say, "Thank you"—nothing more and nothing less. Earlier in my career when I would receive accolades I always had something to say to downplay the compliment. I learned later how invalidating this is to the person who is trying to tell you that you've done something that mattered to them. We all have met people who inspire us, so what is so strange about thinking you might inspire someone else? So now when someone gives me a compliment (and some of these sound really a bit over the top to me) I just humbly say "Thank you." It acknowledges that this is true for them. The second thing I have learned to do is be surrounded by friends who are pretty neutral about what I do on stage—they know the difference between my work and my life. It's healthy to have people who balance what you do on stage with the facts that you're a lousy cook and like watching sitcoms on television.

How do I get to feel comfortable about not being 'perfect'?

Very quickly realise that you're not! And anyway, how would you know if you were? Is there not always some next level that comes to awareness as we reach some level of accomplishment? Being perfect is not an issue if you don't carry the expectation of being perfect. Perhaps being competent is a better ideal to strive for.

**I question whether my knowledge is really deep enough.
I question whether I have taken enough time to check out
the information I am using. How will I ever know?**

I think this plagues most trainers at some time in their career. It can even be strong enough to discourage very talented and knowledgable people from sharing their knowledge. You can certainly be diligent and responsible for testing your knowledge by talking with experts in your field, asking them for feedback. Otherwise, you have to trust your audience responses. You may not ever know everything about a subject, but what you *do* know may be far beyond that of your students, and that is your value to them. Will you ever know? I don't know. Maybe on some days you really have that confidence. Most days, though, I think you'll be like all the rest of us—confident in what you do know, acutely aware of all that you don't know. Just forge ahead and keep trying to improve, but keep working while you are doing that.

How do I develop real confidence, as opposed to merely appearing confident?

Is there a difference? Just joking. Appearing confident is obviously all that is needed for the trainer, just like an actor with stage fright. It doesn't matter to the audience what your subjective experience is, they only care that you appear confident and competent at what you are doing. But if you subjectively want to feel confident, it will come only with experience, if it ever comes at all. Some trainers, like some actors, are plagued with stage fright and lack of confidence for their entire career. One way you might build your inner confidence is to start believing more in what others tell you than in what your inner voice tells you. Stop arguing with people when they tell you that you are very good, or very knowledgeable. Sometimes others have a far more accurate perception of your skills than you do. Start believing them.

I don't have any 'formal' qualifications in training. What courses or other means are available?

Usually trainers don't have formal qualification in training, they have formal qualifications in the content area in which they teach. If you are interested, however, you can consider doing a degree program in adult learning and education; it would be a nice feather in your training career cap.

When is not having a formal education a limitation to a trainer or presenter?

Not having formal qualifications is really only a limitation if your audience or clients perceive it to be a limitation. Of course, this can be overcome with other good credentials and a good story as to why this shouldn't be perceived as a limitation. But if it is expected, it can be easier to go get those credentials than to constantly have to be justifying why you are just as qualified without them.

Another limitation can be in your own mind. I have met many trainers who, through other means, have gained a great deal of content expertise but falsely believe that, because they have no formal qualifications, they won't be perceived as credible. That prevents them from trying. There are hundreds of stories of successful people in every industry who do not have formal academic qualifications. What I'd suggest is you go and read a few good life stories of some of these people—they can be quite inspirational.

What can I do about the physical and emotional drain of a five-day course, either to recover more quickly, or avoid the drain in the first place?

The physical drain is the easy part of this question. How physically demanding training will feel is directly proportional to the physical demands of the rest of your life. If you sit at a desk all week, and watch television in the evening, then standing up all day talking will feel terribly demanding. This is why I encourage trainers to get involved with other physically demanding pursuits. It has the effect of increasing their fitness but, by comparison, their training days aren't so shocking to their systems. When I was preparing to compete in triathlons I found that standing up to talk all day was a pleasant, relaxing relief! It is definitely easier to stand on stage and talk when you compare that with the five-kilometre run you did before work.

But if you will never be convinced that increasing your activity level will in fact make all physical activities easier, you do have other alternatives. You can make sure that you are eating properly and that many other life demands are handled for you by other people. You can monitor what you do after a training session. Anything that relaxes your muscles, like water (drinking it and soaking in it), stretching, getting massaged or meditating will likely keep you going a bit longer. Even in your training sessions you might find you benefit from not being so available to the students on breaks and over lunch. I usually have a private room where I can go to relax during these times.

The emotional drain is a bit more difficult. I used to come out of a session so emotionally strung out that the world looked bleak— it's all the swings from high to low and back again that eventually just wear you out. I learned after ten years of this that I didn't have to go emotionally where my students were going. I just learned to dissociate myself from my students' processes. If the students got really revved up and excited about accomplishing something in class, it didn't mean I had to get revved up too. I thought it was great that they had that experience, but my getting all excited didn't add to their experience, it just made me tired. It was the same if they typically struggled through a certain portion of the training. That was for them to do; I didn't have to feel that along with them. It wasn't going to help them one bit for me to feel the same feelings.

I also learned to not think about my experiences with a group until a few days or even a week had passed. When the training was over, it was over. I went home, cooked dinner and did other things, and wouldn't let myself think about the training. Then, after a few days, I could go back and remember some of the experiences—the problems people expressed, the touching stories, the funny experiences and so on. From a distance I could indulge in a little emotional processing with out the debilitating effects of doing this while working with the group.

I get too emotionally involved in any problems or issues that participants have in my courses. This leaves me mentally and physically exhausted by the end of a day's training. How do I get unhooked?

There is a point in your career when you make a decision about what you can and cannot be engaged in with your students. You may realise one day that your emotional involvement in their process in fact hinders your ability to help them. I know what it is like to want to reach out and help and fix it for a troubled student, but I also know that doing so changes my relationship with that student in a way that is not useful or healthy.

Engaging emotionally certainly leaves you physically and mentally drained; if you see yourself as doing a job and that staying out of these issues is the only way you can continue perform well, you may push yourself over this edge. In my case I care intensely about my students, but I am not engaged at that level with their process. I am outside of it enough to think clearly and maintain my level of service to them.

What is different about presenting in front of cameras instead of a live audience, especially in terms of content, connecting with the audience and presentation?

This question strikes a chord with me. I have done a lot of television and radio interviews and made a good number of videotapes. And I am really not very good at this at all. It is very different to working with a live audience. If you are someone who takes their cues from the audience, like I do, you may find that you perform very poorly in front of the camera. To overcome this I try to have all my tapings done with a live audience in the studio, or at least a handful of people to talk to—even if I have to invite some friends along.

Recently I did a teleconference from a studio in Brisbane to an audience somewhere else. There were several hundred people in the audience on the other end, and me standing in a room talking to a camera. I knew they were there and I knew they were seeing me projected on a large screen, but I felt like I was blind. I had no idea how the audience was reacting. This was really scary and very uncomfortable and I swore I wouldn't do another of these sessions. Of course, I did, but I made sure that there was a camera on the other end taping the audience, which was then fed to a monitor in my studio. This helped immensely.

You will find it helpful to prepare for camera work differently than you do for a training. You want it to be more like a lecture, but yet still keep the inflection in your voice as if there was someone there listening. When I do such sessions now, I actually try to imagine someone is sitting there in front of me listening to the talk. In my preparations I want to be sure that I know the sequence of my key points which are normally triggered by the interaction with the students and my movements on stage. What I mean is I have to work harder to ensure that the presentation is cohesive. I even rehearse (that doesn't mean memorise) my talk for this situation, just to get a feel for how to talk about the subject without the audience cues.

I have a real fear about being 'tall-poppied' (cut down) if I become powerfully visible. This has happened twice in the past. How can I become visible and not get cut down?

What you want from your visibility is a way of developing respect from others: respect for what you know and how hard you've worked to become competent. People do not cut down those they respect, they tend to cut down those they don't understand.

I think your visibility will have a lot to do with how you express yourself. There is a way of being visible that acknowledges what you know at the same time as making it clear what you don't know. You also need a way of expressing yourself that validates the skills and talents and experiences of others around you. Therefore your job is to be very clear about what you know and what you don't know and how you came to know those things. You don't want to fall into the false humility trap; it is a terrible trait for a trainer. There's a real incongruence in a trainer who stands on stage expressing their expertise out of one side of their mouth, while the other side speaks in self-effacing terms. I think, though, it is true that those who choose to be visible run the risk of being scrutinised by others, and sometimes in less-than-flattering terms.

I think there is great wisdom in finding some inner security and a handful of trusted friends and simply ignoring that outside factor. You don't have any control over it, so for me the best approach has been to not think too much about it. Rather than waste my time trying to fix a problem or a potential problem, I just keep studying and learning—getting better at what I do and increasing my knowledge every day.

What is the most useful feedback for a trainer?

If you are truly interested in being an excellent trainer, then the best feedback is honest feedback, from two different sources. The first source is your students. Find a way to compel them to give you honest feedback about your teaching style and your content. The second source is from other industry experts. Invite them to observe your work, especially those experts whose work you reference and teach. Remember, other people's impressions and perceptions of your work matter much more than your own.

I am interested in exploring a move, getting out on my own, leaving the Public Service and picking a topic to specialise in. What's the first step on this path of exploration?

To really be successful and have longevity as an independent trainer, your choices should be guided by your interests. Ask yourself what subject or topic are you fired up enough about that you could wake up every day, seven days a week, and be compelled to talk about and to study. This has to be the criteria because that's what it will take to be a top trainer and remain a top trainer in a particular subject.

I certainly have motivating subjects. When I wake up in the morning, I look forward to spending the next eight, ten or twelve hours doing nothing but exploring or talking about those topics. Remember, when you are on your own you will spend more time studying than you do teaching, and you will spend more time alone than you do with others. What is going to get *you* out of bed and to your desk, and keep you there?

What needs to be considered when making the move to marketing myself as a trainer, as in freelancing?

The goal is to get your name associated with the industry you want to work in. For example, when people think of computer training, you want your name to be the one that comes to mind. To start, you will need to put together whatever portfolio you can from your past experiences, then begin to actively seek new experiences to fill in the gaps. I would start speaking everywhere you can to get your name 'out there'—at community centres, industry conferences, TAFE and so on. I would also start writing articles for industry magazines and to try to get published as quickly as possible.

If I am working full-time as a trainer, how do I build up my credentials?

Remember, credentials are artefacts from our past that allow others to quickly assess our skills. As a trainer, academic credentials can, in time, be important. For this reason I try to get my trainers to think about attending academic courses, even if it is only one evening class per year. Not only might this eventually add up to a degree, but you have the opportunity to meet other people, not only class-mates, but other people who you 'meet' vicariously through the literature. Being familiar with other people's research and being able to speak about it intelligently is another form of credential. The more your work is referenced back to academic sources, the more credibility you will have.

I would also highly recommend that you become of a member of associations in your industry. Not only should you attend conferences, but you might consider submitting papers and becoming a conference speaker. This on a brochure or resume lifts you out of the crowd; you're perceived as someone who speaks *to* your industry. At some point in your career you will want to consider publishing: authorship is a powerful credential. You might also think about taking on contracts simply for the sake of being able in the future to say that you had that experience or that you worked with that client. There have been many times I really didn't want to do another training, or take another trip, but the thought of the future benefit of doing the job was compelling enough.

Lastly, I would begin collecting artefacts now for the sake of using them in the future. I am actually very bad at this myself, but fortunately I have had staff members who took the time to collect newspaper and magazine articles, radio interviews, letters of thanks from clients and so on for me. About ten years into my career, when I was changing direction, I was so happy to have these. I was able to create a portfolio of past experiences that played a big role in the training jobs I was able to procure in that new stage.

255

CONCLUSION

The questions raised and problems discussed in this chapter are by no means conclusive. But that's almost the point: they are merely representative of the *types* of questions and problems that may arise in your own training endeavours. Try to use my responses to spark ideas about how you might solve a particular problem, but extrapolate from these responses to deal with the idiosyncrasies of other problems you encounter.

If nothing else, I hope that this chapter has demonstrated unequivocally that the starting point for all our judgments about what is right or wrong, good or bad, normal or not normal in how we respond as trainers is summarised by the phrase, *it depends*!

epilogue

It is still a source of amazement to me that that which I can communicate in sixty hours during a training course has taken over a thousand hours to structure in a written form. I still find writing difficult and arduous, but I have been well convinced by others of its merits—and therefore deserving of the amount of effort that the task requires. The process of restructuring my own knowledge of the phenomenon of training, such that it would make sense in written form, has been illuminating. As a result, I not only feel I now know this content in a whole new way, but I have also discovered new connections that simply eluded me in the past. I have little doubt that my own abilities as a trainer will eventually benefit from these new insights. They are already sneaking into my life and my most recent work.

My final words are a simple reminder: the development of your skills and artistry as a trainer is an evolutionary process, one that unfolds slowly, over a long period of time. With attention and commitment you will be a better trainer in five years than you are today. I hope that the ideas discussed in this book will in some way provide new insights at each stage of your development—that what you were able to perceive and understand in your first reading has value, but at some time in the future, subsequent readings provide new distinctions unavailable to you today. I wish you great courage tackling all the opportunities that will present themselves to you in this most dynamic career—the career of a trainer.

further reading

One of the things I have greatly benefited from over my career is the reading and reference lists provided by authors of books that have inspired me or which have added significantly to my knowledge. If I found value in a writer's work, then I gained even more when they provided the means by which I could follow up on some of the work they cite as influential. Now it's my turn to do the favour.

Below is a list of work that has influenced my own thinking about the subjects of training, learning and change. It is by no means exhaustive. Many of the references are books quite easily accessible through any good bookshop. Other pieces are journal articles, so you'll need to approach a university library to access them.

Many of the works have been written in a style that requires no special prior knowledge of the subject—try, for instance, Damasio, Goleman, Brookfield or Holt. Of course, some of the writings are academic research papers and will need to be approached from the perspective of a diligent student.

I wish you well in your personal pursuit to expand your own knowledge base.

Argyris, C. (1991a). "Teaching smart people how to learn".
   Harvard Business Review, 99–109.

— (1991b). "Theories of action that inhibit individual learning".
   In Boud, D. and Walker, D. (Eds.), *Experience and learning:
   Reflection at work*. Geelong, Vic.: Deakin University Press.

— (1993). "Education for leading-learning". *American Management Association*, 5–17.

Boud, D., Cohen, R. & Walker, D. (1993). "Introduction: Understanding learning from experience". In Boud, D., Cohen, R., & Walker, D. (Eds.), *Using experience for learning*. Great Britain: Open University Press.

Boud, D., Keogh, R. and Walker, D. (1985). "What is reflection in learning?". In Boud, D., Keogh, R. & Walker, D. (Eds.), *Reflection: Turning experience into learning*. London: Kogan Page.

Boud, D. and Walker, D. (1991). *Experience and learning: Reflection at work*. Geelong, Vic.: Deakin University Press.

— (1993). "Barriers to reflection on experience". In Boud, D., Cohen, R. and Walker, D. (Eds.), *Using experience for learning*. Great Britain: Open University Press.

Brookfield, S. D. (1986). *Understanding and facilitating adult learning*. San Francisco, CA: Jossey-Bass.

— (1987). *Developing critical thinkers: Challenging adults to explore alternative ways of thinking and acting*. San Francisco, CA: Jossey-Bass.

— (1990). *The skillful teacher*. San Francisco, CA: Jossey-Bass.

Bruner, J. S. (1986). *Actual minds, possible worlds*. Cambridge, MA: Harvard University Press.

Candy, P. (1991). *Self-direction for lifelong learning*. San Francisco, CA: Jossey-Bass.

Cantor, N. and Langston, C. A. (1989). "Ups and downs of life tasks in a life transition". In Pervin, L. A. (Ed.), *Goal concepts in personality and social psychology*, 127–67. Hillsdale, NJ: Erlbaum.

Churchland, P. M. (1995). *The engine of reason, the seat of the soul*. Cambridge, MA: The MIT Press.

258

Churchland, P. S. & Sejnowski, T. J. (1992). *The computational brain*. Cambridge, MA: MIT Press.

Covington, M. C. (1992). *Making the grade*. Cambridge, MA: Cambridge University Press.

Covington, M. V. & Omelich, C. L. (1987). " 'I knew it cold before the exam': A test of the anxiety-blockage hypothesis". *Journal of Educational Psychology*, 79, 393–400.

Damasio, A. R. (1994). *Descartes' error: Emotion, reason, and the human brain*. New York: Grosset/Putnam.

Dewey, J. (1938). *Experience and education*. New York, NY: Collier Books.

— (1991). *How we think*. Buffalo, NY: Prometheus Books.

Dunbar, R. (1995). *The trouble with science*. Boston: Faber and Faber.

Dworkin, M. S. (Ed.) (1959). *Dewey on education*. New York, NY: Teachers College Press.

Eisner, E. W. (1991). *The enlightened eye: Qualitative inquiry and the enhancement of educational practice*. New York, NY: MacMillan.

— (1994a). *Cognition and curriculum reconsidered* (2nd ed.). New York, NY: Teachers College Press.

— (1994b). *The educational imagination* (3rd ed.). New York, NY: MacMillan.

— (1994c). "Preparing teachers for the schools of the twenty-first century". In *Teacher Education for the 21st Century*. Inchon, Korea: Inchon National University of Education.

Ekman, P. & Davidson, R. (Eds.) (1994). *Fundamental questions about emotions*. New York: Oxford University Press.

Emmons, R. A. (1990). "Motives and life goals". In Briggs, S., Hogan, R. & Jones, W. (Eds.), *Handbook of personality psychology*. Orlando, FL: Academic Press.

Eysenck, H. J. (1981). *A model for personality*. New York, NY: Springer.

— (1983). "Personality as a fundamental concept in scientific psychology". *Australian Journal of Psychology*, 35, 289–304.

— (1984). "The place of individual differences in a scientific psychology". *Annals of Theoretical Psychology*, 1, 233–86.

— (1990). "Biological dimensions of personality". In Pervin, L. A. (Ed.), *Handbook of personality theory and research*. New York, NY: Guilford Press.

— (1991). "Dimensions of personality: A biosocial approach to personality". In Strelau, J. & Angleitner, A. (Eds.), *Explorations in temperament: International perspectives on theory and measurement*. New York, NY: Plenum.

Eysenck, H. J. & Eysenck, M. W. (1985). *Personality and individual differences: A natural science approach*. New York, NY: Plenum.

Feynman, R. P. (1988). *What do you care what other people think?*. New York, NY: Bantam Books.

Fridlund, A. J., Ekman, P. & Oster, H. (1987). "Facial expressions in emotion: A review of the literature". In Siegman, A. W. & Feldstein, S. (Eds.), *Nonverbal behaviour and communication* (143–224). Hillsdale, NJ: Erlbaum.

Frijda, N. H. (1986). *The emotions*. Cambridge, MA: Cambridge University Press.

Gardner, H. (1985). *The mind's new science*. New York, NY: Basic Books.

Goleman, D. (1995). *Emotional intelligence*. New York: Bantam Books.

Haley, J. (1985). *Conversations with Milton H. Erickson, M. D.* New York, NY: Triangle Press.

Hallanhan, D. P. (1992). "Some thoughts on why the prevalence of learning disabilities has increased". *Journal of Learning Disabilities*, 25, 523–8.

Holt, J. (1964). *How children fail.* New York, NY: Del Publishing.

— (1989). *Learning all the time.* New York, NY: Del Publishing.

Isen, A. M., Daubman, K. A. & Nowicki, G. P. (1987). "Positive affect facilitates creative problem solving". *Journal of Personality and Social Psychology*, 52, 1122–31.

Izard, C. E. (1990). "Facial expressions and the regulation of emotions". *Journal of Personality and Social Psychology*, 58, 487–98.

Jauregui, J. A. (1995). *The emotional computer.* Cambridge, MA: Blackwell Publishers.

Johnson, G. (1992). *In the palaces of memory: How we build the worlds inside our heads.* London: Grafton.

Johnson, J. L. & Bloom, A. M. (1995). "An analysis of the contribution of the five factors of personality to variance in academic procrastination". *Personality and Individual Differences*, 18(1), 127–33.

Kagan, J. (1994). *Galen's prophecy.* New York: Basic Books.

Knowles, M. (1990). *The adult learner: A neglected species* (4th ed.). Houston, TX: Gulf Publishing.

Kosslyn, S. M. (1994). *Image and brain.* Cambridge, MA: MIT Press.

Kosslyn, S. M. & Koenig, O. (1992). *Wet mind: The new cognitive neuroscience.* New York, NY: The Free Press.

Kreitler, S., Aronson, M., Berliner, S., Kreitler, H., Weissler, K. & Arber, N. (1995). "Life events and personal problems: Their physiological and emotional effects". *Personality and Individual Differences*, 18(1), 101–16.

Labouvie-Vief, G. (1982). "Issues in life-span development". In Wolman, B. (Ed.), *Handbook of developmental psychology* (54–62). New York, NY: Academic Press.

Labouvie-Vief, G., DeVoe, M. & Bulka, D. (1989a). "Speaking about feelings: Conceptions of emotion across the life span". *Psychology and Aging*, 4, 425–37.

Labouvie-Vief, G., Hakim-Larson, J., DeVoe, M. & Schoeberlein, S. (1989b). "Emotions and self-regulation: A life-span view". *Human Development*, 32, 279–99.

Labouvie-Vief, G., Hakim-Larson, J. & Hobart, C. J. (1987). "Age, ego level, and the life-span development of coping and defense processes". *Psychology and Aging*, 2, 286–93.

Langer, E. J. (1989). *Mindfulness*. Reading, MA: Addison Wesley.

— (1993). "A mindful education". *Educational Psychologist*, 28, 43–50.

Lazarus, R. S. & Folkman, S. (1984). *Stress, appraisal, and coping*. New York, NY: Springer.

LeDoux, J. E. (1992a). "Brain mechanisms of emotion and emotional learning". *Current Opinion in Neurobiology*, 2, 191–97.

— (1992b). "How scary things get that way". *Science*, 6 November.

Levenson, R. W., Ekman, P. & Friesen, W. V. (1990). "Voluntary facial action generates emotion-specific autonomous nervous system activity". *Psychophysiology*, 27.

Levinson, D. J. (1986). "A conception of adult development". *American Psychologist*, 41, 3–13.

Little, D. (1983). "Personal projects: A rationale and method for investigation". *Environment and Behavior*, 15, 273–309.

— (1989). "Personal projects analysis: Trivial pursuits, magnificent obsessions, and the search for coherence". In Buss, D. M. & Cantor, N. (Eds.), *Personality psychology: Recent trends and emerging directions*. New York: Springer-Verlag.

Mackintosh, N. J. (1986). "The biology of intelligence?". *British Journal of Psychology*, 77, 1–18.

Mathews, A. (1994). "Once more, with feeling". *Cognition and Emotions*, 8(4), pp. 383–91.

Matsumoto, D. (1987). "The role of facial response in the experience of emotion: More methodological problems and a meta-analysis". *Journal of Personality and Social Psychology*, 52, 769–74.

Mattingly, C. (1991). "Narrative reflections on practical actions: Two experiments in reflective storytelling". In Schon, D. A. (Ed.), *The reflective turn: Case studies in and on educational practice* (235–257).

McClelland, J. L., McNaughton, B. L. & O'Reilly, R. C. (1994). *Why there are complementary learning systems in the hippocampus and neocortex: Insights from successes and failures of connectionist models of learning and memory* (Technical No. pdp.cns. 94.1). Carnegie Mellon University.

McCombs, B. L. (1989). "Self-regulated learning and academic achievement: A phenomenological view". In Zimmerman, B. J. & Schunk, D. H. (Eds.), *Self-regulated learning and academic achievement: Theory, research, and practice* (51–82). New York, NY: Springer-Verlag.

McCombs, B. L. (1991). "Motivation and lifelong learning". *Educational Psychologist*, 26, 117–27.

McCombs, B. L. & Whisler, J. S. (1989). "The role of affective variables in autonomous learning". *Educational Psychologist*, 24, 277–306.

Meece, J. L. (1993). "The will to learn". *Educational Researcher*, 22, 35–6.

Mezirow, J. (1990). *Fostering critical reflection in adulthood: A guide to transformative and emancipatory learning.* San Francisco, CA: Jossey-Bass.

— (1991). *Transformative dimensions in adult learning.* San Francisco, CA: Jossey-Bass.

— (1994). "Understanding transformation theory". *Adult Education Quarterly*, 44(4), 222–32.

Mikulas, W. L. & Vodanovich, S. J. (1993). "The essence of boredom". *The Psychological Record*, 3–12.

Moir, A. & Jessel, D. (1995). *A mind to crime*. London: Penguin Publishing.

Monat, A. & Lazarus, R. S. (1991). *Stress and Coping* (3rd ed.). New York, NY: Columbia University Press.

Moore, J. A. (1993). *Science as a way of knowing*. Cambridge, MA: Harvard University Press.

Muris, P., Merckelbach, H. & Bogels, S. (1995). "Coping, defense, and fear in college students". *Personality and Individual Differences*, 18(2), 301–4.

Newman, M. (1994). "Response to understanding transformational theory". *Adult Education Quarterly*, 44(4), 236–42.

Niedenthal, P. M. & Kitayama, S. (Eds.) (1994). *The heart's eye: Emotional influences in perception and attention*. San Diego, CA: Academic Press.

Oatley, K. & Duncan, E. (1994). "The experience of emotions in everyday life". *Cognition and Emotion*, 8(4), 369–81.

Pekrun, R. (1988). "Anxiety and motivation in achievement settings: Toward a systems-theoretical approach". *International Journal of Educational Research*, 12, 299–323.

— (1992). "The impact of emotions on learning and achievement: Towards a cognitive/motivational mediators". *Applied Psychology*, 41, 359–76.

Plomin, R. & Daniels, D. (1987). "Why are children in the same family so different from one another?". *Behavior and Brain Science*, 10, 1–60.

Polloway, E. A., Schewel, R. & Patton, J. R. (1992). "Learning disabilities in adulthood: Personal perspectives". *Journal of Learning Disabilities*, 25, 520–22.

Rim, Y. (1995). "Coping styles, impulsiveness, venturesomeness and empathy". *Personality and Individual Differences*, 18(1), 159–60.

Riskind, J. H. & Gotay, C. C. (1982). "Physical posture: Could it have regulatory or feedback effects upon motivation and emotion?". *Motivation and Emotion*, 6, 273–96.

Roth, S. & Cohen, J. (1986). "Approach, avoidance and coping with stress". *American Psychologist*, 41, 813–19.

Salovey, P. & Mayer, J. D. (1990). "Emotional intelligence". *Imagination, Cognition, and Personality*, 9, 143–66.

Scherer, K. R. (1994). "Affect bursts". In Van Goozen, S. H., Van de Poll, N. E. & Sergeant, J. A. (Eds.), *Emotions: Essays on emotion theory* (161–93). Hillsdale, NJ: Erlbaum.

Schon, D. A. (1983). *The reflective practitioner: How professionals think in action.* Cambridge, MA: Basic Books.

— (1987). *Educating the reflective practitioner: Toward a new design for teaching and learning in the professions.* San Francisco, CA: Jossey-Bass.

— (Ed.) (1991). *The reflective turn: Case studies in and on educational practice.* New York, NY: Teachers College, Columbia University.

Schroth, M. L. (1995). "A comparison of sensation seeking among different groups of athletes and nonathletes". *Personality and Individual Differences*, 18(2), 219–22.

Sedikides, C. (1992). "Mood as a determinant of attentional focus". *Cognition and Emotion*, 6, 129–48.

Seligman, M. (1993). *What you can change and what you can't.* New York, NY: Knopf.

Seligman, M. R. (1990). *Learned Optimism.* Sydney: Random House.

Singer, J. & Salovey, P. (1993). *The Remembered Self: Emotion and memory in personality*. New York, NY: Free Press.

Smith, R. M. (1990). *Learning to learn across the lifespan*. San Francisco, CA: Jossey-Bass.

Sonnemans, J. & Frijda, N. H. (1994). "The structure of subjective emotional intensity". *Cognition and Emotion*, 8(4), 329–50.

Sternberg, R. J. (1988). "Mental self government: A theory of intellectual styles and their development". *Human Development*, 31, 187–221.

Sternberg, R. J. (1994). "Thinking styles: theory and assessment at the interface between intelligence and personality". In Sternberg, R. J., and Ruzgis, P. (Eds.), *Personality and Intelligence* (169–87). New York, NY: Cambridge University Press.

Stipek, D. (1993). *Motivation to learn* (2nd ed.). Boston, MA: Allyn and Bacon.

Strelau, J. & Angleitner, A. (1991). *Explorations in temperament: International perspectives on theory and measurement*. New York, NY: Plenum.

Taylor, D. (1991). *Learning denied*. Portsmouth, NH: Heinemann.

Woodsmall, W. & James, T. (1988). *Timeline Therapy*. Capitola, CA: Meta Publications.

Willis, C. (1993). *The runaway brain: The evolution of human uniqueness*. London: Harper Collins.

Zajonc, R. B. (1994). "Emotional expression and temperature modulation". In Van Goozen, S. H., Van de Poll, N. E. & Sergeant, J. A. (Eds.), *Emotions: Essays on emotion theory*. Hillsdale, NJ: Erlbaum.

Zajonc, R. B., Inglehart, M. & Murphy, S. T. (1989). "Feeling and facial efference: Implications of the vascular theory of emotion". *Psychological Review*, 96, 395–416.

Zuckerman, M. & Como, P. (1983). "Sensation-seeking and arousal systems". *Personality and Individual Differences*, 4, 381–6.

index

FOR UP-TO-DATE BUSINESS BOOK INFORMATION

Woodslane publishes and distributes books on subjects that span the broad range of the Australian and International worlds of work and business.

If you would like to hear more about Woodslane books fill in your details and subject preferences below.

Name

Company

Address

Postcode

Telephone   Fax

Email

(✓) Please send me more information on

( ) Future training volumes by Stephanie Burns

( ) Other training and HRD books from Woodslane

( ) The full range of Woodslane business titles

( ) Business books on the specific subject of

Others from this organisation who should be kept up to date with business book information are:

Name

Name

Either fax this coupon to (02) 9970 5002 or detach and mail it to our postage-free address.
Phone (02) 9970 5111   Email bizbooks@woodslane.com.au

No postage stamp required
if posted in Australia

Reply Paid 30
Woodslane Pty Ltd
PO Box 935
Mona Vale NSW 2103

------------------------------ FOLD HERE ------------------------------

Thank you for reading Artistry in Training... I would like to show my appreciation by sending you a free gift

I trust you gained some useful insights into the world of training. Most importantly, I thank you for investing in your personal education.

I truly believe that to become and remain a good trainer it is important to commit to ongoing education for yourself. That's why I've organised a free educational audio tape for you. Titled *Motivating the Adult Learner* this tape normally retails for $19.95 but is yours free when you complete and return the form below.

Stephanie Burns

Stephanie Burns
Author - Artistry in Training

Other Products and Programs by Stephanie Burns:

For information on any of the following, please tick the appropriate box(es) and return this form to the address below:

- ❏ Skills for Training Mastery (One day Seminar)
- ❏ Training to Train (Four Month program for Training Professionals)
- ❏ Evening Seminars and Lectures (different subjects available)
- ❏ Advanced Skills for Training Professionals (Audio Tape Set)
- ❏ Customised in-house presentations for Trainers

Name _____ Position _____

Company _____

Address _____

_____ Postcode _____

Ph (W) _____ Fax _____

Mobile _____ Email _____

Comments: _____

_____

_____

Return to:
Stephanie Burns Programs, PO Box 1126, Crows Nest NSW 1585
Phone: (02) 9923 1699   Fax: (02) 9923 1799
Email: info@powwowevents.com.au Website: www.powwowevents.com.au

Reply Paid AAA35
PO Box 446
Spit Junction NSW 2088

- FOLD HERE -